ON THE MOTIVE OF THE INCARNATION

EARLY MODERN CATHOLIC SOURCES

Volume 1

EDITORIAL BOARD

Ulrich Lehner
University of Notre Dame
Series Editor

Trent Pomplun
Loyola University Maryland
Series Editor

Paul Richard Blum
Loyola University Maryland

Susannah Monta
University of Notre Dame

Jorge Cañizares-Esguerra
University of Texas at Austin

Felipe Pereda
Harvard University

Wim DeCock
KU Leuven

Jean-Louis Quantin
École Pratique des Hautes Études
(PSL)—Sorbonne

Simon Ditchfield
University of York

Erin Rowe
Johns Hopkins University

Carlos Eire
Yale University

Jacob Schmutz
University of Paris—Sorbonne

Marco Forlivesi
D'Annunzio University of
Chieti—Pescara

Jean-Luc Solère
Boston College

THE SALMANTICENSES

(Discalced Carmelites of Salamanca)

ON THE MOTIVE OF THE INCARNATION

Translated by DYLAN SCHRADER

THE CATHOLIC UNIVERSITY
OF AMERICA PRESS
Washington, D.C.

Copyright © 2019
The Catholic University of America Press
All rights reserved
The paper used in this publication meets the minimum
requirements of American National Standards for Information
Science—Permanence of Paper for Printed Library Materials,
ANSI Z39.48-1984.
∞
Cataloging-in-Publication Data available
from the Library of Congress
ISBN 978-0-8132-3179-2

Davidi, Luciae, et Eleonorae,

ut Verbo nato ac oblato,

cuius gratia sunt facti,

sine fine fruantur

CONTENTS

Acknowledgments · ix
Abbreviations · xi
Introduction · xiii

ON THE MOTIVE OF THE INCARNATION · 3

Doubt I. Whether God would assume flesh by virtue of the present decree if Adam had not sinned? · 5

§ 1. The certain is separated from the uncertain, and the state of the question is opened up · 6

§ 2. The opinion of St. Thomas is preferred and bolstered by a singular foundation · 22

§ 3. The replies of the Scotists are impugned · 37

§ 4. The escapes sought by Suárez and others are cut off · 53

§ 5. The challenge of a serious objection is met and the link between the Incarnation and the remediation of sin is explained · 69

§ 6. Replies against the preceding doctrine and extrication from them · 89

§ 7. The contrary opinion is related and some of its lines of reasoning overturned · 102

§ 8. The challenge of two other arguments for the same opinion is met · 114

Doubt II. Whether, if Adam had not sinned, Christ would come by virtue of another decree that God would have? · 127

§ 1. The true opinion is clarified by some assertions · 128

§ 2. The foundations of the adverse opinions are demolished · 137

Doubt III. Whether, by virtue of the present decree, Christ would come if only original sin existed and actual sins did not exist? 142

§ 1. The certain is separated from the uncertain 142

§ 2. The affirmative opinion is preferred 150

§ 3. The rationales for the contrary opinion are addressed 165

Doubt IV. Whether, by virtue of the present decree, Christ would come if actual sins existed, even if original sin did not exist? 173

§ 1. The negative opinion is preferred and contrary lines of reasoning are torn apart 174

Bibliography 185
Index 199

ACKNOWLEDGMENTS

I am grateful in the first place to almighty God. I am also indebted to the Most Rev. W. Shawn McKnight, bishop of Jefferson City, to the Most Rev. John R. Gaydos, bishop emeritus of Jefferson City, and to the Diocese of Jefferson City, Missouri, for affording me the opportunity to study sacred theology. I also thank Mr. Joseph L. Shetler, the staff of the Catholic University of America Press, the anonymous reviewers, and especially the series editors for their feedback. Finally, I appreciate the loving support of my family and friends.

ABBREVIATIONS

CCCM	Corpus Christianorum, continuatio mediaeualis
CCSL	Corpus Christianorum, series Latina
CSEL	Corpus scriptorum ecclesiasticorum Latinorum
PG	Patriologiae cursus completus, series Graeca (Migne)
PL	Patriologiae cursus completus, series Latina (Migne)
SC	Sources chrétiennes
ST	*Summa theologiae* (Thomas Aquinas)
Super Matt.	*Super Evangelium s. Matthaei lectura* (Thomas Aquinas)
Super II Sent.	*Scriptum super librum secundum Sententiarum* (Thomas Aquinas)
Super III Sent.	*Scriptum super librum tertium Sententiarum* (Thomas Aquinas)
Super IV Sent.	*Scriptum super librum quartum Sententiarum* (Thomas Aquinas)
Super Rom.	*Super epistolam ad Romanos lectura* (Thomas Aquinas)
Super I Tim.	*Super primam epistolam ad Timotheum lectura* (Thomas Aquinas)

INTRODUCTION

The Salmanticenses

In the seventeenth century, the Discalced Carmelites of the College of *San Elias* at the University of Salamanca, customarily referred to by their Latin moniker of *Salmanticenses*, authored a course of theology. Francesco-Saverio Pancheri, OFM, calls this *Cursus theologicus*, originally meant for students of that order, "the most exhaustive and important production of the Thomistic School in the seventeenth century."[1] The final edition of the *Cursus* consists of twenty volumes published in Paris and Brussels from 1870 to 1883.[2] To give a sense of its enormity, the present disputation (tract. 21, disp. 2, *De motivo Incarnationis*) amounts to about 0.5 percent of the total *Cursus*. Its overall structure loosely follows the *Summa theologiae* of St. Thomas Aquinas, OP (1225–74), though the Salmanticenses use this framework to address new questions and argue their own positions.

The composition of the *Cursus theologicus* lasted from around 1625 to 1710. Its principal authors were Antonio de la Madre de Dios, OCD (1583–1637), Domingo de Santa Teresa, OCD (1604–59), Juan de la Anunciación, OCD (1633–1701), Antonio de San Juan Bautista, OCD (1641–99), and Ildefonso de los Angeles, OCD (1663–1737).[3] Given the

1. *The Universal Primacy of Christ*, trans. Juniper B. Carol (Front Royal, Va.: Christendom Publications, 1984), 130n14.

2. The first volume of the *Cursus theologicus* was published in 1631 and the last in 1712, with the volume containing the disputation *De motivo Incarnationis* appearing in 1687. There are no substantial differences between the 1687 and 1878 editions of *De motivo Incarnationis*.

3. Enrique del Sagrado Corazón, "El colegio de San Elías y los *Salmanticenses*," in Luis Enrique Rodríguez-San Pedro Bezares, *Historia de la Universidad de Salamanca*, vol. 1, *Trayectoria histórica e instituciones vinculadas*, Acta Salmanticensia: Historia de la Universidad 61 (Salamanca: Ediciones Universidad de Salamanca, 2002), 699–703.

purpose, scope, and remarkable unity of the work, the *Cursus* must be considered as representative of the views of the order more principally than those of the individual writers.[4] Juan de la Anunciación was responsible for the portion of the *Cursus theologicus* dealing with the Incarnation and thus for the present disputation.

The Salmanticenses saw themselves as disciples and heirs of St. Thomas, as evidenced by their preface to the *Cursus*, which includes an encomium and invocation of the Angelic Doctor:

The most brilliant lamp of your teaching, O star of Theology, now to us entrusted, our hands have received from the very threshold as we compile this, our course of theology, and gladly do we take it up even till the final line and the goal of our course. May Elijah turn toward us the light of heaven and Theresa pour in the virgins' oil. Throughout, we hope to bear this lamp alight, before us brightly burning, if, that is, you shine for us so as to shine for all.... Barefoot, we strive to reach that burning bush, unapproachable more for divine faith's mysteries than for very flames, with you as guide. Theology's veiled chambers, its Holy of Holies, with you as teacher, our shoes stripped off for reverence' sake, we take our steps to enter. We shall tremble not at the bluster of adverse winds nor the rush of many pressing waters, bearing in our hands our lamp, your lamp, the lamp of all.[5]

---

4. Enrique del Sagrado Corazón, *Los Salmanticenses: su vida y su obra. Ensayo histórico y proceso inquisitorial de su doctrina sobre la Inmaculada*, Pontificia Universidad Eclesiastica de Salamanca (Madrid: Editorial de Espiritualidad, 1955), 128–29; and del Sagrado Corazón, "Juan Duns Escoto en la doctrina de los Salmanticenses sobre el motivo de la Encarnación," in *De doctrina Ioannis Duns Scoti*, Studia Scholastico-Scotistica 4 (Rome: Ercolano, 1968), 463.

5. "Concreditam jam nobis, (o Theologiae sidus) tuae doctrinae lampadem fulgentissimam, manibus acceptam nostris a primo limine cursus Theologici, quem aggredimur, usque ad ultimam lineam, seu cursus metam, Elia admovente coeleste lumen, Theresia infundente virgineum oleum, quam accensam accepimus, praefulgidam perlaturos speramus, si tamen sic nobis affulgeas, ut fulgeas omnibus.... Ardentem rubum plus mysteriis fidei divinae, quam flammis inaccessum, te ductore, nudis pedibus adire contendimus. In Sancta Sanctorum arcanorum sacrae Theologiae, te doctore, excalceati reverenter aggredimur introire. Nec adversantium ventorum flatum, nec multarum irruentium aquarum impetum formidantes, lampadem nostram, tuam, omnium manibus gestaturi." Salmanticenses, *Cursus theologicus Collegii Salmanticensis Fr. Discalceatorum B. Mariae de Monte Carmeli ... Summam theologicam angelici doctoris D. Thomae complectens*, editio nova correcta, vol. 1 (Parisiis: Apud Victorem Palmé, 1870), iii–iv. After the invocation, they offer a lengthy apologia for Thomism.

The Disputation on the Motive of the Incarnation in the Middle Ages and Beyond

Many theologians prior to the Salmanticenses contributed to the debate over the motive of the Incarnation, and many more have addressed it since. In the present introduction, it is only possible to sketch some of the more prominent medieval and early modern writers and their theories, especially those leading up to and influencing the Salmanticenses.[6] Therefore, we shall have to bear with oversimplifications of theologians worthy of careful study in their own right.[7]

In his *Cur Deus homo?*, St. Anselm of Canterbury, OSB (ca. 1033–1109), explored the relationship between God's purpose and plan in creating the universe, human will and sin, Christ's obedient suffering and death, and human redemption. His concern was to explain *why* and *how* the Incarnation was necessary or fitting for the salvation of the human race.[8] The influence of Anselm's work eventually led to a finer set of questions as theologians began to explore more precisely *whether* the Incarnation and human salvation were essentially linked in God's plan and what this might mean for the place of Christ, the God-man, in divine providence.[9]

Honorius of Autun (1080–1154) may be the first to raise the hypo-

---

6. The Salmanticenses themselves cite the most important scriptural and patristic authorities. See also Juniper B. Carol, *Why Jesus Christ? Thomistic, Scotistic, and Conciliatory Perspectives* (Manassas, Va.: Trinity Communications, 1986), 12–18, 150–203; Francesco Maria Risi, *Sul motivo primario della incarnazione del Verbo, ossia, Gesù Cristo predestinato di primo intento per fini indipendenti dalla caduta dell'uman genere e dal decreto di redenzione*, vols. 3–4 (Brescia: Tipografia Mucchetti & Riva, 1898).

7. Overviews can be found especially in Carol, *Why Jesus Christ?*; Risi, *Sul motivo primario della incarnazione*, vol. 1; Chrysostome Urrutibéhéty, *Le Motif de l'Incarnation et les principaux thomistes contemporains* (Tours: Librairie Alfred Cattier, 1921); Albert Michel, "Incarnation," in *Dictionnaire de théologie catholique*, ed. Alfred Vacant et al. (Paris: Librairie Letouzey et Ané, 1923), vol. 7.2, cols. 1530–39; Jean-François Bonnefoy, "La question hypothétique: Ultrum [sic] si Adam non peccasset ... au XIIIe siècle," *Revista española de teología* 14, no. 2/3 (1954): 327–68; and Trent Pomplun, "Baroque Catholic Theologies of Christ and Mary," in *The Oxford Handbook of Early Modern Theology, 1600–1800* (Oxford: Oxford University Press, 2016), 104–18.

8. As he has Boso note at the beginning of *Cur Deus homo?* (ed. Schmitt, 2:48).

9. On Anselm's influence, see Pancheri, *The Universal Primacy of Christ*, 14–17.

thetical inquiry ("Would God have become man apart from sin?") in clear form and give an affirmative reply.[10] Nevertheless, his contemporary, Rupert of Deutz, OSB (ca. 1075–1129), is probably the one who popularized this hypothetical inquiry.[11] Rupert's chief concern is to

10. *Libellus octo quaestionum*, chap. 2 (PL 172:1187–88). See Jeremy Moiser, "Why Did the Son of God Become Man?," *The Thomist* 37, no. 2 (1973): 289. Honorius's emphasis on Christ's absolute place in God's plan has a strong precedent in Isaac of Nineveh (d. ca. 680). See Irénée Hausherr, "Un précurseur de la théorie Scotiste sur la fin de l'incarnation: Isaac de Ninive (VIIe Siècle)," *Recherches de sciences religieuse* 22 (1932): 316–20; and Dominic J. Unger, "The Love of God: The Primary Reason for the Incarnation According to Isaac of Nineveh," *Franciscan Studies* 9, no. 2 (1949): 146–55.

Other patristic studies by Dominic Unger on Christ's primacy include "Franciscan Christology: Absolute and Universal Primacy of Christ," *Franciscan Studies* 2, no. 4 (1942): 428–75; "Christ's Role in the Universe According to St. Irenaeus," *Franciscan Studies* 5, no. 1 (1945): 3–20; "A Special Aspect of Athanasian Soteriology: Part I," *Franciscan Studies* 6, no. 1 (1946): 30–53; "A Special Aspect of Athanasian Soteriology: Part II," *Franciscan Studies* 6, no. 2 (1946): 171–94; "Christ Jesus the Secure Foundation According to St. Cyril of Alexandria," *Franciscan Studies* 7, no. 1 (1947): 1–25; "Christ Jesus the Secure Foundation According to St. Cyril of Alexandria: Part II," *Franciscan Studies* 7, no. 3 (1947): 324–43; "Christ Jesus the Secure Foundation According to St. Cyril of Alexandria: Part III," *Franciscan Studies* 7, no. 4 (1947): 399–414; "The Incarnation—A Supreme Exaltation for Christ According to St. John Damascene," *Franciscan Studies* 8, no. 3 (1948): 237–49; "Christ Jesus, Center and Final Scope of All Creation According to St. Maximus Confessor," *Franciscan Studies* 9, no. 1 (1949): 50–62; and "Christ the Exemplar and Final Scope of All Creation According to Anastasios of Sinai," *Franciscan Studies* 9, no. 2 (1949): 156–64.

Further studies include Aloysius Spindeler, *Cur Verbum caro factum? Das Motiv der Menschwerdung und das Verhältnis der Erlösung zur Menschwerdung Gottes in den christologischen Glaubenskämpfen des vierten und fünften christlichen Jahrhunderts*, Forschungen zur christlichen Literatur- und Dogmengeschichte, 18.2 (Paderborn: Verlag Ferdinand Schöningh, 1938), 39–162; Martin Jugie, *Theologia Dogmatica Christianorum orientalium*, 5 vols. (Paris: Letouzey, 1926–1935); Hieronymus Pinna, *De praedestinatione Chisti et Deiparae secundum Theophanem Nicaenum* (Calari: Società Editoriale Italiana, 1948); Mauricius Gordillo, *Mariologia orientalis* (Roma: Pontificium Institutum Orientalium Studiorum, 1954); Gabriele Giamberardini, "Due tesi scotiste nella tradizione copta: Il primato assoluto di Cristo e l'Immacolata Concezione di Maria," in *De doctrina Ioannis Duns Scoti: Acta Congressus Scotistici Internationalis Oxonii et Edimburgi 11–17 Sept. 1966 celebrati*, Studia Scholastico-Scotistica 3 (Rome: Ercolano, 1968), 317–84; and Giamberardini, "La praedestinazione assoluta di Cristo nella cultura orientale prescolastica e in Giovanni Scoto," *Antonianum* 59 (1979): 596–621.

11. Bonnefoy, "La question hypothétique," 331.

uphold divine immutability. Thus, he argues that if God now saves us through Christ, he must always have planned to save us through Christ. Rupert's fear is that if the Incarnation would not have occurred absent sin, then this implies that God has had to think up a "new plan" (*novum consilium*).[12] Rupert's conviction that the God-man always featured in God's design for history leads him, in turn, to emphasize Christ as the reason why God created everything else.[13]

Robert Grosseteste (ca. 1168–1253) also poses the inquiry in hypothetical form, arguing that there is good reason to think Christ would have come apart from sin.[14] Robert's reasoning centers primarily on the nature of God as the supreme good, who would thus communicate himself to humanity in the supreme way. Robert finds it unfitting that God's greatest expression of love should hinge on human evil. He also worries about the identity of the Church, whose head is Christ, with sacraments such as matrimony and the Eucharist. It does not seem right that these would only exist because of sin. In fact, the universe itself would be incomplete without the God-man, who unites in himself every grade of being (from divinity down to matter) and who brings the divine work full circle by connecting man, the last-created, to the first principle.[15]

By the thirteenth century, Henry of Ghent (ca. 1217–93) cites the question of whether the Incarnation would have occurred absent sin as a contemporary theological dispute.[16] While Honorius, Rupert, and

---

12. *In Iohannis Evangelium*, I (CCCM 9:13.155–66).

13. *De gloria et honore*, XIII (CCCM 29:410.491); and *De glorificatione Trinitatis et processione Spiritus sancti*, III, chap. 20 (PL 169:72–73).

14. *De cessatione legalium*, III, chap. 1, no. 2 (Auctores Britannici medii aevi, 7:119.12–18); and the sermon *Exiit edictum*, 1, in Dominic J. Unger, "Robert Grosseteste Bishop of Lincoln (1235–1253) on the Reasons for the Incarnation," *Franciscan Studies* 16, no. 1/2 (1956): 18. It is not clear whether Robert was aware of Rupert's work. See James McEvoy, *Robert Grosseteste*, Great Medieval Thinkers (Oxford: Oxford University Press, 2000), xi. Unger believes that Robert built on the work of Rupert and possibly Honorius of Autun. Unger, "Grosseteste on the Reasons for the Incarnation," 26.

15. *De cessatione legalium*, III, chap. 1, nos. 10–30 (Auctores Britannici, 7:123–33); and *Exiit edictum*, 8–16 (ed. Unger, 20–23).

16. "[C]um moderno tempore dubium sit et hucusque dubium fuerit apud doctores theologiae, an scilicet Christus fuisset incarnatus si Adam non peccasset, quibusdam asserentibus quod sic, aliis vero asserentibus contrarium." *Tractatus super facto*

Robert addressed this in the form of a hypothetical inquiry, other theologians framed the issue differently.

Alexander of Hales, OFM (ca. 1185–1245), for instance, asks whether the Incarnation would still have been fitting apart from humanity's need for redemption.[17] His reply that a nonredemptive Incarnation would still be fitting relies especially on the principle that goodness is diffusive of itself and on a view of completion steeped in numerology.[18]

St. Bonaventure, OFM (1221–74), in turn, asks about the Incarnation's "chief reason" (*ratio praecipua*). He goes through many arguments, including those put forward by the authors mentioned above, and ultimately concludes that the opinion holding that human redemption was the chief reason for Christ's coming appeals more to the "piety of faith," despite the fact that the opposite opinion resonates more with the judgment of reason.[19] Even so, Bonaventure's preference for the opinion that human redemption was the chief reason for the Incarna-

---

praelatorum et fratrum (*Quodlibet XII, quaestio 31*), II, resp. 4 (ed. Hödl and M. Haverals, 17:138.12–15).

17. *Summa fratris*, III, inquisitio unica *de Verbo incarnato*, tract. 1, q. 2, tit. 2 (Quaracchi ed., 4:41.23); and *Quaestio disputata XV*, disp. 2, memb. 4, nos. 45–49 (Bibliotheca Franciscana scholastica medii aevi, 19:207–209). Cf. *Glossa in tertium librum Sententiarum secundum codicem L*, dist. 2, no. 13, a. 1 (Bibliotheca Franciscana scholastica medii aevi, 14:26). Besides inspiring the *Summa fratris*, Alexander may also have overseen the editing of this section. See Christopher M. Cullen, "Alexander of Hales," in Jorge J. E. Gracia and Timothy B. Noone, eds., *A Companion to Philosophy in the Middle Ages*, Blackwell Companions to Philosophy (Oxford: Blackwell, 2003), 105.

18. For example, it is a perfection to have more than one person of a single nature (the Trinity), so it is also a perfection to have a single person of more than one nature. Or, it is a perfection to have three persons of one substance (the Trinity) and three persons of three individual substances (such as three human beings), and so it is also a perfection to have one person of three substances (body, soul, and divinity in Christ). Robert also argues (with Rupert) that human beatitude requires seeing God with the eyes of the body in addition to the beatific vision, but this requires that God become visible.

19. *In III Sent.*, dist. 1, a. 2, q. 2, co. (Quaracchi ed., 3:24). He also remarks that the opinion holding that human redemption was not the Incarnation's chief reason but only the reason for its passible mode seems more sophisticated (*subtilis*). *In III Sent.*, dist. 1, a. 2, q. 2, co. (Quaracchi ed., 3:25). He is careful to qualify his own opinion as probable, not certain, especially since both views are Catholic and foster devotion.

tion does not lessen his emphasis on Christ's primacy as the one who both redeems creation and perfects it.[20]

St. Albert the Great, OP (ca. 1200–1280), also describes his opinion not as an assertion but as resonating more with the piety of faith when he argues that even if man had not sinned, God would still incite humanity to great love through the Incarnation.[21] Albert's main emphasis is on the uncertainty of this matter.[22] Further, Albert is more careful than some others we have already considered, such as Robert Grosseteste, to state that the Incarnation does not fulfill a natural human capacity but is a perfecting gift over and above this. This also allows Albert to express clearly that God is not bound to do the best possible in his works *ad extra*.

Thomas Aquinas addresses the hypothetical inquiry primarily in three places.[23] Like Bonaventure and Albert, he states theology's basic inability to give a certain answer to this question. This is because acts that depend on God's free will alone are made known to us only by being revealed. In this, like his teacher Albert, he stresses God's freedom. Unlike Albert, Aquinas prefers the opinion that the Word would not have become flesh apart from sin. He bases this on the same principle: What Scripture and the saints tell us overwhelmingly is that the Incarnation occurred as a response to sin. Therefore, this opinion is more probable, even though the alternative also enjoys probability.[24]

20. See especially *Breviloquium*, IV, chap. 1 (Quaracchi ed., 5:241); *Collationes in hexaemeron: Redactio B*, III, no. 10 (Quaracchi ed., 5:345); and *De reductione artium ad theologiam*, no. 20 (Quaracchi ed., 5:324). See also Benson, "Christology of the *Breviloquium*," in Jay M. Hammond, Wayne Hellmann, and Jared Goff, eds., *A Companion to Bonaventure*, Brill's Companions to the Christian Tradition 48 (Leiden: Brill, 2014), 261–65.

21. *In III Sent.*, dist. 20, B, a. 4 (ed. Borgnet, 28:361).

22. Donald Goergen, "Albert the Great and Thomas Aquinas on the Motive of the Incarnation," *The Thomist* 44, no. 4 (1980): 527.

23. *In III Sent.*, dist. 1, q. 1, a. 3 (ed. Moos, 3:19–24); *Super I Tim.*, chap. 1, lect. 4 (ed. Cai, 2:219.40); and *ST* III, q. 1, a. 3 (Leonine ed., 11:13–14). He also addresses it in passing in *De veritate*, q. 29, a. 4, ad 5 (Leonine ed., 22:860.5).

24. As Goergen observes, Aquinas holds his opinion with growing firmness over the course of his career. See "Albert the Great and Thomas Aquinas on the Motive of the Incarnation," 530–36.

Subsequent Thomists point—none more fiercely than the Salmanticenses—to Aquinas's principle that revelation is needed for knowledge of God's free acts as their foundation.[25] As we will see, Scotism generally, though not exclusively, challenges Thomism on grounds of logical coherence, while Thomism retorts on grounds of authority. For this reason, as the discussion advances, Thomists tend to embrace the Scotistic logical apparatus, and Scotists tend to cite more and more of the Bible and the Fathers. John of St. Thomas, OP (1589–1644), is a prime example of the former tendency, and Bonaventura Belluto, OFM Conv. (1600–1676), exemplifies the latter.[26]

In the generation following Aquinas, we come to John Duns Scotus, OFM (ca. 1266–1308), destined to be regarded as his great opponent in the present dispute. Scotus frames the discussion in terms of Christ's predestination, and specifically its place within God's plan.[27] Because predestination to glory logically precedes foreknowledge of human acts, *a fortiori* does the predestination of Christ's soul to such great glory as arises from its personal union with the Word logically come before God's taking human actions into account. But this means that God predestines Christ prior to considering Adam's sin. If this is the case, then Christ's predestination cannot depend on the fact of that sin, and thus it is more likely that God wills Christ absolutely, not conditionally.

Further, because God wills in an orderly way (*ordinate volens*), he wills what is closer to the end prior to what is more removed from it.

---

25. Pablo de la Concepción, OCD (d. 1734), a great student of the Salmanticenses' work, remarks of this principle as it relates to the motive of the Incarnation: "[H]aec ratio est adeo solida, ut quamvis millies materiam hanc consideres, non poteris aliam fortiorem, immo nec absolute aliam invenire, pro hac probabilissima sententia." *Tractatus theologici*, tract. 16, disp. 2, dub. 1, § 2, no. 4 (ed. Haeredes Pauli Monti, 4:199). In the present disputation, the Salmanticenses accuse their opponents of "divination" several times.

26. See John of St. Thomas, *Cursus theologicus III*, q. 1, disp. 3, a. 1 (ed. Vivès, 8:90–96); and Belluto, *Disputationes de Incarnatione dominica*, disp. 7, q. 2, nos. 41–48 (ed. Rossus, 108–10).

27. See especially *Lectura III*, dist. 7, q. 3, nos. 74–78 (Vatican ed., 20:213–15); dist. 19, q. 1, no. 21 (Vatican ed., 21:32–33); *Ordinatio III*, dist. 7, q. 3, nos. 55–72 (Vatican ed., 9:284–91); and *Reportatio Parisiensis III-A*, dist. 7, q. 4 (ed. Vivès, 23:301–304).

Hence, if the end is his own glorification, then he wills the existence of that soul that will participate in the divine goodness most fully and that will thus give him greatest glory prior to everything else. After all, since the will is inclined to the good, it is unreasonable for one to intend the greater good (such as Christ) only for the sake of the lesser good (such as human redemption).

Scotus does not originate the typically Franciscan emphasis on Christ's absolute primacy and unconditional predestination, but he does put forward its most robust arguments. He emphasizes logical order, which he clarifies by identifying conceptual stages or moments (*signa* or *instantia rationis*) in God's decision-making process: first, God knows himself under the aspect of the supreme good; second, he knows all creatures; third, he predestines or fails to predestine them; fourth, he foresees that some of his creatures will fall in Adam; fifth, he preordains or foresees the remedy for the Fall through Christ's suffering and death.[28] Christ is the first of the predestined and thus included in the third stage, prior to consideration of sin. Given the divine simplicity and immutability, these *signa rationis* involve no temporal succession but instead reflect logical priority and posteriority among the objects of God's will.

Following Scotus, theologians overwhelmingly apply this instrument to the present discussion. Like the hypothetical form of inquiry, the use of *signa rationis* can polarize the discussion by forcing everything into a linear sequence: *Either* God wills Christ's coming prior to taking human sin into account, *or else* he wills it after taking human sin into account.[29] We will see below that later theologians, particularly

---

28. *In III Sententiarum*, dist. 19, q. 1, no. 6 (ed. Vivès, 14:714). Other schemata can be found in *Lectura III*, dist. 19, q. 1, no. 21 (Vatican ed., 21:32–33); *Reportatio Parisiensis III-A*, dist. 7, q. 4, no. 5 (ed. Vivès, 23:303); and *In III Sententiarum*, dist. 32, q. 1, no. 6 (ed. Vivès, 15:432–33).

29. Theologians often merged the hypothetical inquiry and the question of Christ's logical place within God's plan, as Scotus himself indicates. Francisco Suárez, for example, identifies the following inquiries as functionally equivalent: "Was the work of the Incarnation first intended by God *per se* in the first act whereby he willed to communicate himself *ad extra*, or was it only ordained on the occasion taken from the foreseen fall of human nature?"; "Was Christ, the God-man, pre-ordained and pre-elected and loved before every creature?"; "Was he the first of all predestined men

Luis de Molina, SJ (1535–1600), and those influenced by him, including the Salmanticenses, will try to minimize the number of *signa rationis*, in part to avoid this polarization.

Thomists typically pushed back against Scotus's claim that God predestined Christ prior to consideration of human sin by pointing out that Scotus implicitly distinguishes the *substance* of the Incarnation (the fact of the hypostatic union) from its *modality* (is the God-man passible or impassible?). If God's will touches on these in separate conceptual moments, then there must be two decrees, the former inefficacious and the latter efficacious. However, only the single efficacious decree of Christ is at issue. Therefore, since Christ did, in fact, come in passible flesh, he must have come as a response to sin.

Defenders of Scotus rejected the Thomistic mapping of Scotus's conceptual stages rigidly onto divine decrees. For instance, Scotus's early disciple, Peter of Aquila, OFM (d. 1361), who was nicknamed the "little Scotus" (*Scotellus*), embraces the distinction between the substance of the Incarnation and its redemptive end: If humanity had not sinned, this would itself be due to Christ's coming as "a physician who preserves from sickness."[30] Later, we find Scotists such as Juan de Rada, OFM Obs. (ca. 1545–1608), Bartolomeo Mastri, OFM Conv. (1602–73), and Claude Frassen, OFM (1620–1711), teaching that Christ's initial predestination was to the assumption of human flesh, which is intrinsically passible, but that this passibility was not yet determined by extrinsic factors such as the proximate mortality resulting from the Fall or the immortality resulting from the Resurrection.[31] Juan de Campoverde, SJ

---

and angels?"; "Was Christ's predestination before or after original sin was foreseen?" *Disputationes in Tertiam partem*, disp. 5, sect. 2, no. 1 (ed. Vivès, 17:216).

30. "[M]edicus praeservans ab infirmitate." *Quaestiones in quatuor Sententiarum libros*, III, dist. 2, q. 1, ad 3 (ed. Zenarius), 328.

31. Rada, *Controversiae theologicae III*, contr. 5, a. 3, concl. 3 (ed. Ioannes Crithius, 3:162–63); Mastri, *Disputationes theologicae in tertium librum Sententiarum*, disp. 4, q. 1, a. 5, no. 72 (ed. Balleonius, 219); and Frassen, *Scotus academicus*, vol. 7, *De divini Verbi Incarnatione*, tract. 1, disp. 1, a. 3, sect. 3, q. 1 (ed. Salustiana, 7:276). On Frassen's importance, see Carol, *Why Jesus Christ?*, 321; and Michel, "Incarnation," col. 1495. For an overview of Scotistic treatments of Christ's passibility, see Trent Pomplun, "The Immaculate World: Predestination and Possibility in Contemporary Scotism," *Modern Theology* 30, no. 4 (2014): 525–51.

(1658–1737), makes a similar distinction between passibility *radicaliter* and passibility *formaliter*.³² The former is the liability to suffering rooted in human nature itself unless prevented by a special gift of God; the latter is the state of actually lacking such a gift. Juan Sendín Calderón, OFM (d. 1667), distinguishes between remote and proximate passibility to make the same point.³³

All such Scotistic distinctions aim to show that although God's effective decree extends to the full, concrete modality of the Incarnation, we can still distinguish a prior conceptual stage within that decree for the Incarnation's substance without, at that point, asserting whether its mode would entail actual suffering. The extrinsic factor of human sin is what requires the Incarnation's passible mode. After all, the Incarnation is *per se* good and worthy of love, whereas Christ's suffering is lovable not *per se* but only as a means to redemption. Further, Rada points out that the Incarnation of itself logically tends to take on an impassible mode because of the grace and glory overflowing from the human soul of the Word made flesh. Only the extrinsic factor of human sin has prevented this.³⁴ Thus, "just as Christ's immortality is the exemplar of our immortality, so our mortality can be called the exemplar of Christ's mortality."³⁵

Thomists, in turn, such as Vincenzo Gotti, OP (1664–1742), as well as the Salmanticenses, point out that passibility is not the only sticking point when applying the substance-modality distinction. A similar problem occurs, for example, if we ask why the Son would assume human rather than angelic nature or why the Son rather than the Father or the Holy Spirit would become flesh.³⁶

---

32. *Tractatus de Incarnatione Verbi divini*, disp. 9, chap. 1, no. 2 (ed. Garcia Briones, 2:133).

33. *Opus posthumum*, tract. 6, contr. 1, sect. 2, no. 8 (ed. Bernique, 357–58).

34. Rada, *Controversiae theologicae III*, contr. 5, a. 3, concl. 3 (ed. Ioannes Crithius, 3:162–63).

35. "[S]icut immortalitas Christi est exemplar nostrae immortalitatis: ita mortalitas nostra potest dici exemplar mortalitatis Christi." Rada, *Controversiae theologicae III*, contr. 5, a. 3, concl. 2 (ed. Ioannes Crithius, 3:162).

36. Gotti's remark "[N]e fiat recursus ad carnem passibilem, vel impassibilem, arguo sic" evidences how commonplace the substance-modality argument and counterarguments had become. Gotti, *Theologia scholastica-dogmatica … tomus I in Tertiam partem*, q. 4, dub. 4, § 2, no. 16 (ed. Bononiensis, 12:96).

At this point, we may note that after the early fourteenth century, theologians who use the hypothetical inquiry begin to qualify it as "by virtue of the present decree," meaning in the actual order of reality effectively ordained by God. Those who prefer and defend the hypothetical form explain that it is not a question about entirely unreal circumstances (which would be "another decree") but instead a look into whether God's actual plan has included sin as a *sine qua non* condition for the Incarnation.[37] Further, some theologians have expressed displeasure with the word 'motive' in the present discussion, since it normally means something determining and moving the will, which cannot apply in God's case.[38] The Salmanticenses and others who use 'motive' in this discussion, however, understand it to apply to God only analogously and with reference to the proximate end on the part of his work *ad extra*, not to the ultimate end of all God's works, which is only God himself and his glorification. Hence, they take 'motive' to mean essentially the *reason* or *rationale* for the Incarnation within God's plan.[39]

Returning to an earlier stage in the discussion, we find the "Prince of Thomists," Jean Capréolus, OP (ca. 1380–1444), arguing that Scotus's *ordinate volens* principle is true if it means that God establishes the utmost order among the objects of his will, but that it does not mean that there is real order of priority and posteriority among divine acts or within the same act as extending to successive objects.[40] With the caveat that *signa rationis*, too, must be understood as a purely concep-

---

37. On the framing of this question, see the debate between Reginald Garrigou-Lagrange, OP (1877–1964), and Gabriele M. Roschini, OSM (1900–1977). Garrigou-Lagrange, "De motivo Incarnationis: Examen recentium objectionum contra doctrinam S. Thomae III^a, q. 1, a. 3," in *Acta Pont. Academiae Romanae S. Thomae Aquinatis et Religionis Catholicae*, Nova series 10 (Rome: Academia Romana S. Thomae Aquinatis, 1945), 8–10, 25–44.

38. See Bonnefoy's response to Garrigou-Lagrange in "De motivo Incarnationis," 24–30.

39. Gesualdo Maria Rocca and Gabriele Maria Roschini, *De ratione primaria existentiae Christi et Deiparae: Novum tentamen conciliationis sententiae Thomisticae cum sententia Scotistica circa sic dictum motivum incarnationis* (Rome: Officium Libri Catholici, 1945), 23–24; and Garrigou-Lagrange, "De motivo Incarnationis," 34–35.

40. *Defensiones theologicae divi Thomae in III Sententiarum*, dist. 1, q. 1, a. 3, ad 2 (ed. Paban and Pègues, 5:6).

tual distinction,[41] Capréolus identifies the following stages: first, God wills the manifestation of his goodness in the production of a complete universe; second, he wills there to be blessed angels and human beings; third, he foresees the fall of some of those he had predestined; fourth, he decrees their reparation through the Son's Incarnation; fifth, he wills Christ's soul to have preeminence in grace and glory and that the grace, blessedness, and redemption of others should be ordered to the glory of Christ's soul.[42]

Capréolus holds that the total end of the Incarnation consists of various components, including the redemption of the elect (proximate end) and the perfection of the universe (remote end).[43] He finds nothing wrong with the greater good's being occasioned by the less or ordered to it as to a proximate or partial end. Although he does not use these terms, Capréolus also distinguishes between two kinds of final cause, the end *for-the-sake-of-which* (*finis cuius gratia*) and the end *to-which* (*finis cui*).[44] Like strict Thomists following him, he holds that human redemption is the end *for-the-sake-of-which*, that which the agent is trying to acquire in acting, while Christ is the end *to-which* because glory redounds to him from his redemptive work.[45] This means that Christ's predestination and ours "mutually precede each other."[46] Still, Capréolus only expressly distinguishes these two kinds of final

41. "Si vero dicat prioritatem rationis, non ex parte rationabilis, sed ex parte nostri intellectus ratiocinantis, non est inconveniens." *Defensiones theologicae divi Thomae in III Sententiarum*, dist. 1, q. 1, a. 3, ad 2 (ed. Paban and Pègues, 5:7).

42. *Defensiones theologicae divi Thomae in III Sententiarum*, dist. 1, q. 1, a. 3, ad 2 (ed. Paban and Pègues, 5:7).

43. *Defensiones theologicae divi Thomae in III Sententiarum*, dist. 1, q. 1, a. 3, ad 3 (ed. Paban and Pègues, 5:7).

44. "Nam dupliciter aliquid potest dici finis alicujus, puta A esse finis ipsius B. Primo modo, quia B ordinatur ad acquisitionem vel conservationem ipsius A.... Secundo modo, A potest dici finis B, quia ex ipso B provenit aliqua utilitas vel aliquod bonum ipsi A, vel ipsum A tendit in ipsum B sicut in illud cujus similitudinem et participationem desiderat." *Defensiones theologicae divi Thomae in III Sententiarum*, dist. 1, q. 1, a. 3, ad 3 (ed. Paban and Pègues, 5:7).

45. *Defensiones theologicae divi Thomae in III Sententiarum*, dist. 1, q. 1, a. 3, ad 3 (ed. Paban and Pègues, 5:7).

46. "[S]ua praedestinatio et nostra invicem se praecedunt." *Defensiones theologicae divi Thomae in III Sententiarum*, dist. 1, q. 1, a. 3, ad 3 (ed. Paban and Pègues, 5:7).

cause from the perspective of the order of execution, not the order of God's intention.[47]

After the fourteenth century, the number and length of writings on the motive of the Incarnation increased greatly. Part of this is due to the Franciscans' allegiance to Scotus and the Dominicans' allegiance to Aquinas. The related question of Mary's Immaculate Conception, too, motivated theologians to take sides. In general, those who held that Mary was totally free from any debt of contracting sin from Adam tended to be strictly Scotistic, while those who held that she did have such a debt, whether proximate or remote, tended to hold also that the Incarnation was contingent on sin.[48] Growing magisterial support of the Immaculate Conception as well as the weight of Scotistic argumentation induced many Thomists to adopt a "mitigated" position.[49]

The Thomistic commentator, Tommaso de Vio Cajetan, OP (1469–1534), was the first to distinguish final and material causal perspectives in the present discussion. He grants the primacy of Christ in the genus of final cause but insists on the priority of human sin in the genus of material cause.[50] Further, Cajetan argues, we must not lose sight of the distinct ontological orders. The order of nature is logically prior to the order of grace, and both of these precede the hypostatic order. Since we have the power to sin from our nature, sin occurs at the level of the natural order, though it is also opposed to the gratuitous order. Therefore, says Cajetan, God's providential planning extends first to nature, then to grace, then to the hypostatic order. In other words, it extends first to the creation of nature, then to the elevation of rational creatures, then

---

47. "[P]raedestinatio Christi uno modo potest dici finis nostrae praedestinationis ex parte effectus temporalis." *Defensiones theologicae divi Thomae in III Sententiarum*, dist. 1, q. 1, a. 3, ad 3 (ed. Paban and Pègues, 5:7).

48. Pomplun, "Baroque Theologies of Christ and Mary," 114–15. For an overview of authors and positions, see Juniper B. Carol, *A History of the Controversy over the "debitum peccati,"* Franciscan Institute Publications, Theology Series 9 (St. Bonaventure, N.Y.: Franciscan Institute, 1978).

49. A "mitigated" Thomistic position in this context means one holding that Christ would (more probably) not have become incarnate by virtue of the present decree if Adam had not sinned while also holding that Christ himself is, in some way, primary in God's intention.

50. Commentary on *ST* III, q. 1, a. 3 (Leonine ed., 11:15–16).

to the reparation of fallen humanity through Christ. In this way, Aquinas's position that Christ's predestination takes into account Adam's sin is quite correct, and the alternative is a "Scotistic imagining."[51]

Cajetan also rejects what he sees as unwarranted assumptions hidden in Scotus's *ordinate volens* principle. For Scotus's principle to hold, God would have to be logically compelled to will what is *per se* more "willable" more than what is less willable and even to will it prior to what is less willable. But, says Cajetan, just because Christ is preeminent in dignity does not mean that God has to will him prior to everything else. Cajetan's underlying fear is that the Scotistic approach starts with a preconceived logical framework and concludes to how God must actually have acted in the world instead of relying on scriptural evidence.[52]

Cajetan enjoyed great influence in this discussion. For example, when Juan de Rada says that he is about to address "the opinion of St. Thomas," he moves immediately to Cajetan.[53] Rada himself points out serious flaws in how Cajetan maps the three ontological orders onto divine decrees. Some of Cajetan's problems, according to Rada, are that he confuses the order of intention and the order of execution and that he conflates God's knowledge of what is possible with his knowledge of what is actual. Finally, it is simply not the case that everything in the order of grace presupposes everything in the order of nature. Only a causal connection allows us to establish a conceptual order of before and after.

Rada does believe, however, that he has to clarify Scotus's *ordinate volens* principle.[54] It always holds, he says, if 'closer to the end' means what is more immediately joined to the end in the causal process of attaining it, but it does not necessarily hold if 'closer to the end' only means what resembles the end more. However, Rada adds, in the case

51. Commentary on *ST* III, q. 1, a. 3, no. 6 (Leonine ed., 11:15).

52. "Et hoc est in quo deficiunt argumenta Scotica: quia ex magis et prius causalitate, et prius natura secundum consequentiam volito de possibili a Deo, infert volitum esse a Deo de facto." Commentary on *ST* III, q. 1, a. 3, no. 9 (Leonine ed., 11:16).

53. "Pro intelligentia opinionis Sancti Thomae, observa primo, ex Caietano ... quod ordo rerum est triplex." *Controversiae theologicae III*, contr. 5, a. 3, obs. 1 (ed. Ioannes Crithius, 3:152).

54. *Controversiae theologicae III*, contr. 5, a. 3, obs. 3 (ed. Ioannes Crithius, 3:158).

in question, the end is the manifestation of God's glory, so the two coincide. Claude Frassen interprets the *ordinate volens* principle in the same way: Christ, being most noble and lovable, manifests God's glory better than anything else; therefore, God should decree Christ prior to the permission of sin.[55]

When Filippo Fabri, OFM Conv. (1564–1630), responds to Cajetan, he emphasizes that Scotus is not speaking about possible objects of God's will but about what God actually wills.[56] The whole point of *ordinate volens*, he says, is that when a free agent wills several things, if the agent's will is rightly ordered, it wills more what is *per se* more willable. For example, only a disordered will would prioritize the body over the soul. Hence, when Scotus analyzes the actual objects of God's will, including the God-man, human redemption through him, and all God's other works of nature and grace, Scotus is right to conclude that God's most orderly will extends to Christ in himself more than and so prior to everything else.

Cajetan's importance is evidenced not only by the replies of nearly all subsequent theologians but also by the fact that his attention to different causal perspectives becomes a commonplace. The Salmanticenses' own attempt to harmonize aspects of the Scotistic and Thomistic positions relies on this distinction along with the axiom that causes can enjoy reciprocal and relative priority in different genera.

Luis de Molina addresses the present discussion in the context of his treatment of predestination, not Christology proper.[57] He first outlines Scotus's conceptual stages, noting that more could be added if we were to be totally thorough.[58] Scotus's *ordinate volens* principle applies to Christ's predestination as it does to all decrees of predestination: God

---

55. Frassen, *Scotus academicus*, vol. 7, *De divini Verbi Incarnatione*, tract. 1, disp. 1, a. 3, sect. 3, q. 1 (ed. Salustiana, 7:269).

56. Fabri, *Disputationes theologicae in tertium librum Sententiarum*, dist. 7, q. 3, disp. 20, no. 22 (ed. Ginamus, 108).

57. Molina, *Commentaria in Primam divi Thomae partem*, q. 23, aa. 4–5, disp. 1, memb. 7–8 (ed. Prost, 1:308–15).

58. When he indicates that Scotus has Christ as predestined at a stage prior to God's foreseeing fallen humanity, Molina remarks that Scotus "believes he would have been going to exist, even if Adam had not sinned." *Commentaria in Primam divi Thomae partem*, q. 23, aa. 4–5, disp. 1, memb. 7 (ed. Prost, 1:308).

wills glorification (the end) prior to the means (merit) and thus prior to consideration of human acts. In opposition, Molina relates St. Augustine, whom he takes to teach in many places that God foreknew sin prior to his effective choice to send Christ or to free anyone from sin through Christ. After describing a few other opinions, including Cajetan's, Molina gives his own solution. This consists in affirming that God first knew all future contingents (of whatever ontological order) as merely possible, whether through knowledge of simple intelligence or through middle knowledge.[59] Then, by a single decree, God freely willed the entire order of affairs as he pleased.

In this respect, Molina's solution is a true predecessor of the Salmanticenses', which also posits a single decree in God distinguishing the purely possible from the actual. In fact, Molina finds the multiplication of conceptual stages unpalatable no less than the Salmanticenses.[60] By a single act, says Molina, God freely wills not just the end but all of the determinate means, conditions, and circumstances associated with it. Thus, when God wills the end as to be attained through determinate means, Scotus's *ordinate volens* principle does not apply because God does not will the end *before* the means but altogether simultaneously with the means and other circumstances.

Still, the Salmanticenses differ from Molina not only in the rejection of middle knowledge but also in the fact that they analyze the single divine decree internally from different causal perspectives (final cause *for-the-sake-of-which*, final cause *to-which*, material cause) and assign relative priority from each perspective.[61] The fact that the Salmanticenses distinguish causal perspectives gives them—unlike Molina—a way to affirm not only that God willed Christ as preeminent in dignity but also that, from the most important causal perspective,

59. *Commentaria in Primam divi Thomae partem*, q. 23, aa. 4–5, disp. 1, memb. 7 (ed. Prost, 1:310–11).

60. "[S]ane exterminanda omnino videntur instantia Scoti, & aliorum ... quae certe instantia adeo obscuram reddunt quaestionem hanc, ut vix, aut ne vix quidem, intelligi queat." *Commentaria in Primam divi Thomae partem*, q. 23, aa. 4–5, disp. 1, memb. 7 (ed. Prost, 1:311).

61. Thus, the Salmanticenses should not be reckoned simply as Molinists on this issue, despite the fact that they also propose a single-decree theory. Cf. Carol, *Why Jesus Christ?*, 488–89.

God willed him *first* while, from another perspective, he permitted sin *first*.[62] While Molina's single-decree theory flattens everything into a complex object willed by God all at once, with all the circumstances and means being "parts" of the total end, the Salmanticenses can still speak of priority and posteriority within the single decree.

The difficulty of eradicating *signa rationis* and Molina's own seeming inability to avoid speaking of priority and posteriority in God was pointed out to him when his work was being reviewed for publication.[63] In fact, Molina eventually had to add an appendix to his treatment arguing that he only really rejects conceptual stages when one presupposes or entails the other in some way.[64] The Salmanticenses offer greater clarity by distinguishing between conceptual priority and stages *a-quo* (reciprocal entailment) and conceptual priority and stages *in-quo* (non-reciprocal entailment).

Following Molina, we come to another great Jesuit theologian, Francisco Suárez, SJ (1548–1617). Suárez takes great pains to address how God's will can establish an extrinsic connection between an end and its means (since the Incarnation and redemption are not connected by intrinsic necessity). What is this extrinsic connection exactly? After detailed analysis, he ends up saying that we cannot grasp it fully, but the connection between a chosen end and the freely chosen means leading to it is nothing other than God's own decision about how he himself will apply his own causal power in the future.[65] This is important because Suárez is convinced that Thomists and Scotists have been talking past one another and that both positions are true at their core, if only

---

62. Molina does not apply the distinction of causal perspectives, but he does speak of the world's being for Christ, and Christ's simultaneously being for fallen humanity. *Commentaria in Primam divi Thomae partem*, q. 23, aa. 4–5, disp. 1, memb. 7 (ed. Prost, 1:313).

63. As related in *Ludovici Molina liberi arbitrii cum gratiae donis, divina praescientia, providentia, praedestinatione et reprobatione concordia*, ed. Johann Rabeneck, Societatis Iesu selcti scriptores, (Oña: Collegium maximum S. I., 1953), 47*.

64. *Commentaria in Primam divi Thomae partem*, q. 23, aa. 4–5, disp. 1, memb. 8 (ed. Prost, 1:314–15).

65. "[U]num est ex divinis mysteriis quod humana ratione nec comprehendi, nec declarari posse, existimo." *Disputationes in Tertiam partem*, q. 1, a. 4, disp. 5, sect. 1, no. 22 (ed. Vivès, 17:207).

we were careful enough in our conceptual parsing of the divine acts.

Thus, he proposes a theory (a *tertia via*) affirming what each affirms but in a nonexclusive way. The first component of this theory is that God—or any free agent according to Suárez—can act out of two total and adequate motives simultaneously.[66] In this, he acknowledges that he differs from all the other opinions, which presume there can be only one total, adequate motive. Then, Suárez factors in middle knowledge (which he prefers to call "conditioned knowledge"), which is God's knowledge, prior to the free determination of his will, of the truth value of conditional propositions. Thus, God willed the Incarnation primarily out of the mystery's sheer excellence and willed that it would be accomplished in the best way. However, foreseeing through middle knowledge that Adam would sin in the given circumstances in which God would freely create him, a redemptive Incarnation would be the best way. God then effectively willed the Incarnation both totally because of its own goodness and also totally for human redemption.[67]

As for the hypothetical inquiry, Suárez explains that the expression "if Adam had not sinned" can be understood in two senses.[68] Either it means that in the circumstances in which Adam really existed, God would have foreseen (by conditioned knowledge) that Adam was not

---

66. *Disputationes in Tertiam partem*, q. 1, a. 4, disp. 5, sect. 4, no. 6 (ed. Vivès, 17:240). By a total, adequate motive, Suárez means one that would by itself motivate the agent to the action. In other words, it is a sufficient motive. Later theologians, including the Salmanticenses in the present disputation, will take this to imply that a total, adequate motive must also be *necessary for that particular action*. Otherwise, the lack of that motive would seem to make no difference to the act, in which case it is no motive at all. The difference in approaches seems to be that Suárez has a more tolerant understanding of what constitutes the same action than do the Salmanticenses (and other critics, such as Vásquez). For Suárez, the action remains the same numerically if a second total, adequate motive is added. For the latter theologians, the prior action numerically would cease, and the agent would begin to act from a new total, adequate motive made up of the previous motive and the added one.

67. By this, Suárez means to avoid what he takes to be the problematic substance-modality distinction of the Scotistic opinion while still upholding that God primarily willed the Incarnation because of its intrinsic goodness and not the extrinsic need of fallen humanity.

68. *Disputationes in Tertiam partem*, q. 1, a. 4, disp. 5, sect. 5, no. 7 (ed. Vivès, 17:255).

going to sin, or else it means that God would not have placed Adam in those circumstances so as to avoid his sinning. In the first sense, Suárez says that Christ would have come if Adam had not sinned, since God's free, effective decree would be identical to the present one in this case, Adam having been created in the exact same situation in which he really was created. In the second sense, however, the decree would be distinct from the present one, since God would have chosen differently than he has chosen. Therefore, the Scotists are right in affirming that Christ would have come if Adam had not sinned (in the first sense), while the Thomists are right in denying it (in the second sense).[69]

Suárez notes an alternative to his approach—essentially that of Pedro de Godoy, OP (d. 1677), and later the Salmanticenses—holding that God predestines Christ precisely as Redeemer from the first. Although he is not persuaded by it, Suárez admits that this approach is probable and defensible.[70] Suárez's concern with this theory is that it seems to require God to will sin as the necessary means for the redemptive Incarnation. For this reason, he prefers his own way of harmonizing the Thomistic and Scotistic theses, in which Adam's sin is foreseen through conditioned knowledge.

Others, such as Gabriel Vásquez, SJ (1549–1604), eschewed any concession to the Scotistic camp that Christ was first in the order of final cause. Rejecting Suárez's attempted harmonization and Cajetan's application of final and material causal perspectives, Vásquez repeats again and again that the Incarnation is for redemption and not redemption for the Incarnation. He confesses himself baffled that other Thomists have so easily given any ground to Scotus on this point.[71]

---

69. *Disputationes in Tertiam partem*, q. 1, a. 4, disp. 5, sect. 5, no. 16 (ed. Vivès, 17:260–61).

70. "[E]st probabilis, et potest facile defendi; mihi tamen nunquam satis persuaderi potuit." *Disputationes in Tertiam partem*, q. 1, a. 4, disp. 5, sect. 3, no. 4 (ed. Vivès, 17:234).

71. "[E]go quidem valde miror, hos Recentiores Theologos argumento Scoti convictos, tam facile ei concessisse, Christum praefinitum fuisse a Deo prius in genere causae finalis ante praevisionem peccati originalis, simulque sententiam sancti Thomae in hoc articulo defendere voluisse." *Disputationes in Tertiam partem*, q. 1, a. 3, disp. 11, chap. 4, no. 50 (ed. Sanchez Crespo, 1:163). "Constituunt igitur praedicti Auctores casum chimericum, & figmentum quoddam inane." *Disputationes in Tertiam*

Pedro de Lorca, Ord. Cist. (1561–1612), holds that Christ's predestination was carried out prior to foreseeing Adam's sin, which he claims "not only Scotus but also St. Thomas asserts along with the larger and sounder portion of theologians."[72] In this way, he accepts Scotus's point that God's decree of predestination must precede his consideration of human acts as actually going to occur. What Aquinas is really saying, according to Lorca, is not that God decrees Christ's predestination after foreseeing sin but instead that God decrees that Christ's predestination should be put into execution in its redemptive mode and not otherwise.

Francesco Silvestri de Ferrara, OP (ca. 1474–1528), rejects Scotus's argument from predestination. God, he says, does not first choose the elect for glory and then subsequently foresee human sin—not even in our manner of understanding.[73] This is why the Bible says that God sent Christ because of human sin. Thus, too, Silvestri feels no need to explain or clarify St. Thomas's statement that predestination presupposes foreknowledge of future things. However, he adds, on the part of the objects of the divine will, we can say that Christ's soul is prior to human salvation formally and finally.[74] Crucially, Silvestri says this is because the salvation of human beings yields greater glory to Christ. In this way, Silvestri includes Christ's soul under the end *to-which* (*finis cui*).[75] In other words, "Christ's Incarnation is ordered to the salvation of the human race, while human salvation, as caused through Christ, is ordered to Christ's glory and exaltation."[76] Silvestri is important be-

---

partem, q. 1, a. 3, disp. 11, chap. 5, no. 56 (ed. Sanchez Crespo, 1:165). "[F]inis *cuius gratia*, incarnationis Dei, fuit redemptio, & salus nostra, non contra, finis autem *cui*, fuit homo lapsus, non Christus, aut Verbum." *Disputationes in Tertiam partem*, q. 1, a. 3, disp. 11, chap. 6, no. 64 (ed. Sanchez Crespo, 1:166).

72. "[N]on solum Scotus, sed etiam S. Thomas asserit, & maior, ac sanior Theologorum pars." Lorca, *Commentarii ac disputationes in Tertiam partem*, q. 1, a. 2, disp. 10, memb. 2, no. 25 (ed. Sanchez de Ezpleta, 73).

73. Commentary on *Summa contra gentiles IV*, chap. 55, no. 18.1–2 (Leonine ed., 15:188).

74. Commentary on *Summa contra gentiles IV*, chap. 55, no. 18.3 (Leonine ed., 15:188).

75. Commentary on *Summa contra gentiles IV*, chap. 55, no. 18.3 (Leonine ed., 15:188).

76. "[D]icimus ipsam Christi Incarnationem esse ordinatam ad humani generis salutem; humanam autem salutem, ut causatam per Christum, esse ad Christi gloriam

cause he applies the notion of final cause *to-which* (*finis cui*) to the Incarnation, although he does not explicitly address final cause *for-the-sake-of-which* (*finis cuius gratia*) or final cause *which* (*finis qui*).[77]

Luis de León, OESA (1527–91), professor at Salamanca and teacher of St. John of the Cross, held a strictly Scotistic view and enjoyed wide influence at the university. In fact, his being tried by the Spanish Inquisition seems to have been motivated in part by concern over his anti-Thomistic views.[78] Luis may be the proximate influence for the Scotistic concessions of Godoy and Jean-Baptiste Gonet, OP (1615–81), as well as those made by Antonio de la Madre de Dios, who authored the section in the Salamanticenses' *Cursus* on Christ's predestination.[79] This, in turn, prepared the way for Juan de la Anunciación's work on the motive of the Incarnation.

Godoy and Gonet develop the distinction of kinds of final cause, seen already in Silvestri, in a different direction. They affirm Christ's primacy as the end *for-the-sake-of-which* while simultaneously connecting his coming with humanity's need of redemption as a *sine qua non* condition.[80] Godoy even says that Christ as Redeemer is the *end-for-the-sake-of-which* (*finis cuius gratia*) of God's permitting sin in the first place. This distinction of subaltern genera of final cause is a major key to the Salmanticenses' theory.[81]

---

et exaltationem ordinatam." Commentary on *Summa contra gentiles IV*, chap. 55, no. 19 (Leonine ed., 15:188).

77. He alludes to the latter by referencing Aquinas's Commentary on the *Sentences*, II, dist. 1, q. 2, a. 3, as well as by his statement that the recipient of a benefit is "one way" of speaking about an end. Commentary on *Summa contra gentiles IV*, chap. 55, no. 18.3 (Leonine ed., 15:188).

78. Enrique del Sagrado Corazón, "Juan Duns Escoto en la doctrina de los Salmanticenses," 510.

79. See especially Enrique del Sagrado Corazón, "Juan Duns Escoto en la doctrina de los Salmanticenses," 510–15. He shows that the Salmanticenses were familiar with Luis's work, and yet they never cite him by name.

80. Godoy, *Disputationes theologicae in Tertiam partem*, q. 1, tract. 1, disp. 8, § 10, no. 228 (ed. Hertz, 1:138); and Gonet, *Clypeus theologiae Thomisticae*, III, tract. 1, disp. 5, a. 1, § 6, nos. 52–53 (ed. Vivés, 5:483).

81. On the influence of Godoy and Gonet on the Salmanticenses, see Robert B. Pfisterer, "El motivo de la Encarnación según los Salmanticenses" (doctoral thesis,

We have already noted that John of St. Thomas takes great care to clarify how conceptual stages are to be applied to God's decree of the Incarnation.[82] In his own solution, John notes that no decree of Christ's coming can be called efficacious unless it includes Christ's office of Redeemer, as he has actually come.[83] Christ is indeed the final cause of God's work *ad extra*, but this includes his whole modality (passibility, the office of Redeemer, etc.). Thus, says John, Vásquez is wrong to insist flatly that redemption is the end of the Incarnation, since we are not speaking of redemption as something separate from the Incarnation but instead of the redemptive Incarnation, or the Incarnation considered with its power to redeem.[84] Since John also rejects the theory that God willed to permit sin for the sake of Christ as Redeemer, he has to hold that God had another decree prior to his effective decree for Christ's coming, one that extended to general providence, included the world's creation and the initial elevation of rational creatures to grace, established a finality for the world distinct from that later attained through Christ, and included permission of the Fall.[85] From the loss of this order, as from a material cause, God brought the greater good of the redemptive Incarnation. The Salmanticenses, in contrast, hold that Christ himself is the end *for-the-sake-of-which* of the very permission of sin as well as of all the divine works *ad extra* of whatever ontological order.

Among Scotists, we should note the great commentator, Franceso Lychetus, OFM (1465–1520). His interest is primarily to show why Scotus is right to hold that God first predestined Christ's assumed nature to a certain degree of glory then chose the personal union of this nature with the Word as the means whereby such glory would be (congru-

---

Universidad de Salamanca, 1950), 225–28; and Otho Merl, *Theologia Salmanticensis: Untersuchung über Entstehung, Lehrrichtung und Quellen des theologischen Kurses der spanischen Karmeliten* (Regensburg: J. Habbel, 1947), 157–58.

82. *Cursus theologicus III*, q. 1, disp. 3, a. 1 (ed. Vivès, 8:90–96).

83. *Cursus theologicus III*, q. 1, disp. 3, a. 2, nos. 17–26 (ed. Vivès, 8:100–102).

84. *Cursus theologicus III*, q. 1, disp. 3, a. 2, no. 60 (ed. Vivès, 8:110); and a. 3, nos. 13–14 (ed. Vivès, 8:114). In this sense, too, John accepts Scotus's *ordinate volens*, so long as we bear in mind that it is not the Incarnation's substance in isolation that is willed first but instead the Incarnation as apt to redeem. *Cursus theologicus III*, q. 1, disp. 3, a. 3, no. 15 (ed. Vivès, 8:114).

85. *Cursus theologicus III*, q. 1, disp. 3, a. 2, nos. 48–63 (ed. Vivès, 8:108–111).

ously) attained. This contrasts with the Thomistic view that Christ's predestination is to natural divine filiation, namely, that it is the Word himself, in his human nature, who is predestined. Like Scotus, then, Lychetus situates any discussion of the hypothetical inquiry within a treatment of Christ's predestination. Because Christ's predestination—like that of any of the elect—is to glory prior to any foreknowledge of human acts, God must have predestined him prior to considering Adam's future sin.

Lychetus's interpretation of the *ordinate volens* principle is straightforward: One who wills in an orderly way wills the end first and then what is closest to it. He does not, as later Scotists will do, distinguish between what is closer in the sense of resemblance and what is closer in the sense of causal influence. In fact, Lychetus uses the example of a king who wishes to elevate someone to his royal court and thus appropriately chooses a close relative.[86] On the one hand, it may be that Lychetus implicitly understands that when the manifestation of God's glory is the end, similitude to God and causal ability to glorify God more coincide. On the other hand, Lychetus states that even Christ's theandric acts are only good because of the divine acceptation, not good of themselves.[87] He shares Scotus's worry about the greater's being occasioned by or ordered to the less: How can a king bestow the inheritance on his son only because of a lowly servant's evil deed?

Alfonso de Mendoza, OESA (d. 1591), using Scotus's own conceptual stages as his framework, argues that God predestined Christ prior to foreseeing sin but that his coming nevertheless depended on sin. He compares this to God's predestining someone to glory as a reward for merits, where the merits are not foreseen prior to the predestination but are logically required as a means for its being carried out.[88] The Salmanticenses follow him in this comparison, which they use several times in the present disputation.

---

86. Commentary on Scotus's *Quaestiones in III Sententiarum*, dist. 7, q. 3, no. 11 (ed. Vivès, 14:356).

87. Commentary on Scotus's *Quaestiones in III Sententiarum*, dist. 7, q. 3, no. 9 (ed. Vivès, 14:354).

88. Mendoza, *Quaestiones quodlibeticae et relectio theologica de Christi regno ac dominio*, q. 1, no. 5 (ed. Martinus, 13–15).

The Salmanticenses do not seem to have had access to the work of Bartolomeo Mastri, whom we mentioned above. Mastri holds the Scotistic line firmly. For him, the decree of Christ's predestination preceded the Fall, and at that stage, he was not yet predestined as Redeemer.[89] Therefore, he would have come even if there had been no sin. Mastri rejects the division by strict Thomists, like Vásquez, of the Incarnation's end into Christ as the end *to-which* and redemption as the end *for-the-sake-of-which*.[90] He also holds that mitigated Thomists, wishing to hold Christ's glory as the chief end of the Incarnation, fall into circular reasoning when they assert that Christ was willed only as a means to the further end of human redemption.[91]

While Roman Catholic theologians were engaged in this discussion, the lapsarian controversy was emerging within Reformed theology.[92] This debate, too, centers on the logical sequence involved in God's effective decree. Given that God *de facto* predestines the elect only through Christ, the logical place of the effects of predestination among God's works *ad extra* has Christological implications.[93] Thus, infralapsarians hold that God's sovereign will first (logically) extends to creation, the permission of the Fall, and then election and reprobation. Supralapsarians, on the other hand, hold that election and reprobation come prior to creation and sin in God's intention. In other words, does God first foresee the ruin of sin and then effectively choose to save the

---

89. Mastri, *Disputationes theologicae in tertium librum Sententiarum*, disp. 4, q. 1, aa. 1–2 (ed. Balleonius, 207–12).

90. Mastri, *Disputationes theologicae in tertium librum Sententiarum*, disp. 4, q. 1, a. 4, no. 58 (ed. Balleonius, 216).

91. Mastri, *Disputationes theologicae in tertium librum Sententiarum*, disp. 4, q. 1, a. 3, no. 47 (ed. Balleonius, 214).

92. For an overview of these positions, see Karl Barth, *Church Dogmatics*, trans. G. W. Bromiley et al., ed. G. W. Bromiley and T. F. Torrance, vol. II.2 (London: T and T Clark, 2004), 127–45; Herman Bavinck, *Reformed Dogmatics*, trans. John Vriend, vol. 2 (Grand Rapids, Mich.: Baker Academic, 2004), 361–405; and Joel R. Beeke, *Debated Issues in Sovereign Predestination: Early Lutheran Predestination, Calvinian Reprobation, and Variations in Genevan Lapsarianism* (Göttingen, Germany: Vandenhoeck & Ruprecht, 2017), 165–222.

93. On this point in Calvin and his followers, see especially Richard A. Muller, *Christ and the Decree: Christology and Predestination in Reformed Theology from Calvin to Perkins* (Grand Rapids, Mich.: Baker Academic, 2008).

elect through Christ out of this *massa damnata* (infralapsarianism)? Or, is merciful election together with just retribution first in God's intention and the choice to create, to permit sin, and to redeem through Christ subsequent, just as the choice of the end is prior to the choice of the means (supralapsarian)?

Strictly speaking, the lapsarian debate arose following the initial major reformers. Thus, John Calvin (1509–64) cannot be classified exactly as either a supralapsarian or an infralapsarian.[94] Neither can Martin Luther (1483–1546) or Ulrich Zwingli (1484–1531).[95] While the majority of Reformed theologians are infralapsarians, Herman Bavinck (1854–1921) identifies the following as supralapsarians: Theodore Beza (1519–1605), Johann Piscator (1546–1625), Amandus Polanus von Polansdorf (1561–1610), Paul Ferry (1591–1669), William Whitaker (1548–95), William Perkins (1558–1602), Franciscus Gomarus (1563–1641), Jan Makowski (1588–1644), William Twisse (ca.1577–1646), Johann Heinrich Alsted (1588–1638), Abraham Heidanus (1597–1678), Christoph Wittich (1625–1687), Frans Burman (1628–79), Nicolaus Holtius (1693–1773), and Alexander Comrie (1706–74).[96] The predominance of infralapsarian is evidenced, for example, by the Synod of Dort (1618–19), which remained open to supralapsarianism but endorsed infralapsarianism.[97] The Salmanticenses and their Roman Catholic contemporaries are generally unaware of or uninterested in the lapsarian question as it was discussed by Reformed theologians.

---

94. Bavinck, *Reformed Dogmatics*, vol. 2, 363–65.

95. Barth, *Church Dogmatics*, vol. II.2, 127. Barth argues, however, that if Calvin, Luther, and Zwingli had been presented with the lapsarian debate, they would probably have come down as supralapsarians.

96. Bavinck, *Reformed Dogmatics*, vol. 2, 365n73. On Beza, see also Muller, *Christ and the Decree*, 80–81, 88. On Polanus, see Muller, *Christ and the Decree*, 154–55. On Perkins, see Muller, *Christ and the Decree*, 164–65, 169.

97. Synod of Dort, First Doctrinal Chapter, *On Predestination*, a. 7 (ed. Caninus, 280).

The Disputation on the Motive of the Incarnation: The Salmanticenses

The Salmanticenses' work represents a major contribution to the theological discussion on the motive of the Incarnation, one for which they are rightly esteemed. As Juniper B. Carol, OFM, observes, "This is undoubtedly one of the most satisfactory, influential and lengthy treatments of our subject ever written from the Thomistic viewpoint."[98] Based on what we have observed so far, we can consider the Salmanticenses' work a development and refinement of mitigated Thomistic trends, combining the distinction of causal perspectives developed remotely by Capréolus, Cajetan, and Silvestri and proximately by Godoy and Gonet, with a minimization of the conceptual stages used, an aspiration we saw especially in Molina.

On the Motive of the Incarnation consists of four "doubts," or questions to be considered. The first doubt is whether, by virtue of the present decree, Christ would have become incarnate if Adam had not sinned. The Salmanticenses answer with Aquinas that the negative response to this question is more probable and should be held on the basis of Scripture and the Church's tradition. At the same time, they maintain with the Scotistic tradition that Christ holds the primacy within the created order as the first willed and intended by God.

The Salmanticenses argue for these two seemingly incompatible propositions by distinguishing two aspects of final cause: the end *for-the-sake-of-which* (*finis cuius gratia*) and the end *to-which* (*finis cui*). The former is that which motivates the action because of its sheer desirability; it is that on whose account other things are chosen. The latter is the one to whom the benefit of the action is directed. The end *for-the-sake-of-which* and the end *to-which* are not two ends but instead two aspects of a single, total end. Christ is the first willed and intended as the end *for-the-sake-of-which* because, as the God-man, he is the greatest good willed by God outside of God's own intrinsic goodness. Yet, God also wills Christ precisely as Redeemer of humanity. This makes redeemed humanity the beneficiary of Christ's Incarnation and thus

---

98. Carol, *Why Jesus Christ?*, 70.

its end *to-which*. In this way, Christ has priority as the end for whom all things were made, sin has priority as the matter addressed and destroyed by Christ, and redeemed humanity has priority as the beneficiary of Christ's redemptive Incarnation.

A further aspect of the Salmanticenses' vision is that God arranged these elements of his providential plan in the most comprehensive and simple way. Therefore, in contrast to many of their contemporaries, they assign only two conceptually distinct stages (*signa rationis*) in God's ordering of history. First, they say, God knows all possible things with all their possible circumstances and interdependencies. Then, out of all these possibilities, he freely chooses the entire actual order of history, including creation, elevation to grace, the permission of sin with the inference of humanity's actual fall into sin, and the coming of the Redeemer. Thus, Christ the Redeemer falls within God's first and only intended order of reality as chosen and foreseen from the beginning.

In the second doubt, the Salmanticenses address the question of whether, if Adam had not sinned, Christ would have become incarnate by virtue of another decree that God would then have had. The first doubt looked at the question of whether, in the current state of affairs as actually ordained by God, Adam's sin was a *sine qua non* condition for the Incarnation. In contrast, this second doubt considers the question of whether, if Adam had not sinned, God would then have ordained some other state of affairs in which he would have included the Incarnation. Whereas the first doubt inquired as to the interdependencies extant within the real course of history, the second doubt addresses a nonexistent but possible course of history.

The Salmanticenses respond that we cannot know determinately what God would have done in another possible reality, arguing against theologians who definitively affirm or deny the Incarnation in a merely possible state of affairs. Their approach belies their commitment to the principle that we only know the free will of God through revelation. Since neither Scripture nor tradition says anything about what God would have done in some other nonexistent course of history, there is no theological foundation for a determinate answer.

The third and fourth doubts address converse questions: Would Christ have become incarnate if there had been original sin but no actual sins, and would Christ have become incarnate if there had been actual sins but no original sin? To the third doubt, they respond that the remediation of original sin is the more principal motive of the Incarnation, seeing as this is the sin that infects the whole human race as such. Thus, original sin by itself sufficiently constitutes the matter for the redemptive Incarnation. Therefore, Christ would have become Incarnate if there had been only original sin without further actual sins.

The same principle allows the Salmanticenses to answer in the fourth doubt that actual sins without original sin do not sufficiently constitute the matter of the decree of the redemptive Incarnation. Thus, they hold that it is more probable that in the arrangement of things as actually decreed by God, Christ would not have come if there were actual sins but not original sin.

The Disputation on the Motive of the Incarnation: After the Salmanticenses and Today

In the generation following the Salmanticenses, Pablo de la Concepción summarizes the core of the Salmanticenses' theory in his five-volume synopsis of their *Cursus*.[99] While he accurately identifies Christ as the end *for-the-sake-of-which* of other divine works, he does not insist—as the Salmanticenses do with vigor—that this makes Christ the first willed and intended by God *simpliciter*.[100] In general, Pablo is more interested in showing why Christ's coming depends on sin than in emphasizing Christ's primacy in the divine plan.

Two great Thomistic commentators of the eighteenth century, Charles-René Billuart, OP (1685–1757), and Vincenzo Gotti, already mentioned, enumerate nearly identical conceptual stages for God's decree of the Incarnation.[101] Billuart gives eight and Gotti seven, since the

---

99. Pablo de la Concepción, *Tractatus theologici*, tract. 16, disp. 2, dub. 1, §§ 1–3 (ed. Haeredes Pauli Monti, 4:198–204).

100. See also Enrique del Sagrado Corazón, "Juan Duns Escoto en la doctrina de los Salmanticenses," 510.

101. Billuart, *Summa Sancti Thomae hodiernis academiarum moribus accommodata, Tractatus de Incarnatione*, diss. 3, a. 3 (ed. Palmé, 5:400); and Gotti, *Theologia scholastica-dogmatica ... tomus I in Tertiam partem*, q. 4, dub. 4, § 3, no. 29 (ed. Bononiensis, 12:100–101).

former includes God's knowledge of all pure possibles as a first stage. For these theologians, the last conceptual stage is that in which God subjects everything to Christ.[102] In this way, God's will to liberate from sin precedes his effective decree of Christ, but Christ's own predestination precedes that of the elect, who are chosen in him. They agree that the Incarnation's primary motive was the manifestation of God's glory precisely by way of mercy and justice in human redemption. Billuart, however, notes the distinction of causal perspectives, explaining that Christ enjoys priority as the "perfecting end," while the permission of sin is prior as the "matter to be perfected."[103]

Others, such as José de Araújo, SJ (ca. 1680–1759), maintained the Thomistic view in stricter form, as Vásquez had, insisting that the Incarnation is for redemption, not redemption for the Incarnation.[104] Naturally, Scotists, like Juan de Campoverde, also continue to argue against the mitigated Thomists' application of distinct causal perspectives with relative priority.[105]

In the nineteenth century, we find Matthias Joseph Scheeben (1835–88) teaching that God sent the God-man to manifest the God-man's greatness, which perfects the universe and, above all, glorifies God infinitely. This greatness stands out much better because the God-man has both elevated humanity and rescued it from sin.[106] In fact, says Scheeben, we should view both Christ's coming and his suffering first of all not in relation to humanity's need but in relation to God's glorification.[107] Sin, in fact, can be considered in two ways: as a dishonor to God and as an occasion, or opportunity, that the God-man takes

---

102. We may add that Gotti explicitly says that God subjects everything to "Christ the Redeemer," while Billuart says only "Christ."

103. Billuart, *Summa Sancti Thomae hodiernis academiarum moribus accommodata, Tractatus de Incarnatione,* diss. 3, a. 3 (ed. Palmé, 5:403).

104. *Cursus theologici tomus primus ... De Incarnatione,* disp. 8, sect. 3, aa. 1–4, nos. 289–338 (ed. Rodrigues, 139–148).

105. *Tractatus de Incarnatione Verbi divini,* disp. 9, chap. 3, no. 45 (ed. Garcia Briones, 2:164–65); and chap. 5, nos. 69–70 (ed. Garcia Briones, 2:181–83).

106. Matthias Joseph Scheeben, *The Mysteries of Christianity,* trans. Cyril Vollert (St. Louis, Mo.: Herder, 1954), 400.

107. Scheeben, *Mysteries of Christianity,* 421–25.

up for God's greater glory.[108] Even the cross should not be thought of only as means to satisfy for sins. Christ came primarily for what is above him, not what is below him. Christ is for humanity, to be sure, but even more basically, humanity is for Christ. In his own distinctive style, then, Scheeben articulates a view of the Incarnation in many ways similar to that defended by the Salmanticenses.[109]

Among Reformed theologians, Karl Barth (1886–1968) sees himself as breaking out of the lapsarian debate, noted above, by radically centering the doctrine of predestination on Jesus Christ, himself God who elects and man who is elected.[110] Thus, all other acts of God *ad extra* presuppose Christ's election.[111] "Jesus Christ alone is the content of the eternal will of God, the eternal covenant between God and man."[112] The incarnate Word is the primary object of God's plan—is God's plan—and the rest of creation, including humanity to be redeemed, is constituted part of that plan only in relation to him.[113] Sin, in contrast, is nonbeing and thus does not fall under God's positive will. For this reason, Christ's atonement totally overcomes sin without being merely a reaction to it.[114] We might say that, for Barth, it is precisely because Christ is God's original, unaltered purpose that his coming is redemptive: Human malice does not put God on the defensive. It does not compel a reaction from him. Instead, God inexorably carries out his original covenantal intention through Jesus Christ, and sin cannot thwart this. After Barth and in more recent years, the lapsarian question has again become current.[115]

---

108. Scheeben, 427–28.

109. The most notable difference is Scheeben's lack of insistence that the Word would (most probably) not have become man apart from sin by virtue of the present decree. Still, his emphasis on the primacy of Christ as the one who glorifies God most of all through his redemptive suffering resonates with that of the Salmanticenses.

110. *Church Dogmatics*, vol. II.2, 146–47.

111. *Church Dogmatics*, vol. II.2, 156–58, and vol. IV.1, 66.

112. *Church Dogmatics*, vol. IV.1, 54.

113. See especially, *Church Dogmatics*, vol. IV.1, 51–66.

114. *Church Dogmatics*, vol. IV.1, 46–47.

115. See, for example, the discussions in Oliver D. Crisp, "The Election of Jesus Christ," *Journal of Reformed Theology* 2, no. 2 (2008): 131–50; Richard J. Mouw, "Another Look at the Infra/Supralapsarian Debate," *Calvin Theological Journal* 35, no. 1

In Catholic circles, the neo-scholasticism of the late nineteenth and early twentieth centuries reprised the classic debate. Some theologians, such as Franceso Maria Risi, OH (1834–1907), Jean-François Bonnefoy, OFM (d. 1959), and Chrysostome Urrutibéhéty, OFM (1853–1935), argued detailed versions of the Scotistic thesis, taking the opportunity to include Pope Bl. Pius IX's dogmatic definition of the Immaculate Conception.[116] Some, such as Christian Pesch, SJ (1835–1925), argued a strict Thomistic position, while others, such as Garrigou-Lagrange, favored the Salmanticenses' own mitigated position.[117] Still others, such as Paul Galtier, SJ (1872–1961), tried once again to reconcile the Scotistic and Thomistic camps along the lines set by Molina and Suárez.[118]

In the 1940s, Gesualdo Maria Rocca, OSM, and Gabriele Maria Roschini, OSM, developed what they styled a "new attempt" to reconcile the Thomistic and Scotistic theses.[119] They stress that badly

---

(April 2000): 136–51; Guy M. Richard, "Samuel Rutherford's Supralapsarianism Revealed: A Key to the Lapsarian Position of the Westminster Confession of Faith?," *Scottish Journal of Theology* 59, no. 1 (2006): 27–44; and Edwin Christiaan van Driel, *Incarnation Anyway: Arguments for Supralapsarian Christology* (Oxford: Oxford University Press, 2008).

116. See Risi's tremendous work *Sul motivo primario della Incarnazione del Verbo*, cited above. For the latter theologians, who both wrote extensively, see especially Urrutibéhéty, *Christus Alpha et Omega seu De Christi universali Regno*, editio altera (Lille, France: R. Giard Libraire, 1910); and Bonnefoy *La primauté du Christ selon l'écriture et la tradition* (Rome: Casa Editrice Herder, 1959), translated and abridged by Michael D. Meilach as *Christ and the Cosmos*, first American edition (Paterson, N.J.: St. Anthony Guild Press, 1965).

117. Pesch, *Praelectiones theologicae*, 4th and 5th editions, vol. 4, *De Verbo Incarnato; De Beata Virgine Maria; De cultu Sanctorum*, tract. 1, part 2, sect. 2, prop. 31 (Freiburg: Herder, 1922), 228–37. Garrigou-Lagrange outlines the Salmanticenses' theory favorably in *Christ the Savior: A Commentary on the Third Part of St. Thomas' Theological Summa*, trans. Bede Rose (St. Louis, Mo.: Herder, 1957), and argues for it in "Le principe de finalité," *Revue Thomiste* 26, no. 3 (1921): 418–23; "Motivum Incarnationis fuit motivum misericordiae," *Angelicum* 7, no. 3 (1930): 289–302; and "De motivo Incarnationis," 7–45.

118. Galtier and Chrysostome Urrutibéhéty held a lengthy debate on the subject. For Galtier's mature position, see his book *Les deux Adam* (Paris: Beauchesne et ses Fils, 1947).

119. Rocca and Roschini, *De ratione primaria existentiae Christi et Deiparae*.

posed questions are partly to blame for the divide between Scotists and Thomists. Thus, they proceed first by clarifying their inquiry as: "In the present order, what is the adequate, universal reason for the Word's Incarnation?"[120] Because they take 'Incarnation' here to mean the Incarnation as it has occurred together with each and every one of its concrete circumstances, they identify the primary reason for the Incarnation as God's free choice of the whole present order. In other words, God considers all possible orders and chooses the present one, which includes Christ as the end of all things and also human sin and Christ's redemptive work. Thus, they argue, Christ enjoys an absolute and universal primacy, one independent of sin, as the Scotists hold, such that he is head of angels and men, having merited even the angels' grace and man's original justice.[121] However, this primacy is inextricably connected with the fact of human sin, as the Thomists insist, since God decreed Christ and his redemptive work together with the permission of sin by a single act.

Rocca and Roschini's theory resembles that of the Salmanticenses, but it also differs substantially. We have seen that the Salmanticenses also affirm God's singular choice of the present order out of all possible orders, but they argue for much more than the simple simultaneous coexistence of Christ and the permission of sin within this decree. For Rocca and Roschini, Christ's coming *does not* depend on sin (though they are connected).[122] For the Salmanticenses, however, Christ's coming *does* depend on sin as its *sine qua non* condition, whereas it does not depend on what is merely co-decreed with him or directed to him as the end. After introducing their theory, Rocca and Roschini received critical replies from both Scotists and Thomists.[123]

More recently, Jean Galot, SJ (1919–2008), has argued for the primacy of Christ as Redeemer while rejecting that he is the end *for-the-sake-of-which*. Instead, he explains that God has given humanity redemption

---

120. Rocca and Roschini, 27.
121. Rocca and Roschini, 29.
122. Rocca and Roschini, 29–31.
123. See, e.g., their discussions, including with theologians we have already noted, such as Bonnefoy and Garrigou-Lagrange, in Rocca and Roschini, 43–167.

in Christ as a gift of love, which of its nature calls for a response of love that binds redeemed humanity to Christ.[124]

Among those with greater affinity for the Scotistic view, Karl Rahner, SJ (1904–84), teaches that God made the world to communicate himself to it, a process that culminates in Christ.[125] Rahner cites Scotus approvingly on this point and emphasizes that the Word's Incarnation is not just a response to human sin but *is* God's free (non-necessary), personal self-communication to the world.[126] The Word, in fact, "establishes this world to begin with as the materiality which is to become his own."[127] In this way, creation and the Incarnation are "two moments and two phases of the *one* process of God's self-giving and self-expression."[128]

Hans Urs von Balthasar (1905–88), in turn, writes that in the Father's plan, the life of Christ, "though it does not cause, is nevertheless the very condition for the possibility of there being a Fall, and so of there being a Paradise or indeed any creation at all."[129] At the same time, Balthasar does not want Christ's cross to seem "accidental" to the Incarnation.[130] Hence he emphasizes the Son's cross, the extension of his kenotic descent in taking on human nature, as central to the drama of divine and human freedom.[131] In this way, Balthasar holds that

---

124. Galot, *Gesù Liberatore* (Florence: Libreria Editrice Fiorentina, 1978), 11–31, translated by M. Angeline Bouchard as *Jesus, Our Liberator* (Rome: Gregorian University Press, 1982), 12–26.

125. See especially "Christology within an Evolutionary View of the World," trans. Karl-H. Kruger, in *Theological Investigations*, vol. 5 (Baltimore: Helicon Press, 1966), 184–87; *Mary, Mother of the Lord*, trans. W. J. O'Hara, paperback edition (Wheathampstead, Hertfordshire: Anthony Clarke Books, 1974), 10–12; *Foundations of Christian Faith: An Introduction to the Idea of Christianity*, trans. William V. Dych (New York: Crossroad Publishing Company, 1987), 192–98; and *The Trinity*, trans. Joseph Donceel, Milestones in Catholic Theology (New York: Crossroad Publishing Company, 2004), 28–30.

126. "Christology within an Evolutionary View of the World," 176.

127. *Foundations of Christian Faith*, 197.

128. *Foundations of Christian Faith*, 197.

129. Hans Urs von Balthasar, *A Theology of History*, translator unnamed, Communio Books (San Francisco: Ignatius Press, 1994), 64–65.

130. *Mysterium Paschale: The Mystery of Easter*, trans. Aidan Nichols (San Francisco: Ignatius Press, 1990), 11.

131. Besides the places just cited, see, e.g., *Theo-Drama*, trans. Graham Harrison,

the God-man, precisely through his death, descent, and Resurrection, is the reason for God's other works within the actual world order.[132]

Today, Christian piety is still interested in the primacy and centrality of Jesus. The Second Vatican Council proclaims: "The Lord [incarnate] is the goal of human history, the point on which the desires of history and civilisation turn, the centre of the human race, the joy of all hearts and the fulfilment of all desires."[133] Pope St. John Paul II begins his first encyclical letter with the affirmation that "the Redeemer of man, Jesus Christ, is the centre of the universe and of history."[134] Similarly, on the pastoral level, we note efforts, such as that of the United States Conference of Catholic Bishops, to structure catechetical texts in a Christocentric manner.[135]

It is still worth asking whether Jesus' primacy is absolute and unconditional, that of the one through whom and for whom all things were made (Col 1:16), or a primacy only in the order of seeking out and saving what was lost (Lk 19:10). Is there a logically robust and scripturally faithful way to speak of Jesus as the first willed and intended by God precisely in the work of human redemption? The Salmanticenses' disputation *On the Motive of the Incarnation*, the fruit of a lengthy debate preceding them and a touchstone for future theories, remains worthy of engagement as we consider these questions.

---

vol. 2 (San Francisco: Ignatius Press, 1990), 268–72; *The Theology of Karl Barth: Exposition and Interpretation*, trans. Edward T. Oakes (San Francisco: Communio Books/Ignatius Press, 1992), 327–34; and "Trinity and Future," trans. John Riches, in *Elucidations* (San Francisco: Ignatius Press, 1998), 82–84.

132. Balthasar quotes Pedro de Godoy favorably in *Theology of History*, 66; and *Theology of Karl Barth*, 327. He explicitly distances himself from the Scotistic view in *Mysterium Paschale*, 11; *My Work in Retrospect* (San Francisco: Communio Books/Ignatius Press, 1993), 23; and *Dare We Hope "That All Men Be Saved"?*, trans. David Kipp and Lothar Krauth, 2nd ed. (San Francisco: Ignatius Press, 2014), 184–85.

133. *Gaudium et spes*, no. 45, in Norman P. Tanner, ed., *Decrees of the Ecumenical Councils*, vol. 2 (London: Sheed and Ward, 1990), *1099.

134. *Redemptor hominis*, no. 1, in *Acta Apostolicae Sedis* 71, no. 4 (1979): 257. Translation from the Vatican website: http://w2.vatican.va/content/john-paul-ii/en/encyclicals/documents/hf_jp-ii_enc_04031979_redemptor-hominis.html.

135. *Doctrinal Elements of a Curriculum Framework for the Development of Catechetical Materials for Young People of High School Age* (Washington, D.C.: USCCB, 2008).

Notes on the Text and Translation

Throughout this disputation, the Salmanticenses endeavor to show the harmony of the available scriptural and patristic data, to respond to opponents, and to clarify their own arguments. They employ a dialectical style of argumentation with objections and responses. At times, their passion for their own position comes across rather strongly.

The Salmanticenses usually give truncated citations (e.g., by omitting the title of an author's work). For the reader's convenience, these citations have been expanded. Where it has been necessary to correct or modernize a citation, a note indicates the original as given by the Salmanticenses. The Salmanticenses cite sources directly in the body of the text; all footnotes are proper to the translation. The numbering of sections and paragraphs is identical to that of the Latin text. Manifest typographical errors in the original text (e.g., *humannm* for *humanum*) have been tacitly corrected. Footnotes indicate more subtle cases where the translator has preferred an alternative reading.

A few technical terms pertaining to logic (e.g., *consequentia*) are left untranslated to avoid ambiguity. Footnotes help to explain their meaning. The English translation of scriptural quotations is from the Douay-Rheims version, since this corresponds well to the Latin text. A few brief quotations from liturgical texts (the Nicene Creed and the *Exsultet*) are from the translation of the Roman Missal by the International Commission on English in the Liturgy. All other quotations, whether from the Church Fathers or from other Scholastic authors, have been freshly translated as the Salmanticenses quote them.

The Salmanticenses frequently speak of Christ himself or the event of the Incarnation as a remedy for sin or as meant to provide a remedy for sin. The Latin phrase in question is *remedium peccati*, sometimes in constructions like *in remedium peccati* and, rarely, *ad remedium*, *pro remedio*, or *propter remedium*. Literally, all convey the concrete image of God's sending Christ "as a remedy for sin." However, these expressions often occur in places where English prefers a more active word than "remedy." Hence *remedium* is translated sometimes as "remedy" and sometimes as "remediation."

Finally, given the nature of the subject matter, which deals with the logical order of elements that are temporally simultaneous or entirely atemporal, the reader will notice that the verb tenses the Salmanticenses employ at times become cumbersome. In the translation, this is partly due to the English language's reliance on auxiliary verbs. For example, phrases such as "would be going to be" (*esset futurum*) are not uncommon.[136] In the context of the argument, such a phrase is not the same as "would be" (*esset*) and thus has not been truncated. For the sake of flow and to avoid ambiguity, again due to the problem of auxiliary verbs, the word "exist" is sometimes substituted for "be," so that *esset futurum* becomes "would be going to exist."

---

136. Some English works discussing providence and predestination, in strict imitation of Latin, render phrases such as *esset futurum* as "would be future." The present translation generally avoids using "future" when the emphasis is on the fact of eventual actual existence, viewed as logically posterior to possible existence, rather than on existence at a particular point within time. Technical phrases containing the word *futurum*, especially references to *futura conditionata* ("conditioned futures") when the Salmanticenses address Suárez's opinion, are translated more rigidly. The noun *futuritio* ("futurity"), which appears from time to time in the text, is translated by variations on "the fact that x is going to exist" or "whether x is going to exist," depending on context. The Salmanticenses do not use the term *futurabile* ("futurable") in this disputation.

On the Motive of the Incarnation

After St. Thomas[1] (*ST* III, q. 1, aa. 1 and 2)[2] showed the fittingness and the necessity of the mystery of the Incarnation, in a most well-devised order he proceeded to treat of its causes, both extrinsic and intrinsic. And because the end holds the first place among these causes, for indeed the whole operation and movement proceeds from its being intended, he thus began (from a. 3)[3] to treat of the end or motive[4] of this mystery. But because it had been established that God's primary and chief end in all his works is his own glory—according to the passage: *The Lord hath made all things for himself* (Prv 16:3)—thus omitting or supposing this consideration, he turned his mind instead to the more specific motive on the part of the work. This, in turn, he referred back to the quite serious difficulty of uncovering what God's intention was in decreeing such a great mystery. It is this that we will take pains to examine at length and now present below.

1. St. Thomas Aquinas, OP (1225–74).
2. Aquinas (Leonine ed., 11:6–7, 9–11).
3. Aquinas (Leonine ed., 11:13–14).
4. *Motivum*: The word *motivum* occurs in two senses throughout this disputation. In the first sense, it means the proximate final cause on the part of the work "motivating" God to will the Incarnation. This is an analogous expression, since, as the Salmanticenses note with Aquinas, nothing outside God moves God to act, strictly speaking. Rather, the "motive of the Incarnation" means the proximate reason for the Incarnation, since God's glory is the ultimate reason for all of his works. In this first sense, *motivum* is translated throughout as "motive." See Reginald Garrigou-Lagrange, "De motivo Incarnationis: Examen recentium objectionum contra doctrinam S. Thomae III[a], q. 1, a. 3," in *Acta Pont. Academiae Romanae S. Thomae Aquinatis et Religionis Catholicae*, Nova series 10 (Rome: Academia Romana S. Thomae Aquinatis, 1945), 9–10.

In the second sense, *motivum* means a reason or guiding principle for holding a certain position. Thus, *motivum* occurs in the text when the Salmanticenses are referring to their own or others' argumentation. Throughout, *motivum* in this sense is translated as "rationale," "reason," or "line of reasoning."

Doubt I

Whether God would assume flesh by virtue of the present decree[1] if Adam had not sinned?

Many issues come up here both concerning the legitimate understanding of the present difficulty and concerning the conceptual stages[2] that are usually distinguished in God, though especially concerning this specific point of controversy, not to mention others that do not pertain to it. If these came up and were repeated too often, they would lead

---

1. *Ex vi praesentis decreti* ("by virtue of the present decree" or "by force of the present decree"): in the present state of affairs as actually ordained by God, as opposed to another merely possible state of affairs.

2. *Signa rationis* (also called *instantia rationis*): conceptually distinct aspects of a single simultaneous reality that can be compared as logically prior or posterior to one another. When applied to God, *signa rationis* are a way of speaking about the "interplay" between God's knowledge and will, which in reality are identical and simple, but which must be distinguished from our perspective. For example, God's knowing all things he is free to do (all possible events) is logically prior to his freely acting (all real events). These can be described as two *signa rationis*. *Signum* in this sense is translated throughout the text as "stage." The terminology has its roots in Aristotle's *Physics*, 8.8.263b9–15, where the Greek word σημεῖον, which in this context means a particular point in time, appears in the twelfth-century Latin translation ascribed to James of Venice literally as *signum*. See W. D. Ross, ed., *Aristotelis Physica*, reprinted with corrections, Scriptorum classicorum bibliotheca Oxoniensis (Oxford: Clarendon Press, 1966), 8.8.263b9–15; and Fernand Bossier and Jozef Brams, eds., *Physica (translatio vetus)*, Aristoteles Latinus 7.1 (Leiden: Brill, 1990), 325. Theological usage of this terminology arose toward the end of the thirteenth century.

to obscurity and tedium,³ but if we gather them together in a unified way and summarize them up front, they will shed no small light on the subject. And thus:

§ 1. The certain is separated from the uncertain, and the state of the question is opened up

1 Granted that we can assign no final cause to any divine volition, since God is not moved by anything outside himself as primary, we can assign an end to the things willed by God, namely, the end to which God orders them. For as St. Thomas has wisely taught: *To will the end is not for God the cause of willing what is directed toward the end. Rather, he wills what is directed toward the end to be ordered to the end. Therefore he wills this to be on account of that, but it is not on account of this that he wills that* (ST I, q. 19, a. 5).⁴ Hence, since the mystery of the Incarnation was willed and decreed by God, we can raise the doubt as to what end it was ordered or for what it was willed. And, in fact, it is certain that more than one end for which he could will it did present itself to God. To omit others and so limit our consideration of this doubt, God was able to will this mystery on account of its intrinsic goodness and excellence independently of the redemption of men. This is because, taken in this way, it is quite lovable in itself, and even more so than the creation of men and angels. Also, because it is most fitting for the manifestation of God's perfection and attributes. Also, since the Incarnation is the utmost communication of God *ad extra*, it implies an act exceedingly in harmony with and befitting the nature of the highest good whereby it inclines to such a communication, as we have explained at length with St. Thomas (in our commentary on the

---

3. This remark is reminiscent of Aquinas's preface to the *Summa theologiae*, where he complains of theological lessons that have fostered tedium and confusion in the students by frequent repetition (Leonine ed., 4:5).

4. Aquinas (Leonine ed., 4:239). This is to say that the end does not move God to will the means to this end. Instead, God wills the order of the means to the end. Whereas the desire for health moves a human being to will medicine, God wills that medicine lead to health. Thus, health stands as final cause to medicine, but it does not stand as final cause to God, who is the first among final causes.

first article of this question).⁵ And no reason for us to deny that God was able to have willed this mystery in this way, independently of the redemption of men or of another end extrinsic to the mystery itself, presents itself. Hence in this third article St. Thomas supposes this in these words: *Even so, God's power is not limited to this. For God could have become incarnate even if there had been no sin.*⁶ This will become more apparent from what is yet to be said (no. 4).

And with the same certainty it is established that God was able to will and order this mystery to men's remediation and redemption, supposing sin, namely, in such a way that the divine Word subsisting in our flesh would offer condign satisfaction for the sins of men in accord with the rigor of justice, according to what we have said in the preceding disputation.⁷ This is because decreeing such a remedy through the Incarnation implies no disorder but instead a most appropriate act of divine mercy. Also, because just as God is free to decree the Incarnation or not to decree it, so also he is free to decree it for this or another end. Also, because even though there is no connection between the Incarnation and the redemption of men from the nature of the thing, in his free will, God can, on the part of the thing willed, connect things that do not have a connection by decreeing a dependence between them whereby one does not come about without an order to the other. And finally, also because even if the Incarnation is something better and higher than the redemption of men and it seems inappropriate for the more perfect to be ordered to the less perfect as the end *for-the-sake-of-which* or the end absolutely, that would hardly be the case even supposing this divine decree. For the Incarnation would not be for men's salvation as for the end *for-the-sake-of-which* but instead would regard it as the end effected, which is usually called the end *to-which* or the end of benefit.⁸ And in such an arrangement, no disorder appears in

---

5. Salmanticenses, *Cursus theologicus*, tract. 21, commentary on *ST* III, q. 1, a. 1 (ed. Palmé, 13:5–9).

6. Aquinas, *ST* III, q. 1, a. 3 (Leonine ed., 11:14).

7. Salmanticenses, *Cursus theologicus*, tract. 21, disp. 1, dub. 7 (ed. Palmé, 13:155–80). Condign satisfaction is that which atones for sin in strict justice, as opposed to congruous satisfaction, which God could fittingly accept but which does not offer to God a good strictly proportionate to the offense of sin.

8. Throughout this treatise, the Salmanticenses contrast the end *for-the-sake-of-*

the more perfect's being ordered to the less perfect. For this is the way in which the generation of these lower bodies is called the end of the motion of the heavens, though it is not more perfect than they are. In this way, too, the welfare of a peasant is called the end of the king's providence.⁹ Finally, this is the way in which Scripture says that the angels have been produced and sent for ministry to men, though they are more perfect than men, because God has ordered them to this effect, which is the end *to-which*. Hence there is no doubt that God was able to decree the Incarnation in the aforementioned way, to wit, by ordering it to the redemption of men from sin and not willing it otherwise than with a connection to this end or effect.

2. But you will object *first* that if the Incarnation were decreed as a remedy for sin it would be called an occasioned good.¹⁰ This can-

---

which (*finis cuius gratia*) with the end *to-which* (*finis cui*), which they also call the end of benefit (*finis utilitatis*). The *finis cuius gratia* is that which the agent desires on its own account and on whose account the agent desires the other things he wills. The *finis cui* is the person or subject to whom the agent directs the benefit of the action. The *finis cuius gratia* and the *finis cui* are not two ends but are aspects of a single, total end or motive. For example, a physician cannot actually will health (*finis cuius gratia*) without willing that a given patient (*finis cui*) possess and benefit from that state of health. See the Salmanticenses, *Cursus theologicus*, tract. 8, *De ultimo fine*, q. 1, Preface, no. 4 (ed. Palmé, 5:3). The distinction has its roots in Aristotle, *On the Soul*, 2.4.415b1–3, and was greatly developed by the time of the Salmanticenses.

Here, the Salmanticenses also call human redemption the *finis effectus* ("the end as an effect"), which is distinguished from *finis causa* ("the end as a cause"). When redeemed humanity is considered from the perspective of God's intending it, it is the *finis cui* and part of the overall motive. When considered as what results from the work of the Incarnation, however, human redemption is the *finis effectus*. On these distinctions, see Gredt, *Elementa philosophiae Aristotelico-Thomisticae*, vol. 2, no. 770, pp. 199–201.

9. The most basic meaning of *salus* is "health" or "welfare." In Christian usage, however, it typically means "salvation." Here the example of a king, by his *providentia*, looking after the *salus* of a lowly peasant is well suited to the soteriological context. This example is taken from Aquinas, *Super II Sent.*, dist. 15, q. 1, a. 1, ad 6 (ed. Mandonnet, 2:369–70).

10. The worry about the Incarnation's being an occasioned good, with the implication that its actual occurrence is not willed because of its own goodness but only circumstantially, is found in Scotus, *Ordinatio III*, dist. 7, q. 3, no. 64 (Vatican ed. 9:288),

not be said. Therefore it could not have been decreed in such a way. The *sequela*[11] is shown: That is called an occasioned good which is intended not *per se* but instead on the occasion of or by reason of something else whose attainment it serves. But this is how the Incarnation would be if it were decreed as a remedy for sin, seeing as it would be intended not *per se* but by reason of redemption from sin that was foreseen or that was going to exist and for its remedy. Now the falsity of the consequent is clear. For the goods that are the greatest and that of themselves bear tremendous fittingness cannot be called goods that are only occasioned, but it is obvious that the mystery of the Incarnation is the greatest good below God. *Second*, if God willed the Incarnation as a remedy for sin or for sin's remedy, he could not *not* will sin itself. This is plainly absurd, since God cannot will or intend sin, which is opposed to him and which cannot be referred to him. The *sequela* is shown: This is because in redemption or remediation from sin, sin itself is necessarily included. Therefore one who wills the Incarnation as a remedy for sin is bound to will sin itself. Also, because one who wills the end wills what is directed to the end. But for the end of redemption from sin, sin is necessary, seeing as without it the remedy for it is unintelligible. Therefore if God willed the Incarnation as a remedy for sin, he would have to will sin itself. *Third*, if God decreed the Incarnation or Christ as a remedy for sin, Christ's soul could rejoice at the existence of sin and thank us for having sinned, which is altogether false and unbecoming of Christ's perfection.[12] The inference is shown: Everyone can rejoice at the occasion whereby a great good comes to him and can thank those who afford the occasion of attaining such a good. But, on the aforementioned hypothesis, sin would be the occasion of the Incarnation or the assumption of humanity to a divine person, and sinful men would

---

but it also goes back to Bonaventure before him. See Bonaventure, *In tertium librum Sententiarum*, dist. 1, a. 2, q. 2, s.c. 5 (Quaracchi ed., 3:22–23).

11. *Sequela*: the logical inference.

12. This objection is rooted in Scotus, *Ordinatio III*, dist. 7, q. 3, no. 67 (Vatican ed., 9:289) and taken up by subsequent Scotists, such as Juan de Rada, *Controversiae theologicae* III, contr. 5, a. 3, concl. 4 (ed. Ioannes Crithius, 3:166). The same argument, applied not to Christ and humanity but to humanity and the angels, appears earlier in Anselm, *Cur Deus homo?*, I, chap. 18 (ed. Schmitt, 2:78–79).

afford such an occasion. Therefore Christ's soul could rejoice at the existence of sin and give thanks to sinners.

We have deliberately laid out the aforementioned objections in this place because some use them to impugn the opinion asserting that God has *de facto* decreed the Incarnation as a remedy for sin and as connected to this end. For if the aforementioned objections are valid, they attack not only the act but also the power, since they make the case for an imperfection on the part of the object that is logically incompatible[13] for God in any providence or impossible of itself. And so, if they do not overturn the power of decreeing it in such a way, as we will soon show, there is nothing in them to succeed in proving that God has not acted thus or that touches specifically on the present providence. But as to the fact that God could have so ordered [the Incarnation] absolutely, there is no one who denies this. For what even apparent entanglement[14] is there in God's having decreed the Incarnation as a remedy for foreseen sin or dependently on the condition of sin to be repaired through Christ's satisfaction? Since, then, the aforementioned objections can in no way preclude the power of decreeing it in such a way, they are to be regarded as nothing with regard to the actual decree, whether this or something else is asserted. And everyone ought to put aside or omit these objections in this doubt so as to respect its proper scope.

3 To the first objection, it should be said that "occasioned" can be taken in two ways. First, properly, where it means the same as apart from the intention of the agent and by chance. This is the sense in which a woman is called an "occasioned male" because generation has a tendency to the perfect and results in a woman apart from the agent's

---

13. *Repugnantem*: Throughout, forms of *repugnantia* and *repugnans* are translated as "incompatibility," "logical incompatibility," and "logical impossibility," along with their adjectival versions, depending on what is clearest in the given context. The concept of *repugnantia* is particularly that of a state of logical impossibility arising when trying to hold together two things opposed by contradiction.

14. *Implicatio* ("entanglement"): a logically incoherent situation following from accepting certain premises. The point in this section is that unless the cited objections prove that the Incarnation as conditioned on sin is a logical impossibility, they cannot disprove that God actually willed the mystery in such a way, since God has the power to do anything that is not logically contradictory.

intention.[15] And in this sense, even though it was decreed as a remedy for sin, the Incarnation would hardly be called an occasioned good, since it was a very great good and intended by God. In fact, in this sense nothing is or can be said to be an occasioned good with respect to God. For all things with all their circumstances are subject to his providence and his directing them to their appropriate ends. Hence they are not at all by chance or apart from the intention of the primary agent. In the second sense, that is called "occasioned" which happens on the supposition of some occasion or which is put into being dependently on some condition. And in this sense, there would be no disorder in the Incarnation's being called an occasioned good, since being decreed dependently on some occasion is not at all incompatible with it. But because the former way of taking "occasioned good" is proper, it would not be called an occasioned good absolutely.

Nor does it matter if you offer in opposition to us St. Thomas, where he inquires *Whether in the state of innocence there would have been generation?* and gives the solution: *I answer that, in the state of innocence there would have been generation for the multiplication of the human*

---

15. *Mas occasionatus*: this translates the Greek ἄρρεν πεπηρωμένον, taken from Aristotle, *On the Generation of Animals*, 2.3.737a28. Within the Aristotelian-Scholastic framework, in the generation of offspring, the male was thought to supply the formal principle and the female the material principle. Thus, because the form seeks to reproduce itself completely in the matter of the offspring, generation has a natural tendency or intention to result in male offspring. Therefore, female offspring result because by some circumstance the matter was not disposed so as to receive the form from the male perfectly. This means that a female is an *occasioned male* because some intervening circumstance (an *occasio*) prevented her father's seed from imposing its form perfectly on the matter provided by her mother. However, the Scholastics also understood that what is apart from the tendency of the process of generation is not apart from God's intention. Thus, Aquinas claims that while the male form intends to reproduce itself exactly, God desires for circumstances to result in the creation of females because they are part of his larger intention. See, for example, *ST* I, q. 92, a. 1, ad 1 (Leonine ed., 5:396–97). Analogously, the tendency of a woodcut pattern is to reproduce a print identical to itself on each page. Thus, from the perspective of the individual pattern, an image that differs somewhat from the pattern is occasioned. However, the artist, who governs the whole process and who has in mind not only the pattern in its strict identity on a given page but the whole run of prints, actually intends the slight differences in the resulting prints. Thus, the occasioned print is contrary to the intention of the pattern, but it is in harmony with the intention of the artist.

race. Otherwise, *man's sin, from which such a great good has followed, would have been very necessary* (*ST* I, q. 98, a. 1).[16] In that passage he regards it as unfitting for the generations of men to have been only on the occasion of sin and not otherwise. But it is obvious that the Incarnation is a greater good by far than all the multiplication of men. Therefore it could not have been and could not have been called an occasioned good or one with a dependence on sin.[17]

This, I say, does not matter. For the *consequentia*[18] should be denied on account of the manifest aspect of disparity. For St. Thomas (in the place cited) supposes that the first human beings were produced with a natural order to the multiplication of the human species, as he shows in this way: *On the contrary, it is said: "Increase and multiply, and fill the earth" (Gn 1:28). But such multiplication could not have occurred without new generation, since only two were established at first. Therefore in the first state there would have been generation.*[19] But what is natural or pertains to the natural order of things proceeds naturally and independently of another contingent condition, especially sin, which is apart from that order. Hence on the supposition that God created man and established him in a natural order, it was not becoming for the generation of men to have a dependence on sin or to wait upon this condition. But the Incarnation is a work above every requirement of nature, depending on the sole will of God, who has the power to decree it as he pleases, either absolutely or dependently on a condition and in an order to specific ends. And so he was able to decree it dependently on the condition that sin would exist and for its remedy, without any appearance of incompatibility or disorder in this.

[In response] to the second objection, the *sequela* should be denied. For from God's willing the Incarnation as a remedy for sin, it would only be the case either that his foreseeing of sin preceded the decree

---

16. Aquinas (Leonine ed., 5:436). Cf. Juan de Rada, *Controversiae theologicae* III, contr. 5, a. 3, op. Scot., concl. 4 (ed. Ioannes Crithius, 3:166–67).

17. The Latin text of this edition mistakenly reads: *Ergo non potuit esse, aut dici bonum occasionatum, sive dependenter ab occasionatum, sive dependenter ab occasione peccati.* The 1687 edition has: *Ergo non potuit esse, aut dici bonum occasionatum, sive dependenter ab occasione peccati.*

18. *Consequentia*: the logical "consequence" or entailment of the argument.

19. Aquinas, *ST* I, q. 98, a. 1 (Leonine ed., 5:436).

of the remedy of the Incarnation (which includes no willing or choice of sin but only the mere presupposition of it) or that the intention of the antecedent Incarnation as a remedy for sin entailed the permission of the latter without any influence on its malice (which implies no imperfection incompatible with God but instead the providence of the primary agent). This can also be clarified from what Thomists commonly teach in their tractates on predestination. For God can decree an act of penitence, which necessarily connotes sin, without it following from this that God wills sin, since it is enough either that he supposes foreseen sin before the decree of penitence, as is the opinion of some, or that, supposing the intention of penitence, he permits sin, which is necessitated by consequence, as more say. The same appears proportionately in the imposition of the precept of fraternal correction. We will not, however, spend further time on this because we have explained it at length (tract. 5, disp. 6, dub. unic., § 4, no. 28).[20] This is a doctrine that everyone has to admit in this controversy. For whatever may be the case in this decree as far as the Incarnation's substance is concerned, no one denies that Christ was decreed as passible and as going to undertake death as a remedy for sin. Yet no one gathers from this that God willed sin when he issued such a decree, but either that [the decree] supposed it or entailed the permission for it. Therefore the same should be said if God, as he was able to do, had decreed the substance of the Incarnation in an order to the aforementioned effect and dependently on it.

Hence [the response] to the third objection is also plain. For sin, as far as it itself is concerned, would not entice God to decree the Incarnation but would instead entice him to deny it and other benefits. It is, instead, out of God's utmost mercy and goodness that he would decree so great a good as a remedy for so great an evil. Hence sin would not be an occasion to become incarnate proffered by us but one taken up mercifully by God in his good pleasure.[21] Consequently, Christ's soul

---

20. Salmanticenses (ed. Palmé, 2:368–69).

21. *Beneplacitum* ("good pleasure"): God's will considered as free to act over and above the established order already willed by him. Bonaventure makes the point that God's mercy, not sin *per se*, is what actually brings about the redemptive Incarnation in *In III Sent.*, dist. 1, a. 2, q. 2, ad 6 to the contrary (Quaracchi ed., 3:27).

would not rejoice at the existence of sin but at the divine mercy.²² Nor would his soul give thanks to sinners but to God who shows mercy and, from his intention to heal man of his sins, decrees the Incarnation. Similarly, Blessed Matthias would not be chosen as an Apostle if Judas had not fallen, from which it does not follow that he rejoiced at Judas's sin or had to thank him for having sinned. Rather, Matthias rejoiced at his own dignity and gave thanks to God for having conferred it on him in his mercy, taking the occasion from Judas's sin.

4 Supposing these things, what pertains to the power of decreeing the Incarnation for this or that end is also readily conceded by all. The chief difficulty occurs surrounding the actual ordination, and how we decide the present controversy hangs on this. Furthermore, in our decision we must suppose that God intended the Incarnation for its intrinsic excellence in such a way that he decreed Christ as the first willed, to which all other things, even the very permission and remediation of sin, would be ordered as the end *for-the-sake-of-which*, to the point that our predestination and all its effects depend on Christ and suppose him as previously intended and decreed in the genus of final cause. This doctrine, though not common among Thomists, is nevertheless more frequent with some others who conceive of the order of the divine decrees differently. We have established it already (tract. 5, disp. 4, dub. 1, no. 2; disp. 8, dub. 1, § 7, no. 37; and beginning from dub. 3, § 4, no. 99, and elsewhere),²³ and what we will say on Christ's merit and predestination will further confirm it.²⁴ Now, however, we offer persuasion from sacred Scripture, where that famous passage occurs in the Apostle's Letter to the Colossians. He attributes this priority and preeminence under the aspect of being willed and intended to Christ the Lord quite openly in these words: *Who is the image of the invisible God, the firstborn of every creature: For in him were all things created in heaven and on earth, visible and invisible, whether thrones,*

---

22. As Cajetan argues in his commentary on *ST* III, q. 1, a. 3, no. 10, ad 7 (Leonine ed., 11:16). Cf. Bonaventure's remark at the end of his treatment in *In III Sent.*, dist. 1, a. 2, q. 2 (Quaracchi ed., 3:28).

23. Salmanticenses (ed. Palmé, 2:321–22, 392, 410–11).

24. See Salmanticenses, tract. 21, disp. 28, dub. 9 (ed. Palmé, 16:214–30); and commentary on *ST* III, q. 24, aa. 3–4 (ed Palmé, 16:54–51).

or dominations, or principalities, or powers. All things were created by him and in him. And he is before all: and by him all things consist. And he is the head of the body, the church: who is the beginning, the firstborn from the dead (Col 1:15–18). In this passage it is clear that he is speaking of Christ the God-man. And since this precedence is not preserved in the execution of things, with reference to which Christ is posterior to many others, we must have recourse to priority according to God's intention, whereby he first willed Christ and everything else for him, ordering it all to him as to its end, first willed and intended. The following words of the Apostle have the same force: *He hath made him* (that is, Christ) *head over all the church, which is his body* (Eph 1:22–23). And in the same place: *He chose us in him before the foundation of the world, that we should be holy and unspotted in his sight in charity. Who hath predestinated us unto the adoption of children through Jesus Christ unto himself: according to the purpose of his will: Unto the praise of the glory of his grace, in which he hath graced us, in his beloved son* (Eph 1:4–6). All these denote that, of all the things God willed outside himself, Christ was the first willed and intended. This very same thing is taught by the Fathers. From among these, Our Holy Father Cyril of Alexandria[25] says: *Christ is founded before us and we are founded upon him, by whom we are built up before the beginning of the world in God's foreknowledge such that in the divine order the blessing would come before the curse* (*Thesaurus*, assert. 15). Moreover, he adds: *Christ, the author of our salvation, is founded before the beginning of the world such that if we were to fall by our trespass we would once more be renewed in him.* And Rupert the Abbot[26] hands down that *it should be religiously said and reverently heard that for crowning this man* (namely Christ) *with glory and honor, God created all things* (*De gloria et honore Filii*

---

25. St. Cyril of Alexandria (d. ca. 444). "Our Holy Father": a title applied to certain saints held to have lived the essence of Carmelite spirituality and considered patrons of the order. *Thesaurus de sancta et consubstantiali Trinitate* (PG 75:292). The Latin text gives the citation as: *P. N. S. Cyrill. Alexand. lib. 5 Thesauri, cap. 8.*

26. Rupert of Deutz, OSB (d. 1135). *De gloria et honore Filii hominis* (CCCM 29:410). The Latin text gives the citation as: *Rupertus Abbas lib. de gloria Trinit. cap. 19.* This conflates two references, one to Rupert's *De gloria et honore Filii hominis*, which contains the quotation, and the other to his *De glorificatione Trinitatis et processione Spiritus sancti*, III, chap. 20 (PL 169:72), which contains similar argumentation.

hominis, XIII). And the Angelic Doctor below (*ST* III, q. 24, aa. 3 and 4)[27] gives the solution that Christ's predestination was the exemplar and cause of our predestination, which could not have been the case if Christ had not been first intended and predestined. And (*Super IV Sent.*, dist. 48, q. 2, a. 2) he hands down that the whole motion [of the heavens][28] was made for the predestined and especially for Christ their head and exemplar, in which case it was necessary for him to precede other things in the genus of final cause as the first willed and intended among the others.

A quite appropriate argument, one generally associated with Scotus[29] in this matter, offers persuasion for this: One who wills in an ordered way wills the end prior to the means and, out of the means, wills those that are closer to the end prior [to the others]. But to the manifestation of the divine goodness and the extension of his glory, which is the end intended by God in the production of things, the Incarnation of the Word is related more proximately than all creatures, since it surpasses them all in perfection by far. Therefore, granted that God

---

27. Aquinas (Leonine ed., 11:273–74).

28. Where the Latin text has *modum*, I have read *motum*. In the passage cited, speaking of the motion of the heavens, Aquinas asserts that "that motion was ordained by divine providence for the completion of the number of the elect." *Super IV Sent.*, dist. 48, q. 2, a. 2, ad 6 (ed. Fiaccadorus, 7.2:1175).

29. Bl. John Duns Scotus, OFM (ca. 1266–1308). The doctrine cited is found, among other places, in his *Ordinatio III*, dist. 7, q. 3, no. 61 (Vatican ed., 9:287) and *Lectura III*, dist. 7, q. 3, no. 77 (Vatican ed., 20:214). Later theologians distinguished two interpretations of this *ordinate volens* principle on the basis that "closer to the end" can signify either the order in which one means precedes another in their sequence leading to the attainment of the end, or else it can signify how greatly something resembles the end. See Rada, *Controversiae theologicae* III, contr. 5, a. 3, op. Scot., obs. 3 (ed. Ioannes Crithius, 3:158); Suárez, *Disputationes in Tertiam partem*, disp. 5, sect. 1, no. 12 (Opera omnia, 17:203); and Vásquez, *Disputationes in Tertiam partem*, q. 1, a. 3, disp. 11, chap. 6, nos. 73–74 (ed. Sanchez Crespo, 1:168). Here, the Salmanticenses implicitly address this distinction by emphasizing that the end willed by God is the manifestation of his own goodness and glory, and so the ordering of means to this end includes also the element of resemblance to God. The Salmanticenses also shore up the *ordinate volens* principle in this paragraph by stating that it is a reasonable presumption about how God wills (not a conclusive *a priori* proof) when there is no evidence to the contrary and that, based on the Scripture passages they cite, there is, in fact, positive evidence in favor of its application to this disputation.

was able absolutely not to decree the Incarnation and was able not to preserve the order more connatural to things, nevertheless as one who proceeds in an ordered way (when there is no proof of the opposite), we should consider him as first having intended his own glory as the end, as immediately having intended the Incarnation of the Word as the means closest to that end, and as having intended the rest of what belongs to grace or nature by ordering it in a more mediate way to Christ and, by his mediation, to his own glory, according to the passage: *All are yours, and you are Christ's, and Christ is God's* (1 Cor 3:22–23). And: *It became him for whom are all things and by whom are all things to be the author of their salvation, by his passion* (Heb 2:10).[30]

5 These things, in fact, are easy to understand, and they would prepare an easier way for the solution of the present difficulty if it were well established that the Incarnation was willed in this way for its own sake as the chief end of other things such that it had no dependence on the rest of them in the other genera of causes. In that case, the way to decide this doubt would be straightforward, namely, that the Word was going to assume flesh even if Adam were not to sin, for the mystery would be supposed as independent of this condition both of itself and from the divine ordination. But this is precisely the point on which the difficulty especially hinges as regards the connection coming from God's decree, to wit, whether God established the Incarnation absolutely, independently of Adam's sin, or dependently on it and as its remedy. For if the former is true, we must consequently hold to the affirmative side in this difficulty, whereas if the latter is established, it is the other way around. Hence the whole endeavor comes down to investigating the quality of the present decree whereby God established the Incarnation.

In order to put this forward more easily and at the same time posit the stages, whether natural or conceptual, that are usually employed in this matter, it is to be supposed, lastly, that there is no incompatibility in God's having willed the Incarnation in such a way, for its intrinsic

---

30. The full verse reads: *For it became him for whom are all things and by whom are all things, who had brought many children into glory, to perfect the author of their salvation, by his passion.*

excellence and as the proximate end *for-the-sake-of-which*[31] of all other things, and, nevertheless, that he also willed the same Incarnation as the remedy for sin and the salvation of men as the end *to-which*, the end effected, in such a way that there was mutual dependence between these on the part of the object willed, insofar as the Incarnation was prior to our salvation under the aspect of the end *for-the-sake-of-which*, whereas our salvation was prior to the Incarnation in the genus of the end *to-which* and under the aspect of material cause. For, generally speaking, no entanglement can be assigned in a mutual dependence of this sort between two things,[32] especially if they have this mutual dependence extrinsically by the ordination of God who intends and decrees them not otherwise than as connected between themselves and with mutual dependence, as when he wills glory *per se* as the end of merits. For he wills that merits depend on glory in one genus and that glory depend on merits in another, and he wills that neither come to be without dependence on the other. We have professedly shown by instruction and examples that this is often the case and holds together quite well (tract. 15, disp. 3, dub. 4, § 1, beginning from no. 71).[33] Let the reader recall this so that we may avoid going into what we have already dealt with in another place. Here we only need to designate the conceptual moments or stages that we must distinguish in God for this purpose. In this, some are so liberal as to assign four or five stages, others eight or ten, and still others proceed even past this point, despite the fact that these are not necessary and add obscurity to a matter difficult on its own. We should thus proceed with greater brevity, by clarifying how the Incarnation was able to be intended *per se* after the manner of the end of other things and at the same time, by virtue of the same decree, with a connection to the remediation of sin and dependently on it.

---

31. Where the Latin has *finem proximum ejus gratia*, I have read *finem proximum cujus gratia*.

32. A reference to the Scholastic maxim *causae ad invicem sunt causae* (*sed in diverso genere*), meaning that A can be the cause of B and B simultaneously the cause of A so long as they are causes in distinct (particularly complementary) senses, as in the example given where merits lead to glory as its moral efficient cause, but glory leads to merits as their final cause.

33. Salmanticenses (ed. Palmé, 10:578–79).

6 Hence in conformity with what we have handed down (tract. 5, disp. 4 and disp. 5; and tract. 13, disp. 15),[34] it should be supposed that there are two stages *in-quo* to be distinguished in God and that these suffice.[35] One stage is that in which he knew perfectly all possible things and all their possible connections and combinations under possible being alone through knowledge of simple intelligence.[36] The other stage is that in which, out of all the known possibilities, he chose, approved, absolutely decreed, and saw the order of things along with the combinations and dependencies that he pleased. Now it is obvious that these two stages have to be distinguished, since what can possibly be is independent of what is freely going to be, both in *existence* and *knowledge*. Thus the former precedes the latter not only by the independence or order of nature meant by "priority *a-quo*," but also in existential entailment,[37] which we call "priority *in-quo*." And, consequently,

---

34. Salmanticenses (ed. Palmé, 2:321–60, 8:85–216). For the latter, see especially tract. 13, disp. 15, dub. 2, § 2, nos. 54–58 (ed. Palmé, 8:109–11).

35. Throughout this disputation, the Salmanticenses employ the Scholastic distinction between priority *in-quo* (literally, "in-a-thing" priority) and priority *a-quo* ("from-a-thing" priority). Conceptual stages *in-quo* and *a-quo* are based on these kinds of priority. The qualifier *in-quo* indicates strict, one-way entailment, while *a-quo* indicates two-way entailment. For example, "animal" is prior to "man" *in-quo* because "man" implies "animal" but not vice versa. Conversely, from the perspective of material cause, matter is prior to form *a-quo* because, although prior in its own causal order, matter always bears some reference to form both in real existence and in thought. Thomas Harper points out that the terminology of *in-quo* and *a-quo* emphasizes that the former is intrinsic and the latter derivative in *The Metaphysics of the School*, vol. 2 (London: Macmillan, 1881), 565–66.

36. *Scientia simplicis intelligentiae* ("knowledge of simple intelligence"): God's knowledge considered insofar as he knows himself and thus knows all things that he could create or do, conceived of as conceptually prior from our perspective to the knowledge of vision (*scientia visionis*), whereby he knows the creatures that he has actually chosen to exist.

37. *Consequentia subsistendi* ("existential entailment"): priority *consequentia subsistendi* is priority of nonreciprocal entailment, particularly conceived of as the higher vis-à-vis the lower. In other words, it is priority based on the fact that one thing logically implies another but not vice versa, and hence the *consequentia* does not run both ways. To return to a previous example, "animal" is prior to "man" *consequentia subsistendi* because "animal" does not necessarily entail "man," but "man" does necessarily entail "animal." Hence, priority *consequentia subsistendi* is priority *in-quo*, not priority

the stage in which what is possible is known and the stage in which what is going to be is decreed and known must constitute a twofold stage *in-quo*, and the prior in no way depends on the posterior. Now as for the fact that these two are sufficient, this can also be shown. For if God knows in one single stage all possible things in all combinations in which or with which they are capable of being chosen, he will equally be able, in another subsequent stage, to choose all the things he wills in every combination or with every dependence he pleases and in this way, in the end, to know them as going to be. For just as in one single stage and through one act he can know all possible things, so also in one single stage and through one volition, out of all the possible things previously known, he can decree what he wills, without need for us to multiply other stages that would add nothing but confusion. Yet, we do not thereby exclude that on the part of the objects willed there is mutual priority and different dependencies in the various genera of causes as befits the objects themselves either from their nature or at least from the divine ordination. But this priority that exists on the part of the objects is not priority *in-quo*, whether of existence or of conceiving of one without the other. Instead, it is priority *a-quo*, priority of nature and dependence, in accord with which one thing neither exists nor is known without the other but exists and is known as dependent on the other in a given genus of cause, as we have explained at greater length in the place cited above (tract. 13, disp. 15).[38]

7. Thus, in accord with this doctrine (to confront the point of particular difficulty and close in on it more exactly):[39] In that first stage, God knew that the universe comprised of angels, men, and the other creatures that have really been made was possible. He knew that the first man, Adam, was possible, who would receive original justice with

---

a-quo. Cf. Aristotle, *Categories*, 12.14b9–23; Anthony Goudin, *Philosophia juxta inconcussa tutissimaque D. Thomae dogmata*, vol. 1, *Logica* (Pompei: Urbeveteri, 1859), 362; and Gredt, *Elementa philosophiae Aristotelico-Thomisticae*, vol. 1, no. 206, p. 186.

38. Salmanticenses (ed. Palmé, 8:109–11). The Latin text mistakenly gives the citation as: *tract. 15*.

39. Where the Latin has *ut ad punctum praecipua difficultatis magis accingamur, et approximemur*, I have read *ut ad punctum praecipuae difficultatis magis accingamur, et approximemur*, as in the 1687 edition.

the stipulation that by not sinning he would preserve it for himself and his children, whereas by sinning he would lose it for himself and his children, constituting himself and them as guilty and liable to eternal damnation. He knew that the Incarnation, or the union of the divine Word to human nature, was possible, from which Christ, the true God-man, would arise, who by the dignity of his person would be able to elicit infinitely satisfactory acts and thereby to make equal satisfaction for any offenses and to merit whatever reward he willed. He knew that Christ, on account of his infinite excellence, was most suited to be established as the end of all creatures, for all things to be made for him, and for men to be chosen or predestined to glory in such a way that all these effects would regard Christ as the end and would depend on him in the genus of final cause. He also knew that the sins that he would permit both in Adam and in his children would be the sufficient matter as whose remedy and satisfaction Christ would be predestined, in such a way that his predestination would be bound to the remediation of sin and the redemption of men, seeing as there is no doubt that this combination and connection falls within the bounds of what is possible. Finally (to omit other things not as pertinent to our present consideration), he knew that between the Incarnation and the remediation of sin or the redemption of men the connection and mutual dependence could be established such that the permission of sin and its remediation would be ordered to Christ as the end *for-the-sake-of-which* and depend on him in the genus of final cause while, conversely, the Incarnation of Christ would be ordered to the salvation of men as the end *to-which*, the end effected, would regard sin as the matter to be destroyed through his satisfaction, and would depend on these things in the genus both of material cause and also of final cause *to-which*. Now it is certain that these combinations are possible, that they were the objects of God's simple intelligence, and that they pertained to the first stage *in-quo*, as we were just saying. The doubt, however (one that depends on the will of God alone), is which of these did God choose in the second stage *in-quo* and how? So this is the basis on which we have to track down the legitimate resolution of this doubt. And as to the fact that God willed Christ as the end of other things, to whom the predestinations and benefits of men on the one hand and the permissions of sins (a point on which others are greatly hard-pressed to be persuasive) on the other would be ordered, we readily grant them, and it is established from no. 4 that we should make such a supposition here. But as to whether Christ was willed as the end of other things such that he was at the same time ordered to the redemption of men and had, therefore, a dependence on sin in another genus of cause and, consequently, a connection with it by the divine ordination, this is the special difficulty that we are now going to resolve.

§ 2. The opinion of St. Thomas is preferred and bolstered by a singular foundation

8 It should be said that God decreed the Incarnation as a remedy for sin and, consequently, that the Word would not assume flesh by virtue of the present decree if Adam had not sinned. This second part of the assertion, which directly answers to the question, is manifestly gathered from the first in accord with what we noted up front in the preceding §. Both parts are commonly taught by the holy Fathers, as we will presently show, but especially the Angelic Teacher (ST III, q. 1, a. 3; *Super III Sent.*, dist. 1, q. 1, a. 3; *De veritate*, q. 29, a. 4, ad 3 and 4; and *Super I Tim.*, chap. 1, lect. 4)[40] and frequently elsewhere. All his disciples unanimously subscribe to this: Capréolus[41] (*Defensiones divi Thomae* III, dist. 1, q. 1, a. 1, concl. 1); Ferrara[42] (Commentary on the *Summa contra gentiles* IV, chap. 55, § *Circa praedicta aliud dubium*); Cajetan[43] (Commentary on ST III, q. 1, a. 3); Medina[44] (*Expositio in Tertiam D.*

---

40. ST III, q. 1, a. 3 (Leonine ed., 11:13–14); *Super III Sent.*, dist. 1, q. 1, a. 3 (ed. Moos, 3:19–24); *De veritate*, q. 29, a. 4, ad 3 and 4 (Leonine ed., 22:860); and *Super I Tim.*, chap. 1, lect. 4 (ed. Cai, 2:219.40). The Latin text mistakenly gives the last citation as: *1, ad Corinth. 1, sect. 4*.

41. Jean Capréolus, OP (ca. 1380–1444), *Defensiones divi Thomae* III, dist. 1, q. 1, a. 1, concl. 1 (ed. Paban et Pègues, 5:1–2). The Latin text gives the citation as: *Capreolus in 3, dist. 1, quest. unic. art. 1, concil. 1*.

42. Francesco Silvestri de Ferrara, OP (ca. 1474–1528), Commentary on the *Summa contra gentiles* IV, chap. 55, § *Circa praedicta aliud dubium* (Leonine ed., 13:187.16).

43. Tommaso de Vio Cajetan, OP (1469–1534), Commentary on *ST* III, q. 1, a. 3 (Leonine ed., 11:15–16).

44. Bartolomé de Medina, OP (1528–80), *Expositio in Tertiam D. Thomae partem*, q. 1, a. 3 (ed. Gastius, 74–83).

Thomae partem, q. 1, a. 3); Araújo[45] (*In Tertiam partem Divi Thomae commentarii*, q. 1, a. 3, dub. unic., concl. 1); Álvarez[46] (*De Incarnatione divini Verbi disputationes*, q. 1, a. 3, disp. 9, concl. 2); Cornejo[47] (*Tractatus primus de Incarnatione Verbi divini*, q. 1, a. 3, disp. unic., dub. unic.); Cabrera[48] (*In Tertiam partem Sancti Thomae Aquinatis commentarii et disputationes*, q. 1, a. 3, disp. 1, § 10); Vicente[49] (*Relectio de habituali Christi Salvatoris nostri sanctificante gratia*, sol. q. 6, p. 683); Nazario[50] (*Commentaria et controversiae in Tertiam partem Summae Divi Thomae Aquinatis*, q. 1, a. 3); John of St. Thomas[51] (*Cursus theologicus in Summam Sancti Thomae*, in III, disp. 3, a. 2, concl. 3); Godoy[52] (*Disputationes theologicae in Tertiam partem Divi Thomae*, tract. 1, disp. 8, § 1, no. 14); Gonet[53] (*Clypeus theologiae Thomisticae*, part 3, tract. 1, disp. 5, § 1). Parra[54] (*Incarnationis arcanum scholastice disputationibus et quaestionibus reseratum*, tract. 1, disp. 1, q. 7, a. 2); Juan Prudencio[55] (*Commentarii in Tertiam partem Sanctissimi Thomae*, tract. 2, disp. 1,

---

45. Francisco de Araújo, OP (1580–1664), *In Tertiam partem Divi Thomae commentarii*, q. 1, a. 3, dub. unic., concl. 1 (1636 ed., 95–98).

46. Diego Álvarez, OP (ca. 1550–1635), *De Incarnatione divini Verbi disputationes*, q. 1, a. 3, disp. 9, concl. 2 (ed. Facciottus, 74–80).

47. Pedro Cornejo de Pedrosa, O.Carm. (1566–1618), *Tractatus primus de Incarnatione Verbi divini*, q. 1, a. 3, disp. unic., dub. unic. (ed. Varesius, 2:98–116).

48. Pedro de Cabrera, OESH (d. 1616), *In Tertiam partem Sancti Thomae Aquinatis commentarii et disputationes*, q. 1, a. 3, disp. 1, § 10 (ed. Barrera, 252–58). The Latin text gives the citation as: *Cabrera disp. 1 § 2*.

49. Juan Vicente, OP (1544–95), *Relectio de habituali Christi Salvatoris nostri sanctificante gratia*, sol. q. 6, p. 683 (ed. Dianus, 683).

50. Giovanni Paolo Nazario, OP (ca. 1556–1645), *Commentaria et controversiae in Tertiam partem Summae Divi Thomae Aquinatis*, q. 1, a. 3 (ed. Rossius, 4:116–50).

51. John of St. Thomas, OP (1589–1644), *Cursus theologicus in Summam Sancti Thomae*, in III, disp. 3, a. 2, concl. 3 (ed. Vivès, 8:104–7).

52. Pedro de Godoy, OP (d. 1677), *Disputationes theologicae in Tertiam partem Divi Thomae*, tract. 1, disp. 8, § 1, no. 14 (ed. Hertz, 1:113–16).

53. Jean-Baptiste Gonet, OP (1615–81), *Clypeus theologiae Thomisticae*, part 3, tract. 1, disp. 5, § 1 (ed. Vivès, 5:473–75).

54. Antonio de la Parra y Arteaga, CRM (fl. 1668), *Incarnationis arcanum scholastice disputationibus et quaestionibus reseratum*, tract. 1, disp. 1, q. 7, a. 2 (ed. Sanchez, 94–97).

55. Juan Prudencio, O. de M. (1610–57), *Commentarii in Tertiam partem Sanctissimi Thomae*, tract. 2, disp. 1, dub. 1, sect. 5 (ed. Anisson, 1:282–84).

dub. 1, sect. 5); our Philippe[56] (*Disputationes theologicae in Tertiam partem Divi Thomae*, disp. 1, dub. 6); our Lawrence[57] (*Spicilegium theologicum seu difficiliores controversiae selectae ex Tertia parte Summae Divi Thomae de Verbi divini Incarnatione*, contr. 7, § 14, nos. 132–40); Cippullo[58] (*Commentariorum scholasticorum in Tertiam Partem Summae Theologiae Doctoris Angelici*, q. 1, a. 3, dub. 1, § 2); and many others. The same is also defended by St. Bonaventure[59] (*Commentaria in tertium librum Sententiarum*, dist. 1, a. 2, q. 2), where he observes that the opposite opinion is more in conformity with human reason, whereas ours is more in conformity with the faith, and he himself embraces it; Argentinas[60] (*In tertium librum Sententiarum commentaria*, dist. 1, q. 1, a. 4); Richard[61] (*Super tertium librum Sententiarum*, dist. 1, a. 2, q. 4); the Carthusian[62] (*Commentaria in librum tertium Sententiarum*, dist. 1, q. 2), relating Pierre de Tarentaise[63] as being of the same opinion; Gabriel[64] (*In tertium Sententiarum*, dist. 2, q. 1, a. 3, dub. 3); Marsilius[65]

56. Philippe de la Trinité, OCD (1603–71), *Disputationes theologicae in Tertiam partem Divi Thomae*, disp. 1, dub. 6 (ed. Iullieron, 13–16).

57. Lawrence of St. Therese, OCD (d. 1670), *Spicilegium theologicum seu difficiliores controversiae selectae ex Tertia parte Summae Divi Thomae de Verbi divini Incarnatione*, contr. 7, § 14, nos. 132–40 (ed. Vannaccius, 228–30).

58. Gregorio Cippullo, OP (d. 1646), *Commentariorum scholasticorum in Tertiam Partem Summae Theologiae Doctoris Angelici*, q. 1, a. 3, dub. 1, § 2 (ed. Manelphius, 1:118–22).

59. St. Bonaventure, OFM (1221–74), *Commentaria in tertium librum Sententiarum*, dist. 1, a. 2, q. 2 (Quaracchi ed., 3:24).

60. Thomas of Strasbourg (Thomas de Argentina), OESA (ca. 1300–1357), *In tertium librum Sententiarum commentaria*, dist. 1, q. 1, a. 4 (ed. Ziletti, 2–4).

61. Richard of Middleton, OFM (ca. 1249–1308), *Super tertium librum Sententiarum*, dist. 1, a. 2, q. 4 (1591 ed., 3:12–13). The Latin text gives the citation as: *Ricardus ibidem, art. 1, quaest. 2*.

62. Denis the Carthusian (1402–71), *Commentaria in librum tertium Sententiarum*, dist. 1, q. 2 (Opera omnia, 23:43–45). The Latin text gives the citation as: *Carthusian. dist. 3, quaest. 2*.

63. Bl. Pierre de Tarentaise (Pope Innocent V), OP (ca. 1225–76), *In tertium librum Sententiarum commentaria*, dist. 1, q. 2, a. 2 (ed. Colomerium, 3:5).

64. Gabriel Biel, CRSA (ca. 1420–95), *In tertium Sententiarum*, dist. 2, q. 1, a. 3, dub. 3 (ed. Werbeck and Hofmann, 3:69–74).

65. Marsilius von Inghen (ca. 1340–96), *Quaestiones super tertium librum Sententiarum*, dist. 1, q. 1, a. 3 (ed. Flach, 3:353–54).

(*Quaestiones super tertium librum Sententiarum*, dist. 1, q. 1, a. 3); Abulensis[66] (*Commentaria in Matthaeum*, chap. 4, q. 44); Jean d'Arbres[67] (*Primus tomus Theosophiae*, III, chap. 8); Mendoza[68] (*Quaestiones quodlibeticae et relectio de Christi regno ac dominio*, q. schol. 1, beginning from no. 1); Lorca[69] (*Commentarii ac disputationes in Tertiam partem D. Thomae*, q. 1, a. 3, disp. 10, memb. 3); Vásquez[70] (*Commentarii ac disputationes in Tertiam partem S. Thomae*, q. 1, a. 3, disp. 10, chap. 4); Valencia[71] (*Commentarii theologici*, vol. 4, disp. 1, q. 1, pt. 7); Ragusa[72] (*Commentarii ac disputationes in Tertiam partem D. Thomae*, disp. 28, § 9); Becanus[73] (*Theologiae scholasticae pars tertia*, tract. 1, chap. 1, q. 8); Lessius[74] (*Disputatio de praedestinatione Christi*, sect. 1, no. 2); Maldonado[75] (*Commentarii in Matthaeum*, chap. 9, vers. 13); Salazar[76]

66. Alonso Tostado (Abulensis) (ca. 1410–55), *Commentaria in Matthaeum*, chap. 4, q. 44 (ed. Balleoniania, 18:412). I have been unable to find the relevant doctrine in the place cited. There is possibly an allusion to this opinion toward the end of his commentary on St. Jerome's prologue to Matthew (ed. Balleoniania, 18:121–22). Juniper B. Carol also remarks that he was unable to find this reference. *Why Jesus Christ?*, 40n21.

67. Jean d'Arbres (Arboreus) (fl. 1540), *Primus tomus Theosophiae*, III, chap. 8 (ed. Colinaeum, 97–98).

68. Alfonso de Mendoza, OESA (d. 1591), *Quaestiones quodlibeticae et relectio de Christi regno ac dominio*, q. schol. 1, beginning from no. 1 (ed. Martinus, 1–54).

69. Pedro de Lorca, Ord. Cist. (1561–1612), *Commentarii ac disputationes in Tertiam partem D. Thomae*, q. 1, a. 3, disp. 10, memb. 3 (ed. Sanchez de Ezpleta, 1:80–81). The Latin text gives the citation as: *Lorca disp. 3*.

70. Gabriel Vásquez, SJ (1549–1604), *Commentarii ac disputationes in Tertiam partem S. Thomae*, q. 1, a. 3, disp. 10, chap. 4 (ed. Sanchez Crespo, 1:134–37).

71. Gregorio de Valencia, SJ (1550–1603), *Commentarii theologici*, vol. 4, disp. 1, q. 1, pt. 7 (ed. Cardon, 4:61–76).

72. Giuseppe Ragusa, SJ (d. 1624), *Commentarii ac disputationes in Tertiam partem D. Thomae*, disp. 28, § 9 (ed. Cardon, 221–23).

73. Martin Becanus, SJ (d. 1624), *Theologiae scholasticae pars tertia*, tract. 1, chap. 1, q. 8 (ed. Pillehotte and Cassin, 33–35). Questions 6 and 7 (ed. Pillehotte and Cassin, 17–33) are also germane.

74. Leonardus Lessius, SJ (1554–1623), *Disputatio de praedestinatione Christi*, sect. 1, no. 2 (ed. Delagarde, 564).

75. Juan Maldonado, SJ (1533–83), *Commentarii in Matthaeum*, chap. 9, vers. 13 (ed. Cardon, 206–207).

76. Fernando Chirinos de Salazar, SJ (1576–1646), *Defensio pro immaculata Deiparae Virginis conceptione*, chap. 6, no. 1 (1625 ed., 41).

(*Defensio pro immaculata Deiparae Virginis conceptione*, chap. 6, no. 1); Justinianus[77] (*In omnes Catholicas epistolas*, on 1 Jn 3:5: *He appeared to take away our sins*); Théophile Raynaud[78] (*Christus Deus-Homo*, III, sect. 1, chap. 4, in no. 117); Lugo[79] (*Disputationes scholasticae de mysterio Incarnationis dominicae*, disp. 1, sect. 1ff.); Bernal[80] (*Disputationes de divini Verbi Incarnatione*, disp. 16, sect. 1 and 2); Granado[81] (*In Tertiam Partem S. Thomae Aquinatis commentarii*, tract. 3, contr. 1, disp. 1, sect. 3); and many others, whom it would require too much space to relate.

It is proved by one single yet most weighty foundation of St. Thomas: If the motive or reason for which God has *de facto* decreed the Incarnation ceased, the Word would not assume flesh by virtue of the present decree, seeing as it is known that if the end or the intention of the end is taken away, the choice as well as the execution of the chosen means ordered to it ceases. But if Adam were not to sin, the motive or reason for which God has *de facto* decreed the Incarnation would cease. Therefore, if Adam had not sinned, God would not assume flesh by virtue of the present decree. The *consequentia* is plain. And the minor premise is shown: God has *de facto* decreed the Incarnation as a remedy for original sin and for the redemption of men. Therefore if Adam were not to sin, the motive or reason for which God has *de facto* decreed the Incarnation would cease. Persuasion for the antecedent, in

---

77. Benedictus Justinianus, SJ (d. 1622), *In omnes Catholicas epistolas*, on 1 Jn 3:5: *He appeared to take away our sins* (ed. Cardon and Cavellat, 140–46). The Latin text gives the citation as: *Justinianus 1 Joannis 13, vers. 5 ad aliud* apparuit, ut peccata nostra tolleret.

78. Théophile Raynaud, SJ (1583–1663), *Christus Deus-Homo*, III, sect. 1, chap. 4, in no. 117 (ed. Meursium, 269).

79. Juan de Lugo, SJ (1583–1660). While disp. 1, dealing with the fittingness of the Incarnation, is germane, disp. 7 is directly to the point. It is likely that the citation is meant to refer to the latter. See de Lugo, *Disputationes scholasticae de mysterio Incarnationis dominicae*, disp. 1 (ed. Arnaud and Borde, 1–5); and disp. 7 (ed. Arnaud and Borde, 124–34).

80. Augustín Bernal, SJ (1587–1642), *Disputationes de Incarnatione Verbi Dei*, disp. 16, sect. 1 and 2 (ed. Nosocomius, 125–28).

81. Diego Granado, SJ (1571–1632), *In Tertiam Partem S. Thomae Aquinatis commentarii*, tract. 3, contr. 1, disp. 1, sect. 3 (ed. de Lazcano, 4:66–68).

which the difficulty lies: Since the Incarnation is a work surpassing all natural reason and depending on God's free will alone, who in his good pleasure was able to decree it or not decree it and to decree it for this or that motive and dependently on this or another condition, as we have explained at great length in the preceding §, we cannot gain certain knowledge as to the motive for which it was decreed and willed except from the will of God himself, which is revealed to us in sacred Scripture in accord with the common understanding of the holy Fathers. But the motive proposed by Scripture and the Fathers is the remediation of sin or the redemption of men by the mediation of Christ's satisfaction. And Scripture and the Father propose this so clearly that to the minds of Christians contemplating such a mystery nothing presents itself more frequently than this motive.[82] Therefore God has *de facto* decreed the Incarnation as a remedy for sin or for men's salvation.

9 We could show this principal assumption with great breadth by laying out for consideration many testimonies of Scripture and the Fathers. But we will only include below some more select passages, the ones that seem clearer. *For God so loved the world, as to give his only begotten Son: that whosoever believeth in him may not perish, but may have life everlasting* (Jn 3:16). *They that are whole need not the physician: but they that are sick* (Lk 5:31). *The Son of man is come to save that which was lost* (Mt 18:11). *The Son of man is come to give his life a redemption for many* (Mk 10:45). *God sent his Son, born of a woman, made under the law: That he might redeem them who were under the law* (Gal 4:4–5). *A faithful saying, and worthy of all acceptation, that Christ Jesus came into the world to save sinners* (1 Tm 1:15). *Because the children are partakers of flesh and blood, he also himself in like manner hath been partaker of the same: that, through death, he might destroy him who had the empire of death: And might deliver them, who through the fear of death were all their lifetime subject to servitude* (Heb 2:14–15). And throughout Scripture this same point is hammered home. In fact, to declare for what he had come, even Christ the Lord compared himself to a shepherd who, leaving the ninety-nine sheep in the desert, proceeded to seek after the

---

82. An appeal to the *sensus fidelium*.

one that had gone astray. In this way he explained that he had come for the salvation of men and the reparation of sin.

The Fathers, well learned in Scripture and breaking open its meaning, speak in the same fashion. St. Irenaeus:[83] *They spurn the Incarnation of the Word of God of pure generation, defrauding man of ascent to the Lord and lacking gratitude to the Word of God who was incarnate for them* (*Against Heresies*, III, chap. 19). Origen:[84] *The Word descended into flesh for this: that flesh, that is man believing, might ascend into the Word through the flesh so that many adoptive sons might come to be through the only-begotten natural Son. The Word became flesh not for himself, but for us* (Homily). Tertullian:[85] *As for that man in uncleannesses pieced together in the womb, brought up amid mockery—Christ certainly loved him; for him he descended* (*On the Flesh of Christ*, chap. 4). St. Athanasius:[86] *That you may know that our fault afforded him the occasion to descend and our trespass enticed the humanity of the Word of God to hasten toward us, to appear among men. For we afforded the cause of his embodiment, and for our salvation he has been so humane that he willed to be and to appear in a human body* (*Discourse on the Incarnation of the Word*). St. Hilary:[87] *For the sake of the human race the Son of God was born of the Virgin* (*On the Trinity*, II, chap. 24). St. Gregory of Nazianzus:[88] *Now what cause existed for the humanity assumed by God for us? In truth to prepare our salvation* (*Fourth Theological Oration*, no. 2). St. Basil:[89] *Learn the mystery. God is therefore*

---

83. St. Irenaeus of Lyon (d. ca. 202), *Irenaeus Lugdunensis secundum translationem Latinam – Adversus haereses seu Detectio et eversio falso cognominatae Gnoseos* (SC 211:372–74). The Latin text gives the citation as: *D. Irenaeus lib. 3 contra haeres. cap. 29*.

84. Origen (ca. 185–254). This quotation, however, seems to be from a homily by John Scottus Eriugena (ca. 815–77) on the prologue to John's Gospel (PL 122:295). The Latin text gives the citation as: *Origenes hom. 2 in divers.*

85. Tertullian (ca. 155–240), *De carne Christi* (CCSL 2:878).

86. St. Athanasius of Alexandria (ca. 298–373), *Oratio de Incarnatione Verbi* (PG 25:104). The Latin text gives the citation as: *D. Athanas. serm. 3 contra Arianos*.

87. St. Hilary of Poitiers (ca. 310–67), *De Trinitate* (CCSL 62:60).

88. St. Gregory of Nazianzus (ca. 329–90), Oration 30, Fourth Theological Oration (SC 250:228). The Latin text gives the citation as: *D. Nazianzen. orat. 4 de Theologia*, num. 6.

89. St. Basil the Great (ca. 330–79). This work is falsely attributed to him. Pseudo-Basil, *Homilia in sanctam Christi generationem* (PG 31:1464).

in the flesh because this accursed flesh had to be sanctified (Homily on the Human Generation of Christ, chap. 3). St. Ambrose:[90] *What was the cause of the Incarnation except that flesh, which had sinned, should be redeemed?* (On the Sacrament of the Lord's Incarnation, chap. 6). St. John Chrysostom:[91] *Therefore he assumed our flesh on account of kindness and clemency alone that he might show us mercy. For there is no other cause of the dispensation than this alone* (Homily 5 on Hebrews). And: *This is the only cause of the curing for which he descended into this world* (Homily 66 on Matthew). St. Jerome:[92] *For man stuck in the mire of sin needed a greater help, and so wisdom itself came* (Commentary on Ecclesiastes 7:20). St. Augustine:[93] *There was no cause of the coming of Christ the Lord except to save sinners. Take away the diseases, take away the wounds, and there is no cause for the medicine* (Sermon 9 on the Words of the Apostle, near the beginning). Our Holy Father Cyril of Alexandria: *For he knew that we are mortal because of sin [...] and thus decided in his mercy before the ages that his Word would become man, the beginning of his ways, and the foundation* (Thesaurus, assert. 15).[94] Our Holy Father John Damascene:[95] *Since we obscured and wiped out the notes of the divine image through transgression of the commandment, he becomes a partaker in that which is baser, that is our nature* (On the Orthodox Faith, IV, chap. 4). St. Leo the Great:[96] *Because by the envy of the devil death entered into the world and human captivity could be*

---

90. St. Ambrose of Milan (ca. 340–97), *De incarnationis dominicae sacramento* (CSEL 79:252).

91. St. John Chrysostom (ca. 349–407), *In Epistulam ad Hebraeos homilia V* (PG 63:47); and *In Matthaeum homilia LXVI al. LXVII* (PG 58:626). The Latin text mistakenly gives the citation of the former as: *Chrysos. hom. 3 in Genes*. The confusion probably stems from the similar sentiments found in *In caput primum Geneseos homilia III*, no. 4 (PG 53:37).

92. St. Jerome (ca. 347–420), *Commentarius in Ecclesiasten* (CCSL 72:309). The Latin text gives the citation as: *D. Hieronym. in cap. 2 Ecclesiast.*

93. St. Augustine of Hippo (354–430), Sermon 175 (PL 38:945).

94. *Thesaurus de sancta et consubstantiali Trinitate* (PG 75:292). The Latin text gives the citation as: *S. P. N. Cyrillus Alexand. lib. 5 Thesauri, cap. 8*. The Salmanticenses do not note the omission.

95. St. John Damascene (ca. 676–749), *De fide orthodoxa* (SC 540:164).

96. Pope St. Leo the Great (ca. 400–461), *Tractatus LXXVII: Item alius de Pentecosten* (CCSL 138A:488).

loosed in no other way than that he should take up our cause who, without loss to his majesty, would become true man and alone would not have the contagion of sin, he apportioned for himself the work of our reparation (Tractate 77, Sermon 3 on Pentecost, chap. 2). Similar statements (to avoid prolixity) are offered by St. Epiphanius[97] (*Against Heresies*, I, tom. 1, at the end), St. Gregory of Nyssa[98] (*On the Holy Baptism*, at the beginning), St. Cyril of Jerusalem[99] (Catechesis 6), Theodoret[100] (*Epitome of Divine Dogmas*, Chapter on the Incarnation), Theophylact[101] (Commentary on Jn 3:16: *God so loved the world*), St. Bernard[102] (Homily 3 on *Missus est*, near the end), Guerric the Abbot[103] (Sermon 3 on the Lord's Nativity), and others in general. And finally, the entire Church professes this in the symbol of faith published at the Council of Nicaea and with utmost reverence, falling to her knees, proclaims and sings throughout the whole world: *For us men and for our salvation, he came down from heaven (...) and became man.*[104] Therefore it cannot be denied that, according to sacred Scripture and the common opinion of the Fathers, God intended, chose, and decreed the Incarnation as a

---

97. St. Epiphanius of Salamis (ca. 310–403), *Panarion*, haer. 20, no. 1, in Karl Holl, ed., *Epiphanius*, vol. 1.2 (Berlin: De Gruyter, 2013), 227.

98. St. Gregory of Nyssa (ca. 335–94), *In diem luminum, in quo baptizatus est Dominus noster* (PG 46:577–82).

99. St. Cyril of Jerusalem (ca. 313–86), Catechesis 6, chap. 11, in Guilielmus Carolus Reischl, ed., *S. patris nostri Cyrilli Hierosolymorum Archiepiscopi opera quae supersunt omnia*, vol. 1 (Monaci: Sumtibus Librariae Lentnerianae, 1848), 171.

100. Theodoret of Cyrus (ca. 393–458), *Haereticarum fabularum compendium* V, chap. 11 (PG 83:489).

101. Theophylact of Ohrid (ca. 1055–1107), *Enarratio in evangelium Joannis*, chap. 3, vers. 16 (PG 123:1212).

102. St. Bernard of Clairvaux, O.Cist. (1090–1153), *In laudibus Virginis Mariae*, Homily 3: *super "Missus est"*, no. 14, in J. Leclercq and H. Rochais, eds., *S. Bernardi opera*, vol. 4 (Rome: Editiones Cistercienses, 1966), 45–46.

103. Bl. Guerric of Igny, O.Cist. (ca. 1070–1157), Sermon 3 on the Nativity, no. 1 (SC 166:186).

104. In what is now called the extraordinary form of the Mass, this portion of the Creed is always said or sung kneeling. In the ordinary form of the Mass as described in the Roman Missal promulgated in 1969, these words are said or sung while making a profound bow, with the exception of the solemnities of the Annunciation and Christmas, when they are said or sung kneeling out of special acknowledgment of the Incarnation. The Salmanticenses do not note the omission.

remedy for sin and in connection with the redemption and salvation of men. This is the solid and legitimate kind of argumentation when it comes to the accomplishment of a work thoroughly free to God, where the whole reason why it happens or does not happen is, in the final analysis, reduced to God's decision. As for the things that natural reason thinks up in this case, they are, rather, divinations, as St. Anselm[105] rightly said (*Cur Deus homo?*, I, chap. 1), calling similar patterns of argumentation paintings in the air.

10 A compelling confirmation: Many Fathers of great weight not only teach positively that the Word assumed flesh for the redemption of men from sin but also deny with carefully chosen words that the Word would assume flesh if the necessity or occasion for redeeming men from the miseries of their sins were not present. St. Irenaeus speaks thus: *For if flesh did not have need of being saved, the Word of God would not at all have become flesh* (*Against Heresies*, V, chap. 14).[106] St. Athanasius: *The necessity, in fact, and the need of men is antecedent to Christ's nativity, so that if need and necessity were taken away, he would not have clothed himself in flesh* (*Second Oration against the Arians*).[107] St. Gregory of Nazianzus: *Now what cause existed for the humanity assumed by God for us? In truth to prepare our salvation* (*Fourth Theological Oration*, no. 2). St. Augustine: *The Son of man came to seek out and save what was lost. If man had not been lost, the Son of man would not have come* (Sermon 8 on the Words of the Apostle, not far from the beginning).[108] And: *There was no cause for the coming of Christ the Lord except to save sinners* (Sermon 9 on the Words of the Apostle). And, explicating the passage: *The steps of a man are from the Lord* (Ps 36:23): *But if, O man, you were not to dismiss God, God would not become man for you* (*Expositions on the Psalms*, Psalm 36, addr. 2).[109] And: *If the*

---

105. St. Anselm of Canterbury, OSB (ca. 1033–1109), *Cur Deus homo?*, I, chap. 1 (ed. Schmitt, 2:49).

106. *Irenaeus Lugdunensis secundum translationem Latinam – Adversus haereses seu Detectio et eversio falso cognominatae Gnoseos* (SC 153:182).

107. *Oratio II contra Arianos* (PG 26:261). The Latin text gives the citation as: D. Athanas. serm. 3, contra Arianos.

108. Sermon 174 (PL 38:940).

109. *Expositiones in psalmos* (CCSL 38:357).

integral state of human nature remained, why was it necessary for God to take on our flesh? (*Hypomnesticon*, III).[110] And, on the passage: *Christ Jesus came into the world to save sinners* (1 Tm 1:15), he says: *There was no cause of the coming of Christ the Lord except to save sinners. Take away the wounds, take away the diseases, and there is no cause for the medicine* (Sermon 9 on the Words of the Apostle).[111] St. Gregory the Great:[112] *And indeed if Adam were not to sin, it would not be necessary for our Redeemer to take on our flesh. For he did not come to call the just but sinners to penitence. If, therefore, he came for sinners, then if sinners had been lacking, it would not be necessary for him to come* (Commentary on 1 Sm 8:8). St. Leo the Great: *If man, made after the image and likeness of God, had remained in the honor of his nature and had not deviated through concupiscence and, deceived by the fraud of the devil, from the law laid down for him, the creator of the world would not become a creature and neither would the everlasting be subject to the time-bound nor would God the Son, equal to God the Father, assume the form of a slave and the likeness of sinful flesh* (Tractate 77, Sermon 3 on Pentecost, chap. 2).[113] Our Holy Father Cyril of Alexandria: *If we had not sinned, neither would the Son of God have become like us* (*On the Trinity*, dial. 5).[114] Andrew of Crete:[115] *Why do I linger on these things? If there were no cross, there would not have been Christ on earth* (Homily 1 on the Exaltation of the Cross). By way of metonymy, he understands "cross" as the redemption of men carried out on the cross. St. Bernard: *Why did the Son of God become man except to make men*

---

110. A work falsely attributed to St. Augustine. Pseudo-Augustine, *The Pseudo-Augustinian Hypomnesticon Against the Pelagians and Celestinans*, vol. 2, *Text edited from the manuscripts*, ed. John Edward Chisholm (Fribourg: The University Press, 1980), 121. The Latin text gives the citation as: *Et lib. 3, hypog.*

111. The quotation as given here inverts "diseases" and "wounds" in comparison to that above.

112. Pope St. Gregory the Great, OSB (ca. 540–604), *Expositio in librum primum Regum* (CCSL 144:300–301). The Latin text gives the citation as: *D. Gregor. Magnus in lib. 1. Reg. cap. 1 ad illa verba, juxta omnia opera.*

113. *Tractatus LXXVII: Item alius de Pentecosten* (CCSL 138A:488).

114. *De ss. Trinitate dialogi VII* (PG 75:968).

115. St. Andrew of Crete (ca. 650–726), *Oratio X in venerabilem pretiosae et vivificae crucis Exaltationem* (PG 97:1020).

sons of God? (Sermon 1 on the Vigil of the Nativity).[116] Rupert the Abbot: *The faithful should still call penitent sinners sinners. And if we owe much to you, O Christ our God, because you became man, you, conversely, owe much to us, O man Christ, because for us you were assumed unto God. For if we had not been sinners, there would have been no cause why you would have to be assumed unto God* (On the Works of the Holy Spirit, II, chap. 6).[117] And later on: *If the slaves had not sinned, neither would the nature of a slave have been assumed into the Lord God.* Finally, in the blessing of the Paschal candle taken from St. Gregory, the Church sings: *O truly necessary sin of Adam, destroyed completely by the death of Christ.*[118] It calls sin "necessary" and, as it were, gives it a favorable introduction by the device of prosopopoeia,[119] since if it had not been present, the Word of God would not assume flesh, namely, by negating the occasion in dependence on which it had been decreed by God that he would become man. In this sense, too, St. Ambrose, treating of Adam's sin, said: *O happy ruin which is repaired for the better!* (Explanation of Psalm 39, chap. 20).[120] And St. John Chrysostom: *O envy for the sake of goods, what infinite goods do you collect for us?* (Homily 2 on the Ascension).[121] The Fathers, therefore, are of the opinion that the benefit of the Incarnation was *de facto* decreed and intended by God for men's salvation and redemption from sin and, consequently (which they themselves affirm, not through *consequentiae* but in clear words), that if Adam were not to sin, the Word would not assume flesh, as we affirm in our conclusion.

In this place it is worth observing that the Angelic Doctor puts forward our assertion and resolves the present difficulty in no other way and in no other words than do the other sacred Doctors whose testimonies we have so far been considering, as is clearly established by

---

116. *Sermones in vigilia Nativitatis*, in J. Leclercq and H. M. Rochais, eds., *Sancti Bernardi opera*, vol. 4 (Rome: Ed. Cistercienses, 1966), 199.

117. *De operibus Spiritus Sancti* (CCCM 24:1868).

118. The Scholastics typically attribute the Proclamation of Easter, the *Exsultet*, to Gregory the Great.

119. A rhetorical device of personification.

120. *Explanatio psalmorum xii* (CSEL 64:225).

121. The authenticity of the homily is spurious. *In Ascensionem Domini nostri Jesu Christi sermo II* (PG 52:793–94).

consulting their opinions and words. Since, then, our adversaries consider themselves to be going against St. Thomas in this case, they must also admit that they have the other sacred Doctors against them as well. We, on the other hand, say that we are defending not only the Thomistic opinion but also the common opinion of the Fathers, as we have already stated above. No one is in the dark as to how much strength and prominence this affords in a matter so weighty and dependent on the will of God alone.

11 But before we proceed further, we must dispel two sticking points concerning the previous discussion that come up both in St. Thomas and in the other Fathers. For *in the first place*, St. Thomas does not seem to suppose rightly that what depends on the free will of God alone cannot become known to us with certainty other than from the revelation made manifest through Scripture or the Church's teaching. For the actual creation of the angels was an act free to God and dependent on his will alone, and yet St. Thomas himself (*ST* I, q. 50, a. 1)[122] proves the production of angels by only natural reason and without recourse to Scripture, to wit, because it pertains to the perfection of the universe that there should exist in it complete spiritual substances. Therefore it is possible for the Incarnation and other things that depend on the will of God alone to be proved not from divine revelation alone but also from other principles. *Next*, out of the Fathers, not a few affirm that there was no other cause or motive for the Incarnation than the remediation of sin and the redemption of men. In this, they go too far. For, as is established from what was said (no. 1), God was able to will this mystery for many other ends. In fact, he has *de facto* decreed it on account of its greatest intrinsic excellence, as we established from Scripture and the Fathers (no. 4) and take as a supposition in this difficulty. Therefore we must temper the testimonies of the Fathers we have related so that they do not exclude other ends, as on the surface they seem to do. But if this is the case, they do not succeed in proving determinately that the motive of the Incarnation was the remediation of sin, and they lose the power to prove the assertion of St. Thomas for which they are adduced.

But these issues are easily explained. For, as regards the principle

---

122. Aquinas (Leonine ed., 5:3–4).

taken from St. Thomas, it is most certain and evident, seeing as things above the requirement of nature and depending on the free will of God cannot be asserted in determinate form except from knowledge of the divine decree, which is derived for us in no other way than through Scripture and the Church's tradition in accord with the common understanding of the Fathers. And to conduct oneself otherwise is not to do theology but to commit divination and to give oneself over to rash discourse. And the opposite cannot be gleaned from St. Thomas in the place cited, for the Holy Doctor is not dealing there with the actual creation of the angels, as Suárez[123] and certain others who pose this objection less rightly suppose. Rather, he is considering the essence of the angels and inquiring *Whether an angel is altogether incorporeal?* He gives an affirmative solution to this question and proves it (as well as possible) by the light of natural reason because it pertains to the completion of the universe (which supposes that God has formed it in a perfect manner) to have complete spiritual or incorporeal intellective substances. But when he turns his mind to the actual production of the angels, he is always guided by the light of Scripture, which has revealed this arrangement of God, as is clear both from the passage cited in the argument On the Contrary, where he puts forward the passage *Who makes his angels spirits* (Ps 103:4), and particularly from q. 61,[124] which is *On the production of angels in natural being.* In resolving its difficulties, he proceeds by way of revealed principles and especially adduces the passage *Praise him, all his angels* (Ps 148:2), pondering that it was added afterwards *For he spoke and they were made* (Ps 148:5). Hence no lack of *consequentia* can be noted in the principles taken from the Holy Doctor. From another angle, there is a world of difference between the production of the angels and the fact that the Incarnation was going to occur, such that one could be warranted in proving the former, though not the latter. For the angels are natural substances pertaining to the perfection of this universe, at least as moving the heavens and carrying out other things that cannot be reduced to corporeal causes. Hence from the very universe so produced we are led naturally to knowledge

---

123. Francisco Suárez, SJ (1548–1617). See his *Disputationes metaphysicae*, disp. 35, sect. 1, no. 5 (ed. Vivès, 26:426–27).

124. Aquinas, *ST* I, q. 61, aa. 1–4 (Leonine ed., 5:106–9).

of the production of the angels. And this is the way in which the noble philosophers not enlightened by faith knew of separated substances, intelligences, or angels. On the other hand, the mystery of the Incarnation rises above every requirement of nature and the whole arrangement of the universe and has no connection with the universe either as produced or in the act of production. Hence the determinate fact that it is going to exist can only be reasonably asserted in virtue of the divine decree, whose existence is made known to us in no other way than through Scripture and the teaching of the Holy Fathers. Hence St. Thomas was warranted in assuming this principle in order to address the question.

As regards the other Fathers, they are opposed neither to the truth nor to us when they affirm that there was no other cause of the Incarnation than the remediation of sin and the salvation of men. For the Fathers are not treating of the possible causes or motives, which, as we have observed with St. Thomas (no. 1), could have been many, whichever God willed and of whatever sort. Instead, they treat of the causes that can be assigned with a foundation resting on the sacred text and the Church's teaching, for this is what mattered for their theological consideration, not the mere possibility of things. This is the sense in which they deny causes other than the remediation of sin because this is the only one drawn from Scripture. And this is how St. Gregory of Nazianzus should be taken when he says: *Now what cause existed for the humanity assumed by God for us? In truth to prepare our salvation*, not as an absolute or with respect to the logical nonimpossibility of the affairs in question, but in accord with the teaching of Scripture and the Church, which is what that great theologian was focusing on. And the sense is the same for the other Fathers, as is clear from the fact that they prove their assertion in no other way than by adducing the testimonies of Scripture (no. 9).

But when the matter is pushed further and the objection is raised not only that it was possible for the Incarnation to be willed for another motive, but that *de facto* the Incarnation was willed for another motive—the greatest excellence of the mystery itself, the dignity of Christ, and the exaltation of human nature, as we presupposed (no. 4)—we must say that this is indeed the case but that, even so, the Fathers were right to affirm that there was no other cause of the Incarnation than the remediation of sin. For God did not will the former except as ordered to the latter and in connection with it. For he willed Christ on account of his infinite dignity to be the end of all things *for-the-sake-of-which* in such a way that, by the same act, he willed the remediation of men from sin to be the end *to-which* of Christ's Incarnation, the remedy for sin its end effected, and sin itself the matter to be destroyed through his satisfaction. Hence all these things are brought back to the single adequate cause assigned by the Fathers. Hence St. Thomas (*ST* III, q. 1, a. 2)[125] assigns ten aspects of fittingness or causes of the Incarnation in the advancement of good on the one hand and in the removal of evil on the other, concluding: *But there are many other benefits that have resulted beyond what the human mind can apprehend.* And yet in the present article (*ST* III, q. 1, a. 3, ad 1)[126] he says: *All the other causes assigned pertain to the remediation of sin.* In other words, God, in his wisdom and will, has so chained together these goods on the part of the object willed that they possess a mutual dependence in different genera of cause and that none of them would exist without an order to the remediation of sin, as we have already suggested (no. 7) and will explain further (no. 29). And it is well established that this is the case from the motive proposed in Scripture and by the Fathers, as we have pondered above.

§ 3. The replies of the Scotists are impugned

12 There are various evasions by which our adversaries have tried to lighten the weight of the foundation laid above. First, some of Scotus's disciples respond that Scripture and the Fathers assign the remediation of sin positively as the motive of the Incarnation but that they do not deny or exclude other motives. Hence the argument laid out above is from negative authority, which usually offers nothing conclusive and is therefore rejected. Similarly, it is established from the divine text that angels were made for ministry to men, and yet it is certain that they were made for other ends, for example for the completion

---

125. Aquinas (Leonine ed., 11:9–11).
126. Aquinas (Leonine ed., 11:14).

and beauty of the universe, and, consequently, they were going to be produced even if the end of ministering to men had not been present.

But this response is easily overturned. *First*, because the Fathers, breaking open the meaning of Scripture and well learned in it, not only affirm that Christ came as the remedy for sin but also deny that he would have come lacking this occasion or necessity, as is patently obvious from their clear testimonies related in no. 10, which in no way allow for this explanation but are, rather, directly opposed to it. *Second*, because concerning what depends on the will of God alone, we have no other knowledge and should have no other opinion than in accordance with Scripture, in which the aforementioned will of God is revealed. But to ordain the Incarnation for this or that motive depends on God's will alone, just as ordaining the very substance of the mystery does. Since, then, Scripture only assigns the remediation of sin as the motive of the Incarnation, as the Fathers commonly interpret it, and the present evasion does not deny this, this clearly entails that we can reasonably affirm this motive alone and what concerns it or is connected to it, whereas others can be affirmed only by divination and without solid foundation. The *consequentia* is legitimately inferred from the premises. Of these the major premise is established from what was said in § 1 and the minor in § 2. The same response is refuted *third*, because in the most important matters pertaining to the faith a negative argument from the authority of sacred Scripture in accord with the explanation of the Fathers has the utmost weight and is equivalent to express negation. In this way, we can see that because Scripture mentions only one single world when it recounts the world's creation, even though it does not expressly deny any others, we gather through a legitimate *consequentia* that it is also a matter pertaining to the faith that there are no other worlds. And whoever asserted that there are other worlds would be accused of heresy or at least rashness. In this way, too, because where Scripture treats of the divine persons it names only three, even if it does not deny that there are other persons or more persons, we are warranted in inferring that there are only three persons in God.[127] And someone who affirmed that there are more would be a heretic. Finally, to

---

127. Cf. Gonet, *Clypeus theologiae Thomisticae*, part 3, tract. 1, disp. 5, § 1, no. 8 (ed. Vivès, 5:474).

approach the present matter more closely, because Scripture expressly says that the Word, the Son of God, assumed flesh when it puts forward the mystery of the Incarnation, although it does not expressly deny this of the Father or the Holy Spirit, it is clear to us with certainty that the Son alone has become incarnate. And someone who applied this to the other persons would be manifestly guilty of heresy. Since, then, when sacred Scripture treats of the motive of the Incarnation, it only puts forward the remediation of sin and the redemption of men, even though it does not positively exclude other motives, we must hold precisively[128] to the aforementioned motive as certain, whereas others are affirmed only rashly and without foundation. Now what is said about the angels has no persuasive force both because of what we have said in the preceding number and because it is certain that they are natural substances and thus have claim to their own natural ends apart from ministries to men. Scripture recounts those ends expressly enough in the book of Job and in other places where mention of intelligences who are sphere-bearing and who move the heavens comes up not infrequently, as exegetes commonly observe.[129]

13 Second, they respond that Scripture and the Fathers treat of the motive of Christ's Incarnation not considered in itself and as regards its substance but instead considered according to its mode and the circumstance of passible flesh. On this point they observe that antecedently and independently of all foresight and of the remediation of sin, God efficaciously willed the Incarnation on account of its intrinsic excellence and the perfection of the universe. Then, having foreseen that there would be sin, he willed the circumstance of the Incarnation in a passible and mortal body, or (and it comes to the same thing) he willed that Christ, otherwise previously and efficaciously willed in substance, would be passible and would undergo death for the redemption

---

128. *Praecise* ("precisively"): in logic, to affirm something precisively is to affirm it exclusively. Here the Salmanticenses are saying that even though Scripture does not state that Christ did *not* come for motives other than redemption, we must still affirm redemption as the motive to the exclusion of other motives.

129. In Jerome's Vulgate, Job 9:13 reads: *Deus cuius resistere irae nemo potest et sub quo curvantur qui portant orbem*. "God, whose wrath no man can resist, and under whom they stoop that bear up the world."

of men. Hence even if there were not going to be sin, he would come in substance by virtue of the prior decree so willed. But because there was sin, he came in passible flesh, and he would not have been going to come in passible flesh if there were not going to be sin. And the latter is what Scripture and the Fathers are teaching both in their affirmations and in their negations. But they are not at all touching on the former in the testimonies that we laid out for consideration above.

This response, which contains Scotus's own proper mind and foundation, can be refuted in many ways and quite effectively. And first of all, it does not challenge the argument of St. Thomas if applied to the Incarnation considered in its substance, since we can affirm nothing certainly and determinately of what is above nature and depends on the will of God alone, except from knowledge of the divine will itself, which is revealed to us in Scripture and the teaching of the Church Fathers. And for this reason (to assume what Scotus supposes) because the circumstance of passible flesh as a remedy for sin is above the requirement of nature and depends on God's will alone, we could not affirm for certain that Christ would come in passible flesh as a remedy for sin and would not come in this way lacking that motive, unless we had it from Scripture and the Fathers that God willed this circumstance for the aforementioned motive. But the Incarnation considered in its substance and ordered to other ends or willed for its own sake is a supernatural work depending on God's will alone, as is clear of itself. Therefore, for us reasonably to affirm that it was willed by God for its own sake and was going to exist independently of the motive of the remediation of sin, this will of God must be made known to us through knowledge revealed in the teaching of Scripture and the Church Fathers. And this is not at all what we have. Instead, we have the contrary, since Scripture and the Fathers teach throughout and expressly that Christ was willed and came as a remedy for sin, and they do not assign another end unconnected to this. Therefore rashly and without foundation do we assert determinately that Christ was willed in substance without an order to the remediation of sin and that, so considered, he would come lacking it. For, having left revelation aside, from what source do Scotus and his disciples draw this determinate and thoroughly probed knowledge of the divine determination? For if, without waiting upon revelation, they focus on elements of fittingness alone, these will only be persuasive as to the possibility of the mystery, not the determinate fact that it is going to exist, since it is certain that, notwithstanding the fact that these elements of fittingness present themselves, God could have decreed that it would not be going to exist.

14. Next, from the doctrine stated above and the response, it follows that all the following propositions are false when taken as proper speech: *The Son of man is come to save that which was lost* (Mt 18:11); *God sent his Son [...] that he might redeem them who were under the law* (Gal 4:4–5);[130] *Christ Jesus came into the world to save sinners* (1 Tm 1:15). From the Nicene Creed: *For us men and for our salvation, he came down from heaven, and became man.* And others still more express in their meaning, which we have recalled from the Fathers (no. 9). The consequent is altogether heretical, being directly incompatible with the doctrine of the faith. Therefore the aforementioned doctrine or reply can in no way be maintained. Proof of the *sequela*: The meaning of the aforementioned propositions in proper speech is that the Word assumed flesh and became man for our salvation or redemption, and absolutely assuming flesh and becoming man pertain to the substance of the mystery, as is clear of itself. But, according to the contrary opinion and the response given, it is false that the motive of this mystery considered in its substance was the salvation and redemption of men. Therefore in proper speech it is false that the Word assumed flesh and became man for the salvation and redemption of men, as the aforementioned propositions affirm in proper speech. And, consequently, the aforementioned propositions, as they stand in Scripture and the Fathers, are false if the aforementioned response or doctrine is true. For, according to it, passibility and mortality were assumed for men's salvation but flesh was assumed not for this end but for other motives. Hence, according to this doctrine, it will end up being true that Christ, God become true man, was passible for us men and for our salvation but false that the Son of God, for us men and for our salvation, *came*

---

130. The Salmanticenses do not note the omission in the verse. Including the omitted text, it reads: *God sent his Son, made of a woman, made under the law: That he might redeem them who were under the law.*

down from heaven and became man, as we profess in the Creed. For the motive of the Incarnation absolutely is not the redemption of men but something else according to the opposite opinion.

Furthermore, the aforementioned response is directly incompatible with the testimonies of the holy Fathers we related (no. 10) and cannot at all be applied to them, since several of them imply a universal negative proposition[131] equivalent to this: *The Word of God would nowise assume flesh if man had not sinned.* And this: *There was no motive for God to assume flesh except the redemption of men.* These propositions become totally false[132] according to the opposing doctrine, which admits propositions opposed to the preceding by contradiction, namely: *If man were not to sin, the Word of God would in some way assume flesh*, namely impassible flesh. And likewise: *There was a motive for God to assume flesh other than the redemption of men*, to wit, that for which the Incarnation considered in its substance was first willed and decreed. Now that the testimonies of the Fathers imply a universal negative meaning is clear from the testimonies themselves. For St. Irenaeus says: *For if flesh did not have need of being saved, the Word of God would not at all have become flesh.* Here "not at all" means the same as "in no way." St. Gregory of Nazianzus: *Now what cause existed for the humanity assumed by God for us? In truth to prepare our salvation. What else can be given as the cause?*, as if to say: *Nothing*. St. Gregory: *If sins were lacking, it would not be necessary for him to come*,[133] where he excludes every other cause. Rupert the Abbot: *You owe much to us, O man*

---

131. A universal negative proposition is one that denies every instance of the thing in question without exception.

132. *Falsificantur*: the way the Salmanticenses use the verbs *verificare* ("to make true") and *falsificare* ("to make false") in this text is essentially equivalent to how contemporary philosophers speak of truthmaking and falsemaking. In the present case, the Salmanticenses are saying that the proposition *Christ would have come by virtue of the present decree even apart from sin* is a falsemaker for the two propositions that they take to be implied by what the Fathers have said. Throughout, *verificare* in the active is translated as "make true" and in the passive "become true." *Falsificare* is translated as "make false" in the active and "become false" in the passive. When the Salmanticenses say that a person asserting A makes B true, they mean that A, which the person asserts, is a truthmaker for B.

133. The quotation has been slightly altered from how it was given in no. 10.

Christ, because for us you were assumed unto God. For if we had not been sinners, there would have been no reason why you had to be assumed unto God. Augustine: *If man had not been lost, the son of man would not have come.* And the other Fathers related in that place put forward similar universal negatives, not because other causes and motives were logically impossible but because they are speaking in accord with the present providence of God and the actual decrees revealed in Scripture, as we have observed (no. 11). Therefore those who teach the proposition opposed by contradiction, namely: *Even if man had not sinned, the Son of God would assume flesh in some way and for some other motive*, make the Fathers' teaching false and are directly at odds with them, just as they are opposed to the doctrine of St. Thomas, who established the assertion in this matter no differently and in no different words and who did not articulate any distinction about Christ's coming in passible or impassible flesh. Hence just as our adversaries do not offer interpretations of St. Thomas's testimonies but instead think of themselves in an absolute sense as going against him, so must they conduct themselves in this way with the other sacred Doctors.

15 Nor does it matter if to lower the force of this impugnment it is said that when a thing can happen in two ways, if it does not happen in one of these ways, this is sufficient to deny its happening absolutely or to say that it does not happen. Hence Christ the Lord said: *Go you up to this festival day: but I go not up to this festival day* (Jn 7:8). And yet he did go up, as is obvious from the very same chapter: *But after his brethren were gone up, then he also went up to the feast* (Jn 7:10). For, since he could go up in public or in secret, the fact that he did not will to go up in public is a negation of the sort that suffices for saying truly and absolutely that he did not go up. This is the doctrine that the Gospel itself suggests to preserve Christ's veracity, for it adds: *Then he also went up to the feast, not openly, but, as it were, in secret.* Since, then, Christ would have been able to come in two ways, namely, in passible flesh and in impassible flesh, and since lacking Adam's sin he would not come in passible flesh, the Fathers are warranted in teaching that in that event Christ would not come.

This, I say, is an interpretation of the Fathers that is hardly satisfactory and instead contains a very false doctrine.[134] This is because a proposition negating a given predicate absolutely negates it in every way by the fact that a negation has a malignant nature and destroys whatever it finds after itself.[135] And for this reason, to say truly that *this subject does not possess heat*, it is necessary that it possess no heat: not the heat of fire, not the heat of the sun, not natural heat. And if it does possess any kind of heat, the proposition is rendered false, even if the subject is devoid of a given heat. Also, because when a thing can happen in two ways it is not sufficient for it not to happen in one way in order to be absolutely denied that it happened. For who would deny that the king is going to come into the city because he will not come, as he is able to do, in a chariot, if he really does come on a horse? Or who would deny that Peter was made because he was not made through creation, as he could have been, if he really has been made by generation? And, finally and more compellingly, also because from this opposing doctrine it follows that this proposition is true and should be conceded: *Christ will not come at the end of the world*, which is manifestly heretical as it stands. For our adversaries say that the Fathers asserted absolutely that Christ would not come because he was able to come in passible or impassible flesh and if Adam had not sinned he would not come in passible flesh. But, at the end of the world, Christ could come in passible or impassible flesh. Therefore because he will not come in passible flesh, it will be true that Christ will not come at the end of the world. In fact, it will then be true that *Christ has not come* because he was able to come in passible flesh or in impassible flesh and, *de facto*, has not come in one of these ways, namely, in impassible flesh. For, according to our adversaries, the negation of one of two possible ways suffices for the truth of the proposition denying a predicate absolutely. This will also be true: *God does not generate*, since God, considered in one way, namely as in the Son or in the Holy Spirit, does not generate. And likewise this will

---

134. For this paragraph, cf. Vásquez, *Disputationes in Tertiam partem*, q. 1, a. 3, disp. 10, chap. 4, nos. 42–43 (ed. Sanchez Crespo, 1:135–36); and Godoy, *Disputationes theologicae in Tertiam partem Divi Thomae*, tract. 1, disp. 8, § 1, nos. 24–25 (ed. Hertz, 1:115).

135. A logical maxim meaning that a simple negation denies everything following it in the proposition.

become true: *God has not assumed human nature,* both because God as in the Father or in the Holy Spirit has not assumed human nature and because he has not assumed the human nature that is found in Peter or Paul. All these things are so false and intolerable that they can ask for no greater refutation. And we do not doubt that someone who puts forth the aforementioned propositions and defends them should be punished as a heretic. Now, as for the testimony cited to the contrary, it does not favor the opposing doctrine. For by the words *I go not up*, Christ did not universally deny that he would go up but instead denied going up with the particular determination of going up in public and in a way manifest to the crowds, the way the disciples were asking about, as is plain from the text: *Pass from hence and go into Judea, that thy disciples also may see thy works which thou dost. For there is no man that doth any thing in secret, and he himself seeketh to be known openly. If thou do these things, manifest thyself to the world* (Jn 7:3–4). In this same sense and with reference to the same subject matter he said: *I go not up*, that is, publicly, as you are asking about. Hence it is clear that Christ's proposition was not universally negative and its veracity is not founded on such an absurd doctrine as the evasion desperately tries to defend. Recall what we have said in tract. 17, disp. 2, dub. 1, no. 30.[136]

16 Finally, this distinction of a twofold decree, one regarding the Incarnation's substance and the other regarding its circumstances, on which the given response relies, can be effectively refuted. This is because, according to the doctrine handed down in no. 6, just as God knew in the first stage *in-quo* all possible things under all combinations and possible circumstances and thereby knew the Incarnation in its substance according to the mode of possibility with an order or connection to Adam's sin under the aspect of possible, so also in the second stage *in-quo* (and we need not distinguish any others) he willed the Incarnation with all the circumstances he pleased. For God was able to will all these things by a single act, and such is becoming to his utmost actuality both in willing and in knowing, just as the opposite

---

136. Salmanticenses (ed. Palmé, 11:112). There they explain that "I go not up to this festival day" (Jn 7:8) is not amphiboly by way of strict mental reservation but a different type, i.e., where the words have a clear colloquial meaning in the circumstances.

way of going through a process of several volitions arises in us from potentiality and imperfection. Therefore it is superfluous to distinguish a twofold decree in God whereby in one he willed the Incarnation in its substance and by the other willed the same Incarnation with the circumstance of possibility, since he was able to will these by a single act. For if by a single act he saw that the Incarnation was possible, was possible in passible flesh,[137] and was possible under the aspect of the end of the permission of sin and the redemption of men or connected with this term or motive, why could he not will all these by a single act without the needless multiplication of decrees? In the end, *de facto* he did will all these with all these connections, as is clear from the effect in the execution of the mystery. To what purpose, then, do we posit another prior decree concerning the substance of the Incarnation in itself and taken by itself when it produces no effect?

Further explanation: The first decree that God had concerning the Incarnation did not decree that Christ would be in himself, precisively of the circumstance of passible flesh or impassible flesh, nor did it decree that Christ would be with the circumstance of impassible flesh.[138] Therefore it decreed Christ determinately with the circumstance of passible flesh and, consequently, dependently on sin. This second *consequentia* is plain from the first. For, as our adversaries concede and the testimonies of Scripture and the Fathers explain, Christ would not come in passible flesh except dependently on sin and as its remedy. As for the first *consequentia*, it is necessarily inferred from the antecedent by process of elimination.[139] For it is not apparent what else that first decree could touch on. Now the antecedent as regards the second part seems evident because if God decreed absolutely that Christ would be

---

137. The Latin text has: *et possibilem in carne impassibili*. The 1687 edition of the text has *passibili*, which is clearly correct in this context.

138. This argument is a form of one related by Vásquez in *Disputationes in Tertiam partem*, q. 1, a. 3, disp. 10, chap. 9, nos. 99–110 (ed. Sanchez Crespo, 1:146–49).

139. *Enumeratio partium* (lit. "enumeration of the parts"): a form of argumentation in which the elimination of possibilities (the "parts") enumerated within a proposition allows for a conclusion about the remaining possibility. In this case, God's first decree of the Incarnation vis-à-vis passibility had three possible configurations: A) indifferent; B) determined to impassible flesh; or C) determined to passible flesh. The Salmanticenses are arguing that because A and B are not the case, C must be the case.

in impassible flesh, then Christ would *de facto* have come in impassible flesh, which is heretical. The *sequela* is established: If this were not the case, one of two things would necessarily have to be said, namely, either that God changed and revoked his first decree or that the aforementioned decree was not efficacious. And whichever is said, it argues for a mutability and an impotence incompatible with God. And this is clear from similarity:[140] Because God decreed that the Incarnation would be in passible flesh with dependence on Adam's sin, if, supposing this sin, God had not come in passible flesh, there would be a very good argument that God's will is impotent or mutable. Therefore, it is equally the case that if God had decreed the Incarnation in impassible flesh absolutely and independently of Adam's sin, he would *de facto* have come in impassible flesh absolutely and independently of the remediation of sin. And since this did not happen and will not happen, it follows that the aforementioned will of God was either changed or was impotent. And since we cannot say this, we must say that God did not have such a decree or will.

17 Now the first part of the same antecedent, whose opposite our adversaries seem rather to favor, is also shown. This is because to understand and to will something confusedly and in general and then to will and understand it in particular with all its modes and circumstances is an imperfection of intellect and will arising from the potentiality and imperfection of these faculties, as is the case in us. Therefore since God is purest act in every line,[141] it cannot at all be said that he goes through such a process, first willing (and thereby also understanding) a thing confusedly and in general and then willing it in particular with its specific circumstances. And, consequently, when he

---

140. *A simili* ("from similarity"): the logical ground for an argument because of the essential similarity of two cases.

141. *Actus purissimus in omni linea*: God is complete utmost actuality along any trajectory of possible perfections. This does not mean that God's actuality realizes a perfection only in a fuller degree than do creatures, nor that God and creatures are contained together within a genus. Rather, it only means that, beginning from the perspective of a perfection in creatures and tracing that perfection upward through the hierarchy of being by way of analogy, we arrive at the necessity of affirming the perfection of God in the purest, most realized possible way.

first decreed Christ, he decreed him with the particular circumstance of passible flesh or impassible flesh, not in himself, confusedly, and precisively of the aforementioned modes. Also, because we must attribute to God, both in willing and in knowing, that manner of proceeding which is more perfect and possible absolutely, seeing as the divine perfection demands it. But to will an object with all its circumstances is possible absolutely, no less than to know all these things in their status of logical nonincompatibility by a single act. Again, this is more perfect than to will first in general and then in particular, as we were just saying, because it evidences greater simplicity and actuality. Therefore it should be said that God did not first will the Incarnation in itself by one decree and then by another decree will the Incarnation with the circumstance of passible flesh but, rather, that by a single, simple, and primary volition he decreed the Incarnation with all the modes and circumstances with which it was actually committed to execution. Also, because an absolute and efficacious act of the divine will is terminated in the object as practically capable of being put into execution; in fact, it brings it to execution in its own genus. But the Incarnation in itself or considered as regards the substance alone is not an object capable of being put into execution prescinding from the mode of impassible flesh and passible flesh. For it is logically impossible to have Christ in reality except either in a passible body or in an impassible body. Therefore either God did not have a decree concerning Christ in himself independently of the aforementioned modes, as we would have it, or the aforementioned decree was not absolute and efficacious. And if the latter is said, it becomes patently the case that Christ would not come by virtue of the aforementioned decree, seeing as we are not supposing it to be efficacious or fit to entail the fact that [its] object is going to exist and its existence. It will be then, as regards the resolution of the present difficulty, as if it did not exist. And finally, because the most perfect and comprehensive providence in the line of providence extends not only to the object in itself but also to all the modes and circumstances with which it is committed to execution. For the fact that the case is otherwise in our own providence arises from the imperfection of our intellect, which proceeds from potency to act and from the more universal to the more particular. For if we could, by a single, simple act comprehend and keep before our eyes all the modes and circumstances of an object (as God can), then by intending and decreeing objects with all the circumstances we would provide far better than by proceeding from one to another. But it is obvious that God's providence (especially concerning the Incarnation, which is its most perfect object) is the most perfect providence and provides comprehensively. Therefore it should not be said that it regarded the Incarnation in itself, logically, confusedly, and precisively of the modes under which it is possible, descending through another act to its particular modes and circumstances, but instead that it regarded the Incarnation with all the modes, determinations, and motives that it had in execution.

Confirmation by destruction of the opposing foundation: In this case, the Incarnation would be willed in itself prior to the Incarnation with the mode of passibility, or (and it comes to the same thing) in this case the Incarnation would be willed in itself and for its own sake by the first decree and then by another, second decree the circumstance or mode of passibility in an order to the remediation of sin would be willed. For the Incarnation in itself implies objective[142] priority of independence from the mode of passibility and remedying sin, since it can be conceived of, be intended, and exist without it. But this argument is null. Therefore the argument is null that states that God previously and by one decree willed the Incarnation in itself and independently of the remediation of sin and then by another decree willed the circumstance of the Incarnation in passible flesh as a remedy for sin. The *consequentia* is plain. And the major premise contains the Scotistic foundation. The minor premise, however, is shown: *First*, because the same argument, if valid, militates against the knowledge of possible things. For "animal" is prior logically and objectively to "rational" or "irrational," since it does not depend on these differences but instead can be conceived of objectively without them. Therefore God previously and by

142. "Objective" and "objectively" here and throughout the disputation mean considered as an object of knowledge or will. In this case, the point is that, as an object of thought, the Incarnation itself is prior to its involving suffering and salvation from sin because we can think of the Incarnation without these elements. In contrast, "subjective" and "subjectively" mean considered in the thing itself, i.e., as a subject and not as an object of our minds.

one knowing touches on "animal," then next and by another knowing touches on "rational" and "irrational," which are determinations and differences of "animal." But this is absurd and ridiculous, since it posits that confused, potential, and hardly comprehensive first knowing in God. Therefore from the fact that the Incarnation in itself is logically and objectively prior to the Incarnation with the mode of possibility or impassibility, it is not at all proved that God first and by one act willed the Incarnation in itself and then and through another act willed the Incarnation with the mode of passibility. *Second*, because even if this could be admitted in speculative and precisive knowledge on account of knowing the thing in an objectively precisive way, it cannot be admitted in practical volition entailing the execution of the object.[143] For, in fact, it is not possible to have the Incarnation in reality without either the determinate mode of passibility or of impassibility, as is clear of itself. But the decree of which we are speaking is a practical decree entailing the execution and the existence of the object. Otherwise, the Incarnation would not be entailed by virtue of it, as our adversaries infer. Therefore their discussion does not at all succeed in proving that God first willed the Incarnation in itself by one decree and then by another decree willed the Incarnation in passible flesh. *Third*, because if our adversaries' foundation as given above succeeded in proving anything, by that very fact it would succeed in proving that God first willed the Incarnation in passible flesh without any dependence in respect of the remediation of sin by one decree and then by another decree ordained the aforementioned Incarnation as such a remedy by intending the salvation of men. The consequent is absurd and contrary to our adversaries themselves, both because it multiplies decrees without necessity and because from it we plainly infer that Christ would come in passible flesh if Adam had not sinned, which they deny, being otherwise unable to address the testimonies of Scripture and the Fathers adduced above.

143. In other words, the object has within it the possibility of being known under the more generic aspect without considering the more specific. For example, "animal" can be thought of abstractly without consideration of rationality or irrationality. However, even if we admitted that God can know things in this way speculatively, the same argument could not be made in practical matters. Thus, if God chooses concretely to create "animal," it will have to be either rational or irrational, not indifferent.

Therefore the aforementioned foundation proves nothing. Proof of the *sequela*: Just as the Incarnation in itself is prior objectively to the Incarnation under the circumstance of passible flesh and independent of that object because it could be preserved without it and intended for its own sake, so also the Incarnation in passible flesh is prior objectively to the same Incarnation as ordered to the remediation of sin, not objectively dependent on it by such ordination, since it could be preserved and loved for its own sake and for other ends independently of the motive of the aforementioned remediation, as is clear of itself. But it is for this reason that our adversaries say that God first and by one decree willed the Incarnation in itself and then by another decree willed the Incarnation in passible flesh or willed such a circumstance. Therefore they equally have to say that God first willed the Incarnation in passible flesh by one decree and then willed the Incarnation in passible flesh as a remedy for sin by another decree.

18 From what has been said, the other evasions whereby some more recent thinkers have tried to address the testimonies of Scripture and the Fathers, on which both St. Thomas's assertion and the foundation of that assertion chiefly rely, are overturned *a fortiori*. For some have said that these succeed in proving not that the Word was not going to assume flesh if Adam had not sinned, but that he was not going to assume it for us or as a remedy for sin, for, in fact, this motive would be lacking. Others have said that these testimonies are persuasive not to the effect that the Word would not be going to assume flesh if Adam were not to sin, but that he would not be going to come and dwell among us. Finally, others have said that the Fathers are speaking not of sin contracted or actually committed but instead of impending sin. For it is a sufficient motive of the Incarnation for there to be the aforementioned threat or danger such that God would assume flesh and thus provide a remedy. These and other less important evasions are related and impugned at length by Godoy (*Disputationes theologicae in Tertiam partem Divi Thomae*, tract. 1, disp. 8, § 1, beginning from no. 17).[144] But, as we have said, they are overturned by what was laid out above, so that there is no need to include additional refutations. This is because

144. Godoy (ed. Hertz, 1:114–16).

they have no positive foundation in Scripture and the Fathers, and as a result in a matter depending on God's will alone they are committing divination rashly and without foundation. Also, because according to these evasions it is necessary to concede that the Incarnation taken in its substance was not for the remedy of sin. But this is contrary to Scripture and the Fathers. For they expressly affirm that the Word became man (which pertains to the substance of the Incarnation) for us men and for our salvation, as we have put forth for consideration (no. 13). Moreover, also because the testimonies adduced above are universal negatives or equivalent to them, and so they exclude every Incarnation or an Incarnation with every mode of passibility, of impassibility, of coming, of lacking this, and so forth. For they deny that if Adam had not sinned the Word would become incarnate, as we have pondered (no. 14). But to say that by the term "sin" they understood impending sin or the power to sin is thoroughly ridiculous because the Fathers are speaking of the sin that introduces the miseries suffered by the human race. For it is from these that we are freed through Christ. It is not a mere power or threat of sinning that brings them on, as is clear in the state of innocence. Furthermore, also because, even though the aforementioned explanations taken separately can be applied to one or another testimony out of those adduced, they can hardly be made to suit all of them taken together or the doctrine drawn from all of them. For, although some of them are speaking of Christ's coming, [while] some of them [speak] of our remedy and seem to exclude these effects,[145] all of them taken together (or even not a few of them taken specifically) absolutely deny that the Incarnation would be going to occur lacking Adam's sin and the motive of our redemption, as the reader who recalls them will easily grasp. For what else does St. Irenaeus (to omit the rest) hand down in the first passage related (no. 10)[146] when he says: *For if flesh did not have need of being saved, the Word of God would not at all have become flesh*? What else does St. Gregory the Great mean when he says: *If Adam were not to sin, it would not be necessary for our Redeemer to take on our flesh*? And the same opinion holds for the others. Finally,

---

145. I.e., some of the Fathers' testimonies mention Christ's coming, while others mention human redemption without including Christ's "coming" by express mention.

146. The Latin text gives the citation as: *num. 20.*

because the opposition we made above to a twofold decree, one of the Incarnation and the other of the circumstance of passible flesh, also overturns similar distinctions of a decree concerning the Incarnation in itself and of another concerning Christ's coming, of one concerning the Incarnation for its own sake and of another concerning the Incarnation for us, and whatever else of the same sort that can be thought up. Hence there is no reason to spend any more time on refuting these. But whoever wants more explanatory impugnments should consult the author we related above.[147]

§ 4. The escapes sought by Suárez and others are cut off

19. Suárez has devised another way to demolish the foundation of St. Thomas laid above and more appropriately explain the testimonies adduced in § 2, a way to which not a few more recent thinkers subscribe. To make the case, he observes (*Disputationes in Tertiam partem*, disp. 5, sect. 2)[148] that from his primary intention God willed the Incarnation, or the union of the Word with this nature numerically that he really assumed, in such a way that Christ the God-man would be head and end of all the divine works. This he learnedly proves from Scripture and the Fathers. Next (sect. 3 and 4),[149] he teaches that God had or knew several motives for decreeing Christ absolutely, independently of the remediation of sin, though he does admit that God did not decree that he would be in passible flesh except after foreseeing sin, though in such a way that, supposing this foreknowledge,[150] he decreed not only the circumstance of passibility but also the substance of the Incarnation itself from the motive of redeeming men. For he does not reckon it unfitting that God should have willed this effect for two total and adequate motives.[151] And he thinks that in this way there is

---

147. Namely, Godoy.
148. Suárez (ed. Vivès, 17:216–33).
149. Suárez (ed. Vivès, 17:233–51).
150. Where the Latin text has *haec praescientia supposita*, I have read *hac praescientia supposita*.
151. *Motiva totalia et adaequata*: the cause motivating the agent to act can be a

an explanation for the testimonies of Scripture and the Fathers, which signify that our reparation was the motive of the Incarnation in its substance. This is something the evasion we impugned in the preceding § did not afford so well. Finally (sect. 5),[152] at great length he hands down these two things: that even if man were not going to sin, God still would have willed the Incarnation for other motives independently of the remediation of sin but that, positing conditioned knowledge (middle knowledge)[153] of man's future fall, he did not have the decree of the Incarnation except as dependent on sin and as its remedy. For he has: *Supposing the conditional foreknowledge that God had of man's future fall should he permit it, it seems true that God could not have had the decree of the Incarnation as he then had it without consequently having the will to permit sin, such that by this way he would put into execution the mystery in the most perfect way adapted to his intention* (*Disputationes in Tertiam partem*, disp. 5, sect. 5, no. 15).[154] And his foundation is: God by a primary intention decreed to communicate himself hypostatically in the most perfect way. Now, supposing foreknowledge of future sin, the most perfect way is to assume passible flesh as a remedy for sin whereby, on the presupposition of such knowledge, he would

---

single good by itself (a total, adequate motive), but it can also be a collection of various partial, inadequate goods that the agent takes as a whole so that together they constitute a total, adequate motive of the act. A total and adequate motive is thus the overall reason moving the agent to that individual act. See the Salmanticenses, *Cursus theologicus*, tract. 8, *De ultimo fine*, disp. 4, dub. 1, § 1, no. 3 (ed. Palmé, 5:130).

152. Suárez (ed. Vivès, 17:251–63).

153. *Scientia conditionata, seu media*: God's knowledge was traditionally distinguished (conceptually) as either knowledge of simple intelligence or knowledge of vision. The former encompasses God's knowledge of himself and thus all things he could do, thereby being equivalent to knowledge of all possible things. The latter, following on an act of the divine will, encompasses all the things that actually have been, are, or will be, thereby being equivalent to knowledge of all real things. Luis de Molina, SJ (1535–1600), posited a third type of knowledge between or in the "middle" of these two types. According to Molina, this middle knowledge encompasses God's knowledge of what creatures with free will *would* do in a given set of circumstances, thereby being equivalent to knowledge of the truth value of all subjunctive propositions founded on the free acts of creatures. Suárez prefers to call it "conditioned knowledge" rather than "middle knowledge."

154. Suárez (ed. Vivès, 17:260).

only assume flesh in this way and for this motive. But because it was contingent that he foreknow the contrary, there would be, on that hypothesis, another most perfect way. And so, even without sin, God would become man, not in passible flesh and not as a remedy for sin, but, rather, for other ends, which would then remain precisively, as, for example, for the sheer excellence of the mystery and the completion of the universe. This is, in summary, the aforementioned author's opinion.

20. But the aforementioned manner of speaking can be refuted in several ways. First of all, *ad hominem*.[155] For, on the supposition of middle knowledge that Adam's sin would be going to exist in the hypothesis that *de facto* has been the case, Suárez admits that God only had the decree of the Incarnation in passible flesh and as a remedy for sin. And no decree of God's preceded this knowledge. Therefore in God, *de facto*, there neither is nor was any decree by which he willed the Incarnation except in passible flesh and as a remedy for sin. And, consequently, if Adam were not to sin, God would not assume flesh by virtue of the present decree that he *de facto* has had.[156] Both *consequentiae* are evidently inferred from the premises. Now the author cited teaches the major premise in the passage above. The minor premise, however, is certain on his principles. For the middle knowledge he attributes to God befits God by necessity, or before every decree, since [Suárez] and his ilk have no greater concern than that the foreknowledge of conditioned futures not be founded in God's free determination but instead precede and direct it.

---

155. Argumentation *ad hominem* means responding to the opponent's argument considered precisely as made within the bounds of his larger system of thought. It is not to be confused with the *ad hominem* fallacy.

156. Suárez has a looser sense of what constitutes the present decree than do the Salmanticenses. He explains that the decree predestining Christ remains the same *radicaliter* but not *formaliter* without sin, i.e., that God's effective choice for Christ remains numerically the same at its root but that it is only after foreseeing sin that all the modes and means related to execution are chosen and that these would have been different apart from sin. In contrast, as they repeat again and again in this disputation, the Salmanticenses view all the modes and circumstances related to execution as included from the moment of God's effective choice so that a substantial alteration in these would yield a numerically distinct decree, not the present one. See Suárez, *Disputationes in Tertiam partem*, disp. 5, sect. 5, no. 14 (ed. Vivès, 17:260).

This is confirmed by further clarifying the lack of *consequentia* in the aforementioned conclusions. For, supposing middle knowledge of the fact that sin is going to exist, God had an absolute and efficacious decree of the Incarnation in passible flesh and as a remedy for sin, by virtue of which he would not assume flesh except in this way and for the stated end, as Suárez concedes, agreeing in this with St. Thomas and so explaining the Fathers adduced above (§ 2). Therefore, God *de facto* did not have another decree by which he established the Incarnation absolutely and for other ends. Proof of the *consequentia*: This latter decree, like any other, supposes middle knowledge of the conditioned fact that Adam's sin is going to exist as well as of the fact that all other conditioned futures are going to exist, as those who subscribe to it teach. But supposing this knowledge, such a decree is altogether useless and superfluous, seeing as it is concurrent with another decree whereby God absolutely established the Incarnation in passible flesh and as a remedy for sin in conformity with the foreknowledge possessed. Since, then, we should not identify any useless and superfluous decree in God, it follows that in God there was *de facto* no other decree by which he established the Incarnation independently of the remediation of sin or for another motive not connected with it.

And this can be made more compelling by inquiring of our adversaries: What does the decree by which God willed the Incarnation absolutely and independently of the remediation of sin imply? For if they say that it is an inefficacious will or a simple complacency in the perfection of this mystery in itself, they say nothing.[157] This is because they identify in God this sort of complacency concerning all possible things. Also, because right now we are not speaking of this complacency but of the will absolutely entailing efficaciously the absolute fact that the object is going to exist. For Christ would not be going to come in virtue of a simple complacency alone but rather in virtue of an absolute and efficacious will, as is clear of itself. If, on the other hand, they say that it implies an absolute and efficacious will of the Incarnation inde-

---

157. God's inefficacious will or simple complacency means that when he knows the Incarnation as possible, he knows it as what would be good and thus "wills" or is pleased with its possibility. This differs, however, from an efficacious will, whereby God wills the Incarnation into actual existence.

pendently of Adam's sin, this is not at all coherent with their opinion. For they say that, supposing foreknowledge that is not free to him, God *de facto* had the absolute, efficacious decree of the Incarnation in passible flesh and as a remedy for sin. But these two decrees are mutually contrary and incompatible. For it is logically impossible to will the Incarnation absolutely and efficaciously independently of the remediation of sin and also dependently on the aforementioned remediation, since on the part of the object willed there is a contradiction that is completely impossible to put into practical implementation. Or, if they say that it implies a conditioned efficacious will, as if God established that the Incarnation would be in the case wherein sin would not be going to exist, we plainly infer from this what we were just saying, that such a decree is a useless and idle act, for before it God knew that sin was going to exist through middle knowledge and in conformity with this established the Incarnation as its remedy absolutely. What purpose, then, does this conditioned decree serve? Besides, in the present difficulty we are speaking of the decree by virtue of which the Incarnation would be placed outside its causes, and a decree of this sort is not conditioned but absolute and efficacious. Finally, if they say that we identify such an affect in God to show his utmost affection for this mystery, they are saying nothing and are proving even less. For to show this kind of affect it is enough for God to have decreed Christ for his infinite dignity and willed him as the end *for-the-sake-of-which* of all divine works. Yet, it is coherent with this that he willed him as Redeemer and in a way dependent on the remediation of sin as the end *to-which*. For these latter elements are quite coherent, and they constitute that object as most excellent, one surpassingly glorious for the Word himself, as we suggested above (from no. 5) and will be established more fully from what will be said below (no. 29).

Add to this that Suárez's aforementioned discussion contains many propositions that are false and incoherent among themselves. For *first* he says that from a primary intention God willed that the Incarnation would be in the most perfect way out of those that presented themselves to him. This assertion rests on no foundation. For since God acts *ad extra* freely, he is not obligated to bring things about in the most perfect way but instead as he wills, as theologians commonly teach (*ST* I, q. 19).¹⁵⁸ And this is clear in the very same mystery. For the habitual grace of Christ the Lord could have had a more perfect measure than it *de facto* possesses. For it could have been more intense absolutely than it is, since grace can be intensified to infinity in a syncategorematic¹⁵⁹ sense, as Suárez himself hands down (*Disputationes in Tertiam partem*, disp. 22, sect. 2),¹⁶⁰ and yet *de facto* it has a determinate measure that God decreed and fixed in advance within the line of possible perfection, as we have said (tract. 19, disp. 5, dub. 1)¹⁶¹ and as will be more obvious from what will be said below (q. 7, a. 9, and q. 10, a. 4).¹⁶² Therefore, it is said without foundation that God first intended the Incarnation as to be accomplished in the most perfect way. *Next*, if we grant that he did decree the Incarnation in this way, Suárez fails in *consequentia* when he asserts that, having foreseen Adam's sin as conditionally future, [God] decreed the Incarnation in passible flesh by means of the permission of sin and in an order to its remediation. For by intervening for her in advance¹⁶³ so that she would not contract sin, Christ redeemed the Blessed Virgin in a more perfect way than by freeing her from sin already contracted. Why, then, was the Incarnation not arranged to our advantage in the aforementioned way? This would assuredly have been the case if Suárez's solution, that God willed the Incarnation to be put into execution in the most perfect way, were true. For the aforementioned way is absolutely possible and absolutely more perfect than the opposite, as is clear in the Blessed Virgin. Furthermore, what the author affirms in the *second* place, to

---

158. Aquinas (Leonine ed., 4:231–51). The Salmanticenses refer here to the entirety of *ST* I, q. 19. *ST* I, q. 25, a. 6 (Leonine ed., 4:298–99), is also to the point.

159. The syncategorematic use of a term means its use in a way that precludes fitting as such into any of Aristotle's categories. In the present context, the point is that, while there cannot be an actual infinite intensity of habitual grace (a categorematic infinity), grace can be intensified without limit (to infinity in the syncategorematic sense).

160. Suárez (ed. Vivès, 17:632–37). The Latin text mistakenly gives the citation as: *Tract. de Charit. disp. 22, sect. 2.*

161. Salmanticenses (ed. Palmé, 12:152–60).

162. Salmanticenses, *Cursus theologicus*, tract. 21, disp. 15 (ed. Palmé, 14:526–57); and Commentary on *ST* III, q. 10, a. 4 (ed. Palmé, 15:122–24).

163. *Illam praeveniendo*: i.e., by assisting her with the prevenient grace of the Immaculate Conception.

wit, that it would have been possible for God to have foreseen through middle knowledge Adam as left to himself or, with the helps precisively that he *de facto* possessed, as not going to sin, and that, supposing this foreknowledge (which is not logically impossible), God would have put the Incarnation into execution independently of sin, is altogether false to say nothing else. For, on this hypothesis, Adam had only the helps sufficient to avoid sin, but no one with only sufficient helps avoids or will avoid sin, even though he can avoid it, since the former requires an efficacious help, however this is explained, as we have shown from the common and certain doctrine of theologians (tract. 14, disp. 7, dub. 1).[164] Therefore on every hypothesis in which Adam is foreseen with only the sufficient helps that he *de facto* possessed, he is foreseen as going to sin, even though it is simultaneously foreseen that he can avoid sin. If, then, the final resolution of God in choosing the most perfect way to put the Incarnation into execution depends on this condition or foreknowledge, it was altogether certain that God would not assume flesh except supposing foreknowledge of the fact that sin was going to exist and as its remedy. What purpose, then, does another decree unconnected with sin serve? Or what efficacy has it had?

21 And these all proceed *ad hominem* from the principles proposed by Suárez. But his opinion is furthermore refuted both by St. Thomas's argument and by all the lines of reasoning objected against the Scotists. For our purposes here it is enough to refer to these by way of summary and to direct them against Suárez. Now the decree of the absolute fact that the Incarnation was going to occur depends on God's will alone, which is made known to us in no other way than the teaching of Scripture and the Fathers. And, consequently, whatever in this area is asserted except according to the aforementioned teaching is asserted without foundation. But such is Suárez's opinion. Therefore, it is devoid of foundation. Proof of the minor premise: He himself hands

---

164. "Sufficient" here means "merely sufficient," i.e., a help of God that was truly enough to avoid sin but not one that ensured the actual avoiding of sin. The manner in which a (merely) sufficient help is truly sufficient and what distinguishes it from an efficacious help is a classic dispute in theology. In the present argument, the Salmanticenses prescind from this question. The reference is to Salmanticenses (ed. Palmé, 10:1–20).

down that God primarily willed the Incarnation for other motives than the remediation of sin and, consequently, that even if Adam's sin were not going to exist and were not foreknown as going to exist, God would have been going to assume flesh by virtue of the prior decree. But, in the first place, this is contrary to the Fathers as related (no. 10), who absolutely and universally deny that the Word of God would have been going to assume or would have assumed flesh except as a remedy for sin and supposing this occasion. Next, it is contrary to Scripture, which does not positively present a motive of the Incarnation other than the remediation of sin, and this is the sense in which the holy Fathers commonly explain it, as we have shown (no. 9). Therefore, to assert that the Incarnation was willed for another motive and that it would have been put into execution independently of the remediation of sin has no foundation in Scripture and the Fathers. And in the same way as St. Thomas's argument opposes the opinion of the Scotists, it overturns Suárez's opinion. For the latter and the former both proceed by divining the free will of God without the Light and leadership of Scripture and the holy Fathers.[165]

Nor does it successfully address [our assertion] if it is said that when the Fathers deny that there would be the Incarnation independently of the remediation of sin they are speaking with a focus on the decree that God had supposing the foreknowledge that Adam's sin was going to exist, by virtue of which decree God would not assume flesh lacking such a motive. But, they are not denying that he would come by virtue of all the decrees existing in God, such as the decree that God had prior to this foreknowledge, intending to communicate himself hypostatically in the most perfect way out of those that would occur to him. Now Scripture does most truly present the motive of the Incarnation, even taken in its substance, as having been the remediation of sin, for God certainly had this motive. But it does not deny that he had other motives by virtue of which he would come even if it did not occur. In this, the Scotists' explanation does not proceed as properly and sincerely, since they identify one decree concerning the substance of the Incarnation and another as ordered to the circumstance of passible flesh.

165. *Nam iste, et illi procedunt divinando liberam Dei voluntatem absque Luce, et duce Scripturae, et SS. Patrum.*

22. This, I say, does not successfully address [our assertion] and is easily refuted from what was said (beginning from no. 14). For, as regards the Fathers, their statements are universal negative propositions in which they deny that the Incarnation was going to be or would have been going to be except as a remedy for sin. Now a universal negative has the force of excluding the predicate absolutely, with this or that mode, by virtue of this or another cause, as is clear in this [proposition]: *There is no world besides this one.* For every other world is denied, greater or lesser, with these or those creatures, by virtue of this decree or causality or another. Nor is there any other way to preserve the truth of universal negatives. Therefore just as someone who asserted that there is another world by virtue of another decree or production would make this proposition, which is of faith, false, so also one who asserts that the Incarnation was going to be or would have been going to be by virtue of another decree existing in God makes false the universal propositions of the Fathers wherein they deny that the Incarnation was going to be or would have been going to be lacking the motive of the remediation of sin. For the Fathers are speaking *de facto* with a focus on everything in God as far as this is made known to them and to us from Scripture. And it is astonishing that Suárez should have seen into more things in God and comprehended him more than the sacred Doctors so that he might affirm more than they do and declare an opinion contrary to them.

Now as regards Scripture, even though it proceeds absolutely or positively by establishing that the motive of the Incarnation was the remediation of sin, this manner of proceeding in matters of such great importance as the Incarnation is equivalent to express negation of other causes or motives. And, for this reason, because sacred Scripture affirms that there are three divine persons, we necessarily gather the denial of more divine persons. And because (Rom 5 and 6) it is said that death entered the world through sin, though it does not deny another cause, we rightly gather that death would not have existed if there had been no sin. And we have clarified the same by other examples (no. 12). And so in this way because when treating of the motive of the Incarnation it affirms that it was the remediation of sin, we must hold absolutely that there was no other motive or at least that there was no other motive unconnected to this one. And, in fact, if it was really the case, as Suárez describes it, that by a primary and absolute intention God willed the Incarnation for its own sake and as to be accomplished in the most perfect way of those presenting themselves and then, supposing foreknowledge of future sin, willed the Incarnation as its remedy, Scripture could not sincerely affirm (as it does) that God became man as a remedy for sin. For this kind of speech presents the first motive of intention. So, too, if someone who had decided to go to Rome from the intention of carrying out some business of his then realized that his friend was in the same place and were moved thereby to visit him or to bring him something,[166] he could not sincerely say to his friend: *I came to Rome for your sake.* But he would truly say: *Because I was coming to Rome, I wanted to speak with you, or to bring you these things.* For really the primary motive for coming to Rome, as the first proposition understood sincerely and in the usual way presents it, was not the friend but rather something else, to which another motive was joined by consequence. Therefore the same lack of sincerity would occur in the statements of Scripture if Suárez's doctrine were true.

Now you will say that in Scripture it is not new or unusual that when a given thing happens out of a twofold motive or end, it is said to happen absolutely for that which is less chief or which occurs by consequence, obscuring that which is principally intended. For, to omit other examples, when Samuel was prepared and moved by God's command to go to Bethlehem to anoint David as king, he feared Saul and God said to him: *Thou shalt take with thee a calf of the herd, and thou shalt say: I am come to sacrifice to the Lord* (1 Sm 16:2).[167] It is indeed certain that the intention of anointing David as king was the chief intention, whereas the intention of offering the sacrifice was less principal and, as it were, secondary. This notwithstanding, it was sincerely and truly said that Samuel came to offer sacrifice, concealing or not mentioning the principal motive. And so it is in this way that Scripture presents and frequently teaches that the motive of the Incarnation was men's redemption or the

---

166. The Salmanticenses are here addressing an example that Suárez uses in *Disputationes in Tertiam partem*, disp. 5, sect. 4, no. 22 (ed. Vivès, 17:246–47).

167. The example is from Suárez, *Disputationes in Tertiam partem*, disp. 5, sect. 4, no. 23 (ed. Vivès, 17:247).

remediation of sin, even though this was really less chief, obscuring or not making explicit the other, which was more principal.

But this is nothing. This is because in the example given by the objection, Scripture itself openly declares that the chief end of Samuel's journey was anointing David as king, and this is made known to us from Scripture. Hence we suffer no deception from the other words: *I am come to sacrifice to the Lord*. Rather, the preceding words readily instruct us that these latter words are presenting a real cause, really assumed, though not primary or principal. Yet Scripture acts otherwise in its presentation of the Incarnation's motive, seeing as it frequently asserts that it was men's reparation and does not put forward another motive distinct from this or at least unconnected with it, as is clear from the testimonies related above. And thus the holy Fathers, to whom it belongs to explain Scripture's meaning, interpret it for us as they do, denying in carefully chosen words that the Word of God would assume flesh if the aforementioned motive were lacking, as is clear from what was said (no. 10). But these things could not be put forward and said sincerely if God had had another primary and principal motive for the Incarnation by virtue of which he would send his Son independently of the motive of men's reparation. Also, because the necessity of covering up the primary motive obliged Samuel to say: *to sacrifice to the Lord*, lest Saul should impede the anointing of David as king or slay Samuel. For if a necessity so grave did not compel him, Samuel would hardly have to conduct himself in this way. Instead, he would have made manifest the principal motive of his coming, as the sincerity of speech requires when no reason to cover things up or to observe secrecy presents itself. But since God has proposed the motive of the Incarnation to us by the mediation of Scripture and the teaching of the Fathers, there was no need or appropriateness for obscuring the primary or principal motive and of presenting precisively one willed less principally and by consequence. For what reasonable cause can be assigned for him to have conducted himself this way? What is obvious is that with greatest frequency he presents the remediation of sin as the motive and puts forward no other end that is not connected with this. Therefore it must be said either that this is really the case, as we would have it, or that the statements of Scripture are not sincere, which is absurd.

23 Third, the same opinion of Suárez is refuted because, according to it, the Incarnation considered in its substance and under the same aspect was willed for two total, adequate ends not subordinated between themselves.[168] First, for its own sake independently of the remediation of sin. Second, supposing the foreknowledge of future sin, as a remedy for sin. This differs from Scotus's opinion in the fact that the latter posits one decree concerning the substance of the Incarnation and another concerning the circumstance of passible flesh. Suárez, on the other hand, identifies both decrees or both intentions in an order to the selfsame substance of the Incarnation, regarding it as absurd (as we have shown above that it really is) that only the circumstance of passible flesh and not the substance of the mystery should have been intended for the redemption of men. Yet it is impossible for the same effect to depend on two total, adequate final causes not subordinated between themselves. Otherwise, it would depend and not depend on either of them taken determinately.[169] Now it would depend [on a given one], as supposed, for, in fact, it regards it as a total, adequate end for which it is intended. And, it would not depend on it, since it has another adequate and total end not subordinated to the former in an order to which it is possible. Therefore Suárez's thought cannot stand. And even though the aforementioned author denies the minor premise of this discussion, in our persuasion for it we need not lay out more extensive proof than is included in the same. For, professedly, we have shown it broadly (tract. 8, *On the Last End*, where this difficulty has its proper

---

168. See Suárez, *Disputationes in Tertiam partem*, disp. 5, sect. 4, no. 6 (ed. Vivès, 17:240).

169. The Salmanticenses conceive of a total, adequate end as the overall reason motivating the agent to act. Suárez, however, speaks of a total, adequate end as one that would of itself be enough to motivate the agent to act. Hence Suárez sees no difficulty in adding a second total, adequate end for the selfsame action of the agent, while for the Salmanticenses adding another end would give rise to a numerically distinct action with a new total, adequate end comprised of the previous end and the additional one. In other words, Suárez only ever speaks of the total, adequate end as *sufficient* to motivate a given act, but the Salmanticenses view the total, adequate end as *necessary*, which is why they argue from the incoherence of simultaneous dependence and nondependence. Cf. Gonet, *Clypeus theologiae Thomisticae*, part 3, tract. 1, disp. 5, § 3, no. 23 (ed. Vivès, 5:477); and Vásquez, *Disputationes in Tertiam partem*, disp. 10, chap. 8, nos. 75–86 (ed. Sanchez Crespo, 1:142–44).

place, disp. 4, dub. 1ff.; tract. 14, disp. 2, from no. 135; and tract. 15, disp. 2, no. 115, where we have refuted various of Suárez's replies).[170] And so we refrain from such an endeavor for the present, since the reader can go back over the passages cited.

Confirmation: Let it be the case that there be no entanglement in having one and the same effect depend on two total, adequate causes with no subordination between them.[171] Even so, this is impossible connaturally. Hence we see that philosophers commonly face the aforementioned difficulty with respect to God's absolute power, on the supposition that it is impossible by the ordinary law and according to the natures of things.[172] But we must speak of the divine intention and disposition concerning this mystery in conformity to the natures of things and the gentle[173] providence of God when the opposite is not shown from a firm and certain revelation of God that manifests how he has arranged things. Therefore God did not decree the aforementioned mystery for two total, adequate ends not mutually connected. And thus if he decreed this mystery as a remedy for sin, as Suárez admits, this end pertained at least inadequately to the primary and principal motive for which the Incarnation was willed and intended. And thus, lacking it, it would not have been committed to execution.

24 And the examples that the aforementioned author uses to argue for the opposite do not weaken the strength of this impugnment. His first example is that wherein someone is already efficaciously determined to go to Rome to see his son and a friend then comes and entrusts him with some errand. Hence from this motive he again in-

---

170. Salmanticenses (ed. Palmé, 5:128ff.); tract. 14, disp. 2, dub. 4, § 2, no. 135ff. (ed. Palmé, 9:210ff.); and tract. 15, disp. 2, dub. 4, § 3, no. 115ff. (ed. Palmé, 10:378ff.).

171. Cf. Gonet, *Clypeus theologiae Thomisticae*, part 3, tract. 1, disp. 5, § 3, no. 24 (ed. Vivès, 5:477).

172. *Potentia absoluta* ("absolute power"): God's power considered as able to do anything not entailing a logical contradiction, i.e., anything possible absolutely. This is contrasted with his "ordained power" (*potentia ordinata*), meaning his power as actually having determined to do this or that. The relationship between these two was an important point of dispute for the Scholastics.

173. Discussions of divine providence often allude to Wis 8:1: [*Wisdom*] *reacheth therefore from end to end mightily, and ordereth all things sweetly.*

tends to make the same journey. The second is that of Samuel, who as we saw (no. 22) first intended to go to Bethlehem from the motive of anointing David as king and then intended the same from the motive of offering sacrifice. For in the aforementioned examples the same effect is intended for two adequate and total ends possessing no subordination. This is confirmed further (sect. 4, § *Cujus rei exemplum*)[174] where he asserts that: *Christ rose again for our justification* (Rom 4:25), signifying that our justice was the adequate end of Christ's Resurrection, and yet it is certain that the aforementioned Resurrection was willed for another total end, namely, for Christ's glory. And many Fathers, especially St. Anselm (*Cur Deus homo?*, I, chap. 16)[175] and St. Bernard (Sermon 2 on the Feast of All Saints)[176] affirm that men were elevated to glory to repair the places of the angels, and yet besides this motive there was another distinct end for men to be chosen for glory.

These examples, I say, do not matter and are not favorable to Suárez's understanding. This is because, as Vásquez has rightly observed (*Commentarii ac disputationes in Tertiam partem S. Thomae*, q. 1, a. 3, disp. 10, chap. 8, no. 81),[177] although it sometimes seems as if several total ends concur for the same effect, one of these alone is the end moving and influencing the work, whereas the other is only an impelling end superadding a new fittingness. And this is the case in the first example of someone who was ready to go to Rome because of his son and then simultaneously wills some fittingness of his friend's by consequence. And the same can be said of the last example. For it is certain that the reparation of the places of the angels was not the principal motive of men's predestination but, rather, added a kind of fittingness. And the Fathers affirm nothing further than this. Also, because even if several ends were to concur for the same work, by the very fact that they occur together they are not taken as total but as parts of

---

174. Suárez, *Disputationes in Tertiam partem*, disp. 5, sect. 4, no. 23 (ed. Vivès, 17:247). The Latin text mistakenly gives the citation as: *sect. 5, § Cujus rei exemplum.*

175. Anselm (ed. Schmitt, 2:74–75).

176. The Salmanticenses, following Suárez, cite Bernard, *Sermo II in festivitate omnium sanctorum* (ed. Leclerq and Rochais, 5:342–48), but Bernard, *Sermo I in festivitate omnium sanctorum*, no. 8 (ed. Leclerq and Rochais, 5:333–34), is more relevant.

177. Vásquez (ed. Sanchez Crespo, 1:143).

the same total motive that comes together from them all or unites their aspects, as is the case in the present matter and in the two examples of Samuel and the Resurrection that Suárez adduces. And finally, also because in all the examples that occur in human matters, it can be the case that a man first intend something for one total motive and then intend the same thing for another total motive.[178] For he does not foresee all these motives' elements of fittingness from the beginning. Also, because he can change his first will and motive. Or finally, because he can subordinate his first volition and its end to another motive. And the fact of his intending several total motives successively is reduced to these roots. But there is no ground[179] for these arguments in God, who in the first stage *in-quo* knew most perfectly all possible elements of fittingness as well as their mutual combinations and dependencies, as we have observed (no. 6), and who is immutable and unable to revoke or improve an intention already held, as is shown (*ST* I, q. 19, a. 7).[180] Therefore there is no reason to say that God willed and decreed the Incarnation out of two total and adequate motives. On this point, Suárez's opinion is patently far more difficult than the opinion of Scotus. For the latter distinguishes the things willed and asserts that the substance of the Incarnation was willed for one end and the circumstance of passible flesh for another, which is not as unsound an understanding. The former, however, not distinguishing the aforementioned, affirms that the selfsame substance of the Incarnation was willed for two total ends. This (besides being obviously false based on what was said) can scarcely be understood to be the case in God's most perfect manner of proceeding both in understanding and in willing. For if he knew all the possible elements of fittingness in the first stage *in-quo* (and all regard this as an established point), he was certainly able to intend those he pleased and to regard them all together as a single object willed and a single adequate motive. If, however, this was not the case, and, having uncovered some new fittingness through middle knowledge, he intended some-

---

178. Cf. Gonet, *Clypeus theologiae Thomisticae*, part 3, tract. 1, disp. 5, § 3, no. 25 (ed. Vivès, 5:477).

179. *Locus* (lit. "place"): the Latin equivalent of the Greek τόπος used by Aristotle (e.g., in his *Topics*). In logic, it means the basis for the argument (*sedes argumenti*).

180. Aquinas (Leonine ed., 4:242–43).

thing new, then in this very fact an argument is made for his mutability and imperfection in willing, which is completely inadmissible.

Add to this that everything we said above (beginning from no. 16) against the evasion of the Scotists, who multiply decrees concerning the substance of the Incarnation and the circumstance of passible flesh, also militates against this response of Suárez, as will be readily obvious to one who considers it. For if the first decree was the sole intention of the Incarnation in itself, prescinding from the mode and the circumstance of impassible or passible flesh, it plainly follows that the aforementioned decree was not efficacious and not apt such that by virtue of it the Incarnation would be placed outside its causes as an event. For the Incarnation considered in this way is not a performable object, since it cannot be realized without one of these modes. Now if it was the intention of the Incarnation in impassible flesh, this is the mode in which the Incarnation would have been accomplished. Otherwise, we would have to say one of the following two things: either that such an intention was not efficacious, contrary to what we supposed, or that God carried out the Incarnation otherwise than he had decreed. Finally, if it was the intention of the Incarnation in passible flesh, then it would have happened in this way even if Adam had not sinned, if indeed this first decree regarded the Incarnation independently of the remediation of sin. But the consequent is contrary to all theologians, who deny that God would have assumed mortal flesh lacking the motive of man's reparation. Now if to avoid these we said that the Incarnation was willed through the first decree in none of the aforementioned modes but rather that this Incarnation concretely was willed with the most fitting mode out of those that would later present themselves and be uncovered through middle knowledge, then by this very fact the argument is made that the first decree was not efficacious simply and did not regard a total motive independent of others. For it remained in suspense, awaiting other things to be uncovered through middle knowledge so that God would decree the mode of the Incarnation and its adequate motive in conformity to what was uncovered. And since, on the supposition of this knowledge's direction and counsel, in the end the decree was that the Incarnation would happen in passible flesh and as a remedy for sin, the entire process of divine providence was finally completed concerning this mystery, lifting that suspension that it had by virtue of the present decree regarding the Incarnation as dependent on the more perfect mode's occurrence and approbation. And thus we clearly infer that by virtue of the present decree finally resolving this matter, in fact by virtue of all decrees actually existing as they have *de facto* been determined, God would not assume flesh except passible flesh as a remedy for sin. And this is the common assertion of St. Thomas and his disciples, in whatever way the divine decrees are explained, a matter that we will shortly address. But in the way that Suárez has invented, besides everything else, there is the contradiction put forward (no. 20) that is incompatible with his own principles, when he identifies a decree in God prior to middle knowledge, since this precedes every free exercise of the divine will, as his supporters assert and as we have considered at greater length in the place cited.

§ 5. The challenge of a serious objection is met and the link between the Incarnation and the remediation of sin is explained

25. But before we relate the opposite opinion, we must disencumber ourselves from a serious difficulty, one not to be glossed over, which arises from what was said in no. 4, where we supposed that among all the objects willed by God Christ was the first willed, intended, and predestined as the end of all others. For this seems unable to be coherent either with our assertion or with its foundation. It seems to be incoherent with our assertion, for if Christ was intended after the manner of an end, he had to precede the fact that other things were going to exist and the choice of them. And, consequently, by virtue of the decree whereby he was willed, he would exist, even if other things were not going to exist. And thus he would come even lacking Adam's sin. Nor does it seem to be coherent with this assertion's foundation, for, if he was willed after the manner of an end antecedently to other things, he could not have not been intended for his own excellence and dignity. And, consequently, the motive of his being intended was something else distinct from the remediation of sin. And so it will be false that only this latter motive is gathered from Scripture and the Fathers,

as we have frequently hammered home in the preceding discussions in order to overturn our adversaries' various replies.

Thomists are divided in resolving this difficulty. For some are directly opposed to our supposition and affirm that the permission of Adam's sin, the fact that it was going to occur, and foreknowledge of it preceded simply and objectively the decree or efficacious intention of the Incarnation. Hence they do not admit that Christ preceded it after the manner of an end primarily intended. And they identify the order of decrees differently from us in this matter. In this we have Cajetan's rather famous opinion (Commentary on *ST* III, q. 1, a. 3, § *Ad evidentiam*),[181] ordering these elements in the following way: *If we consider more clearly the three orders that are* de facto *found in the universe, to wit, the order of nature, the order of grace, and the order of God and the creature,*[182] *we will simultaneously see that the second supposes the first and the third presupposes both. Likewise, the preordination and foreseeing of the first is presupposed by the preordination and foreseeing of the second. Likewise, the preordination and foreseeing of the third presupposes the preordination and foreseeing of both. This is in such a way that God first ordained the universe according to the order of nature and since, according to such an order, the universe does not attain to the enjoyment of God, he superadded the order of grace. Yet such an order does not arrive at union with God in the highest mode possible. Concerning this, sins partly pertain to the order of nature and partly to the order of grace as opposed to it. The consequent is that the predestination of Jesus Christ to be the Son of God presupposes foreseeing future sins, as belonging to the presupposed orders in the genus of material cause.* According to this opinion, at least four stages *in-quo* concerning this mystery are distinguished: First, that in which God knew the possibility of it and other things. Second, that in which he decreed that the natural order would be and knew the deficiencies, both natural and moral, that were going to exist in it. Third, that in which he decreed the order of grace and knew the sins opposed to it. Fourth, that in which he predestined Christ as a remedy for sins and chose those whom he willed in him for future glory. And, consequently, according to this order, Christ was

---

181. Cajetan, commentary on *ST* III, q. 1, a. 3, no. 6 (Leonine ed., 11:15).
182. By "God and the creature," Cajetan means the hypostatic union.

not the first willed and intended by God. Instead, the decree intending him supposes simply the foreknowledge and fact that sin was going to exist, with him being predestined as its remedy, so that lacking it, he would not have come by virtue of the present decree or providence. To this same opinion of Cajetan other weighty Thomists subscribe: Araújo (*In Tertiam partem Divi Thomae commentarii*, q. 1, a. 3, dub. unic., concl. 5, no. 57);[183] Álvarez (*De Incarnatione divini Verbi disputationes*, q. 1, a. 3, disp. 9, concl. 1);[184] our Cornejo (*Tractatus primus de Incarnatione Verbi divini*, q. 1, a. 3, disp. unic., dub. unic., § *Tertius modus*);[185] John of St. Thomas (*Cursus theologicus in Summam Sancti Thomae*, in III, disp. 3, a. 2, concl. 4).[186] And the same is defended by Vásquez, Ragusa, and not a few others of those related in no. 8, although some of them vary in how they designate and multiply the stages or decrees.

Now they prove what they agree on *first* from the line of reasoning implied in the words of Cajetan, that the order of nature is supposed for the order of grace and that both are supposed for the hypostatic order. Therefore, preserving the connatural providence of things, the order of nature and the order of grace had to be decreed and foreseen with the deficiencies opposed to them before the hypostatic order could be decreed. *Second*, from Scripture, which plainly presents the decree of the Incarnation as a work of divine mercy intending to lift us up from the misery of sin, e.g.: *But God (who is rich in mercy) for his exceeding charity wherewith he loved us even when we were dead in sins, hath quickened us together in Christ (by whose grace you are saved)* (Eph 2:4–5). And there is the same sense for nearly all the Fathers related by no. 9. Now it is obvious that mercy necessarily supposes a misery [from which] to be lifted up, since the exercise of mercy is to lift up another from his misery.[187] Therefore the decree of the Incarnation supposes the permission and foreknowledge of sin simply. *Third*, specifically from St. Thomas in the present article in the response to objection 4, where he says: *It should be said that predestination presupposes foreknowledge*

---

183. Araújo (1636 ed., 100–101).
184. Álvarez (ed. Facciottus, 73–74).
185. Cornejo de Pedrosa (ed. Varesius, 2:111).
186. John of St. Thomas (ed. Vivès, 8:107–111).
187. *Sublevare alienam miseriam.*

of what is going to exist. And thus just as God predestines the salvation of a man to be accomplished through the prayers of others, so also he predestined the work of the Incarnation as a remedy for human sin.[188] But the things that are going to exist whose foreknowledge is presupposed for predestination are not effects of the predestination itself, nor are they constituted through it. Rather, they precede it simply. Therefore sin, for the remediation of which Christ has come, was supposed as going to be and foreseen simply before he was intended or predestined. And these proofs proceed positively. But they furthermore argue *fourth* from the unfitting conclusions that are inferred from the opposing opinion, and we will lay these out more conveniently below.

26 This manner of speaking is very probable, both because of the lines of reasoning on which it relies and because of the authority of the Doctors by whom it is defended. And we admit that in it there are two things particularly deserving of praise: *First*, that it is directly opposed to Scotus's opinion, in the assertion as well as in the principles (what is assumed in the opposing objection comes from these principles, so by not admitting them they resolve it with ease). *Second*, that it explains the passages of Scripture and the Fathers adduced above in a very proper and straightforward way. But, even so, we think we must persist in the manner of speaking proposed in no. 4, which appears more probable and more comprehensive to us and which we had already chosen before all the other passages related there. In accord with this manner of speaking it should be said that Christ was the first willed and intended as the end of all divine works and that he thus preceded the order of nature and of grace as well as the sins opposed to them, for whose remediation he was predestined, in the genus of final cause. This is sufficiently proved from the authorities and lines of reasoning put forth in that place. But we find two other foundations convincing in their persuasion. *First*, because to give an explanation for the present difficulty two stages *in-quo* are sufficient: one, in which God knew all possible things as well as their possible combinations and mutual dependencies; the other, in which he decreed those things he pleased out of these and knew that they were going to be with the mutual depen-

---

188. Aquinas, *ST* III, q. 1, a. 3, ad 4 (Leonine ed., 11:14).

dencies that he willed, as we declared in no. 5. Therefore, just as in the first stage *in-quo* he knew the possibility of original sin, knew the possibility of the Incarnation, and knew that it was possible for Christ to be the end *for-the-sake-of-which* of the permission of sin, of its reparation, and of all things, and he likewise knew that it was possible for the reparation of sin or man to be redeemed to serve as the end *to-which*, so also in the second stage he decreed all these things and foreknew them as going to be with the aforementioned mutual dependence. And this is the way in which they have been *de facto* put into execution, without having to have recourse needlessly to the multiplication of other stages. And no one denies that this was indeed possible, nor is there any argument that obliges us to deny that it has *de facto* been the case. Rather, the testimonies of Scripture and the Fathers that seem to be opposed to one another are in this way easily reconciled.

Second, it cannot be denied that there were some sins for whose remediation Christ was predestined that could not have been going to be or could not have been foreseen as going to be in any stage prior to his predestination.[189] For the blasphemies, injustices, and other sins committed specifically against the person of Christ could not have been foreseen as going to be prior to Christ simply, since they depend on Christ himself as their object and their matter *concerning-which*. And yet he was decreed as a remedy for the aforementioned just as he was for other actual sins, since he is the universal Redeemer, according to the passage: *And he is the propitiation for our sins: and not for ours only, but also for those of the whole world* (1 Jn 2:2). Hence he must have preceded the permission of these as well as their reparation in some genus of cause, and especially in the genus of final cause, after the manner of the end *for-the-sake-of-which* both of the permissions themselves, as well as of the reparation and the other effects proceeding from it. In this

---

189. The Salmanticenses here agree with a standard objection to the approach of Cajetan, who is understood to hold simply that sins, which pertain to the natural order and are opposed to the gratuitous order, must all be taken into account in God's plan prior to decreeing the hypostatic order, which presupposes the natural and gratuitous. Cf. Suárez, *Disputationes in Tertiam partem*, disp. 5, sect. 1, no. 3 (ed. Vivès, 17:198–99); and Vásquez, *Disputationes in Tertiam partem*, q. 1, a. 3, disp. 11, chap. 1, nos. 10 and 11 (ed. Sanchez Crespo, 1:129–30).

way, too, he was able to be intended and foreseen in an order toward other sins or the permissions of them.

Now it is the case that we must speak of the divine arrangement and its motives with greater conformity to the natures of things where the opposite is not established through divine revelation. But it is more in harmony with the natures of things that Christ should have been the first intended as the end of all things that God has arranged. For where several willed objects come together, it is in harmony with reason and the natures of things for that which is the most perfect among them all to be regarded more principally, more immediately, and after the manner of the end. Now Christ far surpasses everything that God has arranged in perfection and dignity. Therefore, if we focus on the natures of things and the divine providence that plans them out, it rings truer that he was the first intended as the end *for-the-sake-of-which* of divine works and that all things were willed on his account. Or, from the other angle, the opposite is not established from divine revelation. In fact, the testimonies of Scripture adduced in no. 4 argue for this in no obscure manner. And those we have considered in no. 9 do not teach the opposite but only succeed in proving the precedence of sin in the genus of material cause and of reparation in the genus of final cause as the end *to-which*. The precedence of Christ as the end *for-the-sake-of-which* is coherent with this priority, as we will further clarify below. Therefore we should hold the opinion that this is how God has arranged these matters. And this is what very many disciples of St. Thomas teach: Capréolus, Medina, and Cabrera, whom Araújo relates (*In Tertiam partem Divi Thomae commentarii*, q. 1, a. 3, dub. unic., no. 53);[190] Vicente (*Relectio de habituali Christi Salvatoris nostri sanctificante gratia*, sol. q. 6, Page 629);[191] Herrera[192] (in manuscript, on this article); Nazario (*Commentaria et controversiae in Tertiam partem Summae Divi Thomae*

---

190. Araújo (1636 ed., 94).

191. Vicente (ed. Dianus, 629).

192. Pedro de Herrera, OP (1548–1630). Herrera's work on the Incarnation remains unpublished. Luis Alberto Diez relates that copies of the manuscript *De Incarnatione* are kept in the General Archive of the Dominican Order in Rome and in the Biblioteca Nacional in Madrid. Diez, "Inéditos mariologicos Salmantinos: El primer teólogo de la Realeza: Pedro de Herrera, OP. (1548–1630)," *Ephemerides Mariologicae* 19 (1969): 420.

Aquinatis, q. 1, a. 3, concl. 2);[193] Cippullo (*Commentariorum scholasticorum in Tertiam Partem Summae Theologiae Doctoris Angelici*, q. 1, a. 3, dub. 1, § 15ff.);[194] Godoy (*Disputationes theologicae in Tertiam partem Divi Thomae*, tract. 1, disp. 8, § 6, concl. 2);[195] our Philippe (*Disputationes theologicae in Tertiam partem Divi Thomae*, disp. 2, dub. 6);[196] Juan Prudencio (*Commentarii in Tertiam partem Sanctissimi Thomae*, tract. 2, disp. 2, dub. 1, sect. 4);[197] Parra (*Incarnationis arcanum scholastice disputationibus et quaestionibus reseratum*, tract. 1, disp. 1, q. 7, a. 3);[198] Gonet (*Clypeus theologiae Thomisticae*, part 3, tract. 1, disp. 5, § 6);[199] our Lawrence (*Spicilegium theologicum seu difficiliores controversiae selectae ex Tertia parte Summae Divi Thomae de Verbi divini Incarnatione*, contr. 7, § 12, no. 122);[200] and others. With these agree Granado (*In Tertiam Partem S. Thomae Aquinatis commentarii*, tract. 3, contr. 1, disp. 2, sect. 4);[201] Mendoza (*Quaestiones quodlibeticae et relectio de Christi regno ac dominio*, q. schol. 1, beginning from no. 1);[202] Lorca (*Commentarii ac disputationes in Tertiam partem D. Thomae*, q. 1, a. 3, disp. 10, memb. 3);[203] and many others.

27 And supposing this opinion, we are needled by the objection given in no. 25, to wit, how Christ was the first willed and intended by God as the end of all things and yet nevertheless had a dependence on the sin of Adam such that lacking it he would nowise have come by virtue of the present providence or decree. These two things do not seem to be mutually coherent, as we pondered above. Hence the authors we related found various ways of explaining this connection, out of which we will relate one or another more principal way, so that

---

193. Nazario (ed. Rossius, 4:131–34).
194. Cippullo (ed. Manelphius, 1:132–33).
195. Godoy (ed. Hertz, 1:126–28).
196. Philippe de la Trinité (ed. Iullieron, 13–16).
197. Prudencio (ed. Anisson, 1:279–81).
198. De la Parra y Arteaga (ed. Sanchez, 97–102).
199. Gonet (ed. Vivès, 5:483–85).
200. Lawrence of St. Therese (ed. Vannaccius, 226). Nos. 123–26 go on to explain the opinion (ed. Vannaccius, 226–27).
201. Granado (ed. de Lazcano, 68–72).
202. Mendoza (ed. Martinus, 1–54).
203. Lorca (ed. Sanchez de Ezpleta, 1:80–81).

by refuting them it will be easier to arrive at the way that we think truer and less cumbersome. Thus, Master Vicente taught that God first efficaciously intended and decreed the three modes of communication,[204] namely, that of nature, that of grace, and that of hypostatic union, not by determining the person to assume, nor by determining the concrete individual of the nature to be assumed, but by willing vaguely the Incarnation and that the person resultant from it would be the end of all things. And he taught that God then permitted and foresaw that there was going to be original sin, for whose remedy he distinctly decreed that the person of the Word would assume human nature with this passible flesh concretely. Hence he holds together both that the person incarnate is the end of all things by virtue of the first intention and that he nevertheless depends on the permission of sin, such that if the latter did not exist he would not exist.

But all the authors related for either opinion are warranted in their displeasure with this manner of speaking. This is because it proceeds by divination and without foundation in Scripture and the Fathers. For we gather this much from them: that the Incarnation was willed by God as a remedy for sin. Therefore it is rash to say that it was first willed independently of this motive vaguely and confusedly. Indeed, the Incarnation considered even in this way cannot become better known to us independently of the light of divine revelation than the same Incarnation concretely together with the circumstance of passible flesh, as we pondered in § 3 against the Scotists. Also, because, as Capréolus says quite well (*Defensiones divi Thomae* III, dist. 1, q. 1, a. 3),[205] the virtual order among divine decrees is commensurate with the real order among the objects willed with reference to their dependencies or causalities. Hence if one object is prior to another in the genus of final or efficient cause, we say that in that genus it is willed by God prior to the other. Now where we do not find a corresponding order among objects, there is no foundation for us to identify an order of prior and posterior in the divine

---

204. That is, ways in which God can grant a share in his being to creatures. See especially Vicente, *Relectio de habituali Christi Salvatoris nostri sanctificante gratia*, sol. q. 6, pp. 683–84.

205. Capréolus (ed. Paban et Pègues, 5:5–7).

decrees as touching on the aforementioned objects. However, making the comparison between the general concept of the person assuming and the nature assumed on the one hand and the particular concept of the person assuming and the nature assumed on the other, we find no real order or order of causality between the aforementioned objects, since there is no real distinction between these concepts. Therefore it is less rightly said that God first willed the Incarnation vaguely and in its general aspect and then willed the Incarnation in the particular aspects that it now has and that the first willing regarded the Incarnation as an end independently of sin while the second ordered the Incarnation to the remediation of sin. So, too, it would be inappropriately said that with respect to Peter God first willed the general aspect of man or of the human person and then the particular and individual aspect of Peter. Furthermore, because this manner of willing confusedly and by proceeding from general aspects to particular ones suggests the imperfection of potentiality both in knowing and in willing, which is altogether foreign to the utmost perfection of divine providence, as we have shown at length above (no. 17). And finally, because Vicente multiplies the stages and decrees in vain, since we can easily disencumber ourselves from this difficulty with greater simplicity, as we will see below.

28 Mendoza and Lorca, in the places related above, teach that God first efficaciously intended Christ, taken in particular, as the end of all things, such that Christ was willed in the order of intention independently of sin. Next, he chose, as a means, the permission of sin so that the Incarnation would be put into execution as dependent on it, not because this means was necessary for the aforementioned end from the nature of the thing, but because God chose it and bound the execution of the available end to this determinate means. So, too, if someone decrees for himself that he should make a journey absolutely, by virtue of this intention he does not remain bound to make the journey determinately on a horse or determinately in a carriage, but if he later chooses a carriage as the determinate means to this end, then if the carriage is lacking he will not make the journey. And so, too, God intends absolutely to give glory to someone, without remaining determined by virtue thereof to a certain kind of means, to wit, that

the attainment of glory should be through merits or independently of these. But if he then chooses merits as the determinate means out of his will [for glory], glory will not be given lacking merits. In this way, therefore, it is coherent that the intention for the Incarnation regarded it as the end of all things and independently of sin, as the objection posed in no. 25 purports, and that nevertheless the execution of the Incarnation had a dependence on the permission of sin as on the only means chosen for the end, such that, if it were lacking, the Incarnation would not occur, as our conclusion affirms.

Still, this manner of speaking, too, is insufficient and false. *First*, because it posits in God a kind of intention that is potential and confused concerning Christ. For, in fact, the aforementioned intention wills him absolutely in such a way that, by virtue of it, it does not determine the mode and means of his existence and another act determining these things is instead necessary. But this is something we have already criticized in the preceding manner of speaking, since it would posit in God a manner of proceeding from potency to act and from what is general and confused to what is particular and determinate. For this manner of intending comes about in us from the imperfection whereby we cannot infallibly unify these. Instead, we proceed from the intention of the end to the choice of the means. In God, however, the case has to be otherwise, since by his utmost actuality he can intend the end as to be attained through certain determinate and infallible means, without its being necessary for the intention to remain, as it were, in suspense and dependent on the choosing of the means. Nor is this the sense in which the order of intention is distinguished from the order of execution, as some falsely understand and explain it, since the order of divine intention does not stop precisively at the thing willed but extends even to the means, without which the intention would not be infallibly efficacious, just as no divine knowledge stops at the principles but extends to the conclusions, comprehending them in the principles. We do speak of [the order of intention] as distinct [from the order of execution], however, because, supposing these things, there is the command as well as the other concurrences pertaining to use or execution.[206] *Second*

206. As the Salmanticenses see it, the steps in the process of voluntary action begin with *iudicium, simplex volitio (benevolentia), simplex complacentia, dilectio, imperfecta*

(whereby the preceding line of reasoning is more fully explained), because it is not coherent for the divine intention of the fact that Christ was going to exist to be infallibly efficacious and for it to have had a dependence on the subsequent choice of the means of the permission and reparation of sin such that if these were lacking Christ would not be going to come. But, in point of fact, God's intention is infallibly efficacious, for otherwise it would not be warranted in being called an intention but would instead have to be called antecedent will or simple complacency.[207] Therefore, etc. Proof of the major premise: By the very fact that the aforementioned intention is infallibly efficacious, it entails infallibly what it intends, whether through this means or through another, where no means is necessarily connected with the intended end from the nature of the thing. It is established, however, that the permission of sin and reparation from it is not a means necessarily connected with Christ from the nature of the thing. For indeed, Christ was absolutely possible independently of this means, as is clear of itself. Therefore even if God had not chosen the aforementioned means, Christ would still come by virtue of the preceding efficacious intention, which would be put into execution through another means to be chosen by God. And, consequently, it would become true that even if Adam had not sinned and a remedy for original sin were not chosen,

---

fruitio, iudicium concerning the attainability of the end through certain means, and *intentio*. These complete the first order of intention. Next come *consilium, consensus, iudicium* in the strict sense, and *electio*. These complete the order to the means as related to the intention. Finally come *imperium, usus passivus* (the carrying out of the means), *consecutio et possessio finis*, and *fruitio perfecta*. These latter acts pertain to the order of execution. See Salmanticenses, *Cursus theologicus*, tract. 12, *De virtutibus, Arbor praedicimentalis*, § 1, no. 6 (ed Palmé, 6:418).

Here, the Salmanticenses reject the idea that our conceptual distinction in God's acts between the order of intention and the order of execution is based on distinguishing God's first intention of the end from a subsequent ordering of the means to the end. Instead, they explain that *imperium, usus*, etc., which occur in the actual carrying out of the will's effective intention, are what warrants the distinction between the order of intention and the order of execution in God's acts.

207. God's antecedent will is distinguished from his consequent will. The former means his will as abstracted from concrete circumstances. Thus, it represents a general wish, all things being equal, that may not come to pass in the concrete reality. The latter, in contrast, means his will as actually realized in the actual circumstances.

Christ would still be going to come by virtue of the first intention that regarded him, which we are presupposing is efficacious. Hence while the aforementioned authors are opposed to Scotus's opinion, they fall back into it by how they explain themselves, when they identify in God an absolute and efficacious intention concerning Christ antecedently to all choice and foreseeing of the means. For the aforementioned intention must be fulfilled independently of any means taken determinately and thus independently of the permission and reparation of sin. Recall what we said in tract. 5, disp. 9, dub. 3, § 8.[208]

A further clarification: If, antecedently to the foreseeing of sin and independently of all means and motives, God decreed becoming incarnate absolutely and afterwards bound the aforementioned intention to the means or motive of the remediation of sin, we ask of our adversaries: By virtue of this first intention, lacking sin or if Adam had not sinned, would God have become man or would he not have become man? If they choose the first, they plainly abandon their assertion and ours. If they say the second, we clearly infer either that the aforementioned intention was not efficacious, contrary to their supposition, or that it was changed through the subsequent choice of determinate means, which is incompatible with God's immutability. For if the aforementioned intention were efficacious and would remain, then even if one means were lacking, another would have to be assumed to account for its efficacy and to attain the intended end. Through this, the examples that the related opinion would marshal for its support are overturned. *The first* is taken from human affairs. For man's intention is neither infallibly efficacious nor immutable. Hence a man can later bind a preceding intention of making a journey to a determinate means. And if the aforementioned means is lacking, without any unfitting conclusion we say that his intention of making a journey was not efficacious or that it ceased. And if the man still intends to make a journey, he will have this not by virtue of the first intention, which he had bound to one means

---

208. Salmanticenses (ed. Palmé, 2:455–56). There they explain how predestination is not just to glory in any sense but to glory precisely as a crown for merits. This initial intention to give glory as a crown is totally gratuitous on God's part, not a response to merits. In fact, it is the intention for the crown of glory that gives rise to merits, as the end gives rise to the necessary means.

that then did not present itself, but by virtue of another intention, succeeding the first due to the lack of means. In this a change necessarily intervenes. Now all this is foreign to the efficacy and immutability of divine intention. Hence the aforementioned example should be turned back on those authors. *The second* has a false supposition. For God does not intend glory as an end independently of all means on the part of the object willed, since he would be subject to all the imperfections we have presented up to this point. Rather, proceeding independently of the means or merit on the part of the intention or divine act, he has established to give glory through determinate means and with glory's dependence on them. Nor is it necessary for there to succeed another act choosing or prescribing the determinate means, although command and other acts pertaining to execution follow.

29 Therefore, leaving behind these and other less important manners of speaking (which end up going back to those given above), there is one easier, truer, and more common with the authors related in no. 26, which we have already introduced in no. 6 and the places cited there. According to it, it should be held that God, by a primary intention, decreed Christ not only in substance but also in the circumstance of passible flesh and the aspect of Redeemer from Adam's sin and by the same act simultaneously willed the permission of the aforementioned sin and the redemption of the human race through Christ. This was in such a way that among the aforementioned objects, not of themselves connected, he decreed and established the mutual dependence in different genera of cause whereby Christ would be the end *for-the-sake-of-which* of the passive permission of the aforementioned sin, the redemption of the human race, and of all the divine works pertaining to the order of nature and of grace, that the sin permitted would be the matter *concerning-which* of the redemption, and that the human race would be the end *to-which*. Hence in the genus of final cause *for-the-sake-of-which*, he willed and saw Christ prior to the others, but in the genus of material cause and in the genus of final cause *to-which*, he willed and saw the permission of sin, its remedy, and the other things pertaining to it prior to Christ. Here, "prior" does not designate an order of divine acts, which we do not suppose to be more

than one as far as the present matter is concerned. Instead, it falls to the objects willed with the mutual dependence in the different genera of cause.

This solution will be more easily understood if we make some brief observations. *First*, that it is frequently the case that there is a mutual dependence among things in different genera of cause, as we have explained from general philosophy in tract. 15, disp. 3, beginning from no. 74.[209] And this mutual dependence can be preserved within the same genus of cause when it is subaltern or contains under itself several modes and quasi-species of causality. For this reason, the subject is prior to the accidents in the genus of receptive material cause, whereas the latter are prior to the former in the genus of dispositive material cause. And the same is the case in the genus of final cause when making the comparison between the end *for-the-sake-of-which* and the end *to-which*, as if we said that beatitude is the end *for-the-sake-of-which* of man and man is the end *to-which* of beatitude and that, with reference to these aspects, they mutually depend on and precede each other within the same genus of final cause. *Second*, that in the first stage *in-quo* God foresaw, among other possible things, everything that we have proposed in our solution. For it cannot be denied that they were possible, not only in themselves but also with the mutual dependencies we have described, and God was able to establish these between them, as we said in no. 5. Hence it was not logically incompatible that in the second or subsequent stage *in-quo* he should efficaciously decree and foresee as going to be all these things also with their foreknown dependencies, as we have explained further in no. 6. *Third*, granted that God willed them all by one single act of efficacious intention, and granted that in the divine acts there is no real order of prior and posterior, causality, or dependence, whether among themselves or from the objects, nevertheless where we find an order among the objects and priority in different genera of cause, we rightly conceive of and say that the divine act regards one object in a genus prior to another and vice versa in a different genus of cause. Here the whole order of prior and posterior refers to the causality and the dependence that the objects have either

---

209. Salmanticenses, *Cursus theologicus*, tract. 15, disp. 3, dub. 4, § 1, beginning from no. 74 (ed. Palmé, 10:580ff.).

of themselves or from the will of God, who chains them together and decrees them in no other way. This is as if we said that God wills matter prior to form in the genus of material cause and that he wills form prior to matter in the genus of formal cause. For he wills that in the genus of material cause the matter be the cause and that the form be an effect dependent on it, and vice versa in the genus of formal cause. And priority and posteriority of nature, priority and posteriority *a-quo*, designates nothing other than causalities and dependencies of this sort. Now a single act and a single stage *in-quo* are sufficient for God to decree the aforementioned together with this sort of priority and posteriority with reference to the different genera of causality on the part of the object, as we have said in tract. 5, disp. 9, no. 110.[210]

30 Supposing these things, which are true and easy to understand, our solution's proper understanding appears clearly enough. For we say that, supposing the knowledge of possible objects and possible dependencies in this matter, God decreed the mystery of the Incarnation in the manner described, to wit, in such a way that Christ was willed as Redeemer after the manner of the end *for-the-sake-of-which*, the permission of sin after the manner of the matter *concerning-which*, and the human race as to be redeemed after the manner of the end *to-which*. Hence in the genus of final cause *for-the-sake-of-which*, Christ was the first willed and the rest are something posterior and dependent on him. But in the other genera, the case was otherwise, for the others were willed prior as matter or as the end *to-which*, while Christ is considered as something posterior and dependent on them. But because the final cause has priority among them all, since it has the first influence, and because in a given reality the genus of final cause *for-the-sake-of-which* is of greater account than the end *to-which*, we therefore say that Christ, who was intended as the end *for-the-sake-of-which* of the rest, is the first willed and decreed among all things. Yet this does not prevent his having been willed with a dependence on the others in other genera of causality and, consequently, does not establish that the Incarnation would be independently of other causes or motives, such

---

210. Salmanticenses, *Cursus theologicus*, tract. 5, disp. 9, dub. 3, § 6, no. 110 (ed. Palmé, 2:453).

as the remediation of sin. And it is quite coherent for a thing to be the first willed simply in no other way than with a dependence on others, for this is the way in which the end precedes the means on which it depends and the way in which the substantial composite precedes its accidents, though it cannot exist without them.

But if you inquire by what foundation we affirm that what is presented as possible was *de facto* so willed and arranged by God, we respond that it is sufficiently established from what has been said in this doubt up to this point, without need of opening up other foundations or adding on new proofs. For that Christ the Redeemer was the first willed and intended by God after the manner of the end *for-the-sake-of-which* of the permission of sin, the reparation of man, and all other things, is established from what was said in nos. 4 and 26, his most excellent dignity especially requiring this. But that Christ was willed and intended as a remedy for sin and dependently on this matter and end *to-which* is established from what was said beginning from no. 8, where we proved this part at length from Scripture and the Fathers, cutting off various evasions. Now these two elements are reconciled to each other in no other way nor more aptly than in the way we have laid out by establishing among the aforementioned objects the mutual dependence of causality we have explained, as is clear from the refutation of other opinions beginning from no. 27. And in this way everything that must be preserved here fits together very well, which is no small sign of the truth, for the true resonates with the true, as the common saying goes.[211] Now it happens that what we affirm of the manner of Christ's predestination is consistent with what the more frequent and truer opinion of theologians holds of the manner of predestination of men to glory as a crown.[212] For, granted that the divine intention was altogether gracious and drew no origin from merits that were previously going to be or foreseen, [God] nevertheless willed primarily to confer glory on men as a crown and dependently on merits, this entire dependence falling to

---

211. *Verum vero consonat.*

212. Cf. Rada, *Controversiae theologicae* III, contr. 5, a. 3, op. Scot., concl. 4 (ed. Ioannes Crithius, 3:164–65); Suárez, *Disputationes in Tertiam partem*, disp. 5, sect. 1, no. 34 (ed. Vivès, 17:211–12); and Mendoza, *Quaestiones quodlibeticae et relectio theologica de Christi regno ac dominio*, q. 1, no. 5 (ed. Martinus, 15).

the thing willed, namely glory. Hence by virtue of the aforementioned intention he established such a link between glory, the crown, and merits, that glory was willed in the genus of final cause prior to merits and had no dependence on them in this genus. But this independence was not altogether absolute or in every genus, for merits were willed as prior to glory in the genus of moral efficient cause, and God did not will glory as a crown in a way other than as to be given dependently on merits in the aforementioned genus. Thus, it becomes true that by virtue of such an intention glory would not be given if there were no merits, as we have professedly said (tract. 5, disp. 9, dub. 3, nearly throughout, and especially § 10).[213] In this way, then, in the present matter, God's first intention regarded Christ as Redeemer and as a remedy for sin, the former as the principal end, the end *for-the-sake-of-which*, the latter as the matter and the end *to-which*. Hence he established such a dependence and order of causality between the aforementioned that Christ is prior in one genus and at the same time posterior in another, and he has not been realized nor would he be realized other than dependently on remediation, just as glory is not given as a crown except dependently on merits, since this is how it was decreed on the part of the thing willed. St. Thomas expresses this dependence and order of ends *for-the-sake-of-which* and *to-which* quite well in these words: *It should be said that God loves Christ not only more than the whole human race, but even more than the whole universe of creatures in that he willed for him a greater good, since he gave him the name that is above every name, in his being true God. Nor does his excellence suffer loss from the fact that God gave him up to death for the salvation of the human race, for, in fact, he has thereby become a glorious conqueror. For "the primacy has been laid upon his shoulders" (Is 9:6)* (ST I, q. 20, a. 4, ad 1).[214]

31 From these words we easily gather a response to the objection posed in no. 25. It is to solve this that we have put forth all this for consideration, without needing to add anything additional. For it is quite coherent that Christ was thus the first willed and intended in the genus of final cause and that he was nevertheless willed as a remedy

---

213. Salmanticenses (ed. Palmé, 2:457–59).
214. Aquinas (Leonine ed., 4:256).

for sin and dependently on it, in such a way that by virtue of the aforementioned intention he would not be realized lacking Adam's sin, as we have just explained. Second, granted that Christ was willed and foreseen prior to other things in the genus of final cause, and that among them those were prior in the aforementioned genus which are more perfect and come closer to God and Christ, as, for example, the glorification of the predestined, we nevertheless gather that in the genus of material cause and in the order pertaining to execution, the production of men was willed first, then elevation to the state of grace, further the permission of sin, and afterwards the remedy through Christ the Redeemer and the efficacious election of the predestined and their glorification. In this sense we admit the opinion of Cajetan related in no. 25, and perhaps he himself did not intend anything other than to identify the aforementioned order not in an absolute way but in the genus of material cause and with a focus on the execution of the aforementioned objects. In fact, he seems to subscribe to our opinion and to be the first to introduce it (Commentary on *ST* III, q. 1, a. 3, § *Ad secundum vero*).[215] Third, we gather that in the aforementioned genus of material cause and in the order pertaining to execution, not only Adam's sin but also the sin of the angels was permitted and foreseen before Christ, or (which is the same thing) independently of him in the aforementioned genus. For the sin of men was foreseen as going to be from the temptation of the devil. Hence in the genus in which the fact that Christ is going to exist supposes the sin of men, it also presupposes the angels' sin. Concerning the latter, as far as it is concerned, Christ could be decreed for its remediation, although *de facto* this has not been the case for other reasons. Fourth, we gather that when we discover in Scripture and the Fathers that Christ was willed and predestined *as our remedy* or *for our salvation*, the aforementioned phrases do not denote the end *for-the-sake-of-which*, seeing as this aspect belongs to Christ in respect of our salvation and remediation. Rather, they denote the end *to-which*, the end effected or of benefit, since this great good comes to us from the Incarnation and Christ was predestined in an order to it.

Finally, we gather a response to the lines of reasoning put forward

---

215. Cajetan, Commentary on *ST* III, q. 1, a. 3, no. 8 (Leonine ed., 11:16).

in no. 25 for the contrary manner of speaking. The first only succeeds in proving that the order Cajetan describes was foreseen in the genus of material cause and in the order of execution. For this is the way in which nature precedes grace and both precede the hypostatic union. But it is coherent with this that in the genus of final cause *for-the-sake-of-which* the Incarnation was willed and foreseen prior to the others, since all things were ordained for the glory of Christ the Redeemer. So too, in the genus of final cause, glory as a crown precedes merits, though in the genus of moral efficient cause and in the order of execution merits precede the crown of glory.

To the second, we respond that the intention for the Incarnation as our remedy was an act of the remarkable liberality of God, who was not moved by any preceding merits but who intended our being raised up and our exaltation out of his surpassing charity. Moreover, for such an intention of raising up [from] human misery, it was not necessary to presuppose that misery was foreseen and going to be by virtue of another antecedent decree. Rather, it was enough that on the part of the object willed it would entail the permission of sin and its remedy. For misery preceded Christ predestined in a given genus by the very fact that out of divine mercy he would be its remedy. Similarly, the intention of giving glory as a crown and on account of merits is an act not of justice but of divine liberality, since such an intention does not draw its origin from merits, and yet merits as foreseen and as going to be do precede glory as a crown in a certain genus. Hence the aforementioned intention, subjectively gracious and without merits, regards the act objectively out of justice and dependent on merits.

To the third, it should be said that predestination is taken in two ways. In one way, less properly for the efficacious election of someone for glory and of the means leading to this end. In the other, most properly for the act of command directing the use or execution. In this way it signifies the dispatching to the aforementioned end and supposes both the end and the means as foreseen and going to be, with at least the inchoate, though infallible, fact that they will exist, as is established from what was said (tract. 5, disp. 1, dub. 1; and disp. 2, dub. 2).[216] It is

---

216. Salmanticenses (ed. Palmé, 2:239–42, 2:263–89).

a sign of this difference that intention and election are formally acts of the will, whereas predestination, take most formally, is a practical act of the intellect directing and entailing the execution of the preintended good, as we showed in the last passage. When, therefore, St. Thomas in the place cited affirms in an objection that *predestination presupposes foreknowledge of what is going to exist*, gathering thereby that Christ was predestined as a remedy for sin and that, lacking this, he would not have come, he is speaking, as is appropriate, in the most formal sense and not using "predestination" as meaning intention or election but as meaning the act of command presupposing them and directing the use or execution in an order to the aforewilled end. Hence he is warranted in affirming that Christ's predestination supposes foreknowledge of future sin, since this arises by virtue of the first intention of Christ as Redeemer in the way clarified above. And in this way he meets quite well and directly the challenge of argument 4, which proves that the Incarnation would occur even if there were not going to be sin on the basis that Christ's predestination is eternal and infallibly to be fulfilled. For he replies that although that predestination does not suppose existing sin, it does suppose foreknowledge of it or of the fact that it is going to exist, as the end also generally supposes the willing of the means. Yet we do not at all thereby infer that the first intention of Christ the Redeemer (which is called predestination broadly and less properly) supposes, in the opinion of the Holy Doctor, foreknowledge of future sin by virtue of another decree or antecedent providence. For it is enough that, by virtue of such an intention, its permission and the fact that it is going to exist follow and that these precede Christ himself objectively in some genus of cause, as we clarified above. Godoy hands down another response and continues at length (*Disputationes theologicae in Tertiam partem Divi Thomae*, tract. 1, disp. 8, § 7, beginning from no. 140).[217] But the given response seems to us to be truer and to stick more closely to the text of St. Thomas.

---

217. Godoy (ed. Hertz, 1:129–31).

§ 6. Replies against the preceding doctrine and extrication from them

32 Yet there are still some points of opposition one can raise against the manner of speaking we have chosen that we ought to resolve. And in the first place, the objection is made: Even granting that two given things can be compared to each other as the end *for-the-sake-of-which* and the end *to-which* and have a mutual dependence in the same subaltern genus of final cause, we are less right to assert that with respect to the divine intention decreeing the Incarnation, Christ was characterized as the end *for-the-sake-of-which* and the human race as to be redeemed was characterized as the end *to-which*. For we can show that the situation was the other way around:[218] This is because the particle "for" [*propter*] implies a habitude to the end *for-the-sake-of-which*, as when we say that a sick man takes a bitter drink for health. But the testimonies of Scripture and the Fathers adduced in § 2 manifestly denote that Christ was predestined and came as our remedy. Hence in the Creed of the Council of Nicaea it says: *For us men and for our salvation, he came down from heaven, and [...] was incarnate [...] and became man.*[219] Therefore our remedy or passive redemption[220] was the end *for-the-sake-of-which* with respect to Christ. Also, because that is called the end *to-which* to which particular benefit is intended and accrues. But from the redemption of the human race particular glory and exaltation is intended and accrues to Christ more than to men.[221] Therefore Christ was the end *to-which* of the aforementioned intention. And, consequently, since in our opinion he is also the end *for-the-sake-of-which*, it follows that he is the end *to-which* and the adequate end [composed] of these aspects. From this, [it follows] that

---

218. Cf. Vásquez, *Disputationes in Tertiam partem*, disp. 11, chap. 6, no. 64 (ed. Sanchez Crespo, 1:166).

219. The Salmanticenses do not note the omissions.

220. "Passive redemption" means humanity's being redeemed, in contrast to "active redemption," which is God's act of redeeming. Similar expressions, such as "passive salvation" or "passive predestination" occur throughout.

221. Cf. Vásquez, *Disputationes in Tertiam partem*, disp. 11, chap. 6, nos. 66–67 (ed. Sanchez Crespo, 1:167).

he had no dependence on the remediation of sin in the genus of final cause.—Confirmation: It is not fitting for what is more perfect and prominent to be ordered to what is less perfect as to an end. But Christ is a good more perfect simply than the whole human race to be redeemed. Therefore, he should not have been ordered to its remediation as to an end. And thus in the genus of final cause he was willed and predestined independently of it.

We respond to the objection by denying the antecedent or the assumption. To its first proof it should be said that, although the expression "for" signifies frequently enough a habitude to the end *for-the-sake-of-which*, it nevertheless also denotes in more than one case a respect to the end *to-which*, the end of benefit. But where there is a doubt as to which end or which aspect of the end it signifies, we should focus on and consider which of the present aspects when contrasted with one another is the more perfect. For the more perfect will be signified as the end *for-the-sake-of-which*, while the less perfect will be signified as the end *to-which*, even though the expression "for" is applied to it. For, when comparison is made among the aforementioned aspects, the end *for-the-sake-of-which* is more prominent than the end *to-which*, or that of the subject to whom the benefit comes, as is clear in grace and glory when comparison is made to the subject, as is established from what was said in tract. 14, disp. 4, dub. 7.[222] Since, then, it is certain that Christ the Lord is a good more perfect by far than the human race, when we discover in Scripture and the Fathers that Christ was predestined and came *for us men and for our salvation*, the expression "for" (which is either indifferent or more frequently denotes the end *for-the-sake-of-which*) is taken in accord with the subject matter to which it is applied as signifying only the end *to-which*, that of benefit. This doctrine is taken from St. Thomas, where, resolving a similar difficulty, he says: *Something can be for something else in two ways. In one way, because it is ordered to it as to a proper and principal end. And in this way it is unfitting to say that something is for something baser than itself, as that the moon and stars are for night owls and bats, since the end is of greater account than the things that are directed toward the end. In*

---

222. Salmanticenses (ed. Palmé, 9:581–96).

the other way, something can be said to be for something else to which some benefit comes from it, in the way that a king could be said to be for a peasant, since peace comes to him from the king's rule. And this is the way in which what is said in the text should be understood. For all the benefits that come about in lower bodies from heavenly bodies are foreseen by God, who established those bodies (*Super II Sent.*, dist. 15, q. 1, a. 1, ad 6).[223] And in the same sense, he says: *The good of the multitude, to which the one is ordered, is less than the external good to which the multitude is ordered, as the good of the order of an army is less than the good of the commander* (*ST* II-II, q. 39, a. 2, ad 2).[224] In this way, then, although it is said that Christ came for men's salvation, the word "for" presents not a habitude to the end *for-the-sake-of-which*, the more principal end, but instead a respect to the end *to-which*, that of benefit. For Christ is more perfect than men and men's passive salvation.

To the second proof, it should be conceded that Christ was also the end *to-which* as in its ultimate state, the one to whom the greatest glory has redounded from the work of redemption. But this does not prevent the human race's having been the end *to which* salvation through Christ the Redeemer was proximately intended and decreed. Similarly, in the example just adduced from St. Thomas, the peasant is the end *to which* benefit and peace from the king's rule proximately come, and yet, in the end, the benefit and peace of peasants yields an advantage to the very same king, as is clear of itself. Now the connection willed by God suffices for Christ to have been predestined in a manner connected to our salvation and in such a way that he would not come lacking this motive. Confirmation of this is plain from what was just said, that Christ was not ordered to our salvation as to the end *for-the-sake-of-which*, the more principal end, but only as to the end *to-which*, the end of benefit. In this there is nothing unbecoming or any disorder. Hence the aforementioned difficulty should be directed to the authors of the contrary manner of speaking, who affirm that our salvation was the end *for-the-sake-of-which*, the end simply, of the Incarnation.

---

223. Aquinas (ed. Mandonnet, 2:369–70).
224. Aquinas (Leonine ed., 8:309).

33 The second objection: If the Incarnation were prior to the permission of sin in the genus of final cause simply, there would be no reason why it would have a connection with this permission of the sort that, lacking sin, the Incarnation would not be going to occur. But we have established this latter as a conclusion. Therefore we fail in *consequentia* when we teach that the Incarnation was the end of the permission of sin and precedes it in the genus of final cause. Proof of the *sequela*: Given and supposing this arrangement, the connection of the Incarnation with the permission of sin and its dependence on it can arise from no other source than that both terminate the same intention of God. But this is not at all sufficient. Otherwise, by the same argument it would be proved that, lacking even a fly, the Incarnation would not be going to occur, since by a single act of intention God willed them both, which is plainly absurd and ridiculous.[225] A further clarification: For two given things, one of which is prior in one genus, to have a mutual dependence and for one to be unable to subsist without the other and vice versa, it is necessary that they have between themselves an order either of means to end or of cause to effect. But this is not at all preserved between the Incarnation and the permission of sin, for, in fact, neither is the permission of sin necessary for the Incarnation, nor is the Incarnation required for the permission of sin, as is clear of itself. Therefore they do not have the mutual dependence and connection we have described. And, consequently, if the Incarnation is prior to the permission of sin after the manner of an end, it will be prior in all modes and independent in every genus of cause and thus will be going to exist even lacking sin.

We respond by denying the *sequela*. For it is quite coherent that the Incarnation is prior to the permission of sin in the genus of final cause *for-the-sake-of-which* and that it nevertheless depends on it in other genera, as we explained in the preceding §. Now as for the proof to the contrary, the major premise should be denied. For the reason for this connection and mutual dependence is not founded on the fact that the Incarnation and the permission of sin were willed in the same act, as

---

225. The example of the fly, invoked to slightly different effect, appears in Rada, *Controversiae theologicae* III, contr. 5, a. 3, op. Scot., concl. 4, prob. 3 (ed. Ioannes Crithius, 3:165–66).

the objection falsely supposes. Rather, it is founded on the fact that they were willed with a mutual dependence on the part of the object.[226] For God knew in the first stage *in-quo* that the aforementioned dependence between them was possible, and he decreed in the second stage *in-quo* that it was going to be. Hence, lacking sin, there would not be Christ, whereas there would be Christ lacking a fly or this or that particular being. For even though it was by one act that God decreed that Christ and everything else was going to exist and willed that Christ would be the end *for-the-sake-of-which* of everything, he did not will that Christ would depend on everything in other genera of cause. Rather, he restricted this dependence to certain things, such as the remediation of sin and men's redemption, as we are taught from Scripture and the Fathers. So too, all things are for the glory of the elect, and yet this glory does not depend on individual things, for example, a fly, but depends instead on merits or on other determinate principles that God has decreed as he pleased.

In this way, [the response] to the expansion[227] and explication of the difficulty is plain. For in order that there be a mutual dependence between given objects in different genera of cause, this need not befit them from the nature of the thing. Rather, it suffices that this be determined for them from the will of God intending and decreeing them in this way. So too, glory does not depend necessarily on merits, for it could be conferred by a miracle without them. But God willed that it not be conferred on adults in any other way than through merits. Hence in this way glory is the cause of merits after the manner of the end while at the same time depending on the same in another genus, and it would not be conferred without them by virtue of the present providence. So too, the Incarnation does not depend on sin as on the matter *concerning-which* or on the remediation of the human race as on the end effected, that of benefit, from the nature of the thing. And yet,

---

226. The core of the reply to the objection is that found in Suárez, *Disputationes in Tertiam partem*, disp. 5, sect. 1, nos. 35–39 (ed. Vivès, 17:212–14); and Vásquez, *Disputationes in Tertiam partem*, q. 1, a. 3, disp. 11, chap. 2, nos. 18–23 (ed. Sanchez Crespo, 1:157–58). The Salmanticenses develop it within their own framework of precisely two conceptual stages and of Christ as the end *for-the-sake-of-which* of all creatures.

227. *Augmentum*.

God willed the Incarnation as the end of other things in such a way that he simultaneously willed that it would depend on the aforementioned in other genera, and thus that, lacking them, it would not be put into execution. This is especially since the first intention of Christ regarded him as Redeemer, in passible flesh, and with all the circumstances that he had in execution, as was shown in § 3 and § 4. Now it is only with dependence on the aforementioned in these genera of cause that Christ was able to exist or to be decreed as going to exist in this way, just as glory as a crown can only be given or decreed dependently on merits on the part of the object willed. Therefore it is enough that in matters of this sort there be a mutual connection (which no one will deny is possible, as we said before in no. 5), if not from the nature of the thing, then at least from the divine will.

34 The third objection: If the permission of sin is an effect of Christ's predestination in the genus of final cause, as we assert, it follows that the decree of the Incarnation and of Christ's predestination is supposed as altogether complete before the permission and foreknowledge of sin. Yet from this we plainly infer that Christ's Incarnation and predestination did not have a dependence on the permission of sin in any genus of cause, as will be readily obvious to one who considers it. Therefore, it does not at all fit together that God decreed Christ for the remediation of sin and dependently on this motive and that the permission of sin was for Christ and dependent on him in the genus of final cause. The *sequela* is shown: A decree that on the part of the object is the cause of another has to be understood as altogether complete before its effect is understood. For otherwise it could not be conceived of as its cause. Therefore, if the decree predestining Christ is the cause of the permission of sin, it has to be understood as altogether complete before the fact that [the permission] would exist and foreknowledge of it.

We respond by denying the *sequela*: Since this decree regarded Christ as Redeemer of men from sin and in an order to this end effected, it is only understood as altogether complete on the part of the object willed, if, on the part of this object, Christ as Redeemer, the permission of sin, and finally the passive redemption of men from it are understood.

The reason is that all these things were willed by God through the intention to constitute one adequate end, coming together from the aspect of *for-the-sake-of-which* and the aspect of *to-which*, with the mutual dependence of them among themselves in the different genera. Hence such a decree touching on Christ is only understood as complete with an addition, namely, "in the genus of final cause *for-the-sake-of-which*," with which it is coherent that in another genus it would regard the permission of sin and its reparation as something prior. For they all pertain to the total end intended by God. So too, divine causality touching on matter, which is prior in the genus of material cause, is not understood as complete absolutely prior to its touching on form, and vice versa. For matter and form constitute the substantial composite, which is the adequate term of the divine causality. And likewise, the intention of giving glory as a crown is not understood as complete without merits at the same time foreseen, even though they depend on glory in the genus of final cause. For it stands with this dependence in this genus that glory as a crown should depend on merits in another and that it not be intended by God except dependently on them on the part of the thing willed. Through this, the matter is sufficiently established as regards the proof of the *sequela*. For it only succeeds in proving that God's decree is in itself subjectively the complete cause for entailing both Christ and the permission of sin. But it is not persuasive that, as touching on Christ, this decree is altogether complete on the part of the thing willed. For it extends to more than one thing, as is explained by the examples related.

Nor does it matter if you say, then, that the decree of men's predestination would precede as altogether complete the decree pertaining to the effects of predestination, such as the means through which the predestined person attains the end. For it is their cause and is supposed as altogether complete before the predestination of the effects. Therefore, if the decree of the Incarnation was the cause of the permission of sin and men's passive redemption, if not the whole order of nature and grace (for, in fact, we affirm that all of these were willed by God from the end of the Incarnation, or for Christ), it follows that the decree of the Incarnation was altogether complete on the part of the thing willed antecedently to all these things as going to be and foreseen. And, consequently, [it follows] that Christ, who is the end willed through such a decree, was intended and predestined independently of them. This is directly opposed to our opinion and gives foundation for the contrary opinion.

This, I say, does not matter but is instead easily resolved. For of the effects of predestination, some are mere effects in the order of final cause, since they nowise share in the aspect of the end. And we admit that these suppose the intention or decree of the end as altogether complete, at least in the genus of final cause. But others are effects of predestination in such a way as to pertain at the same time to its end *to-which* and to fill out the total end. And it is not necessary for these latter to presuppose the decree of predestination as altogether complete, since they regard its adequate end. This is how it is with the substance of the predestined subject.²²⁸ For in this way, it is the effect of glory in the genus of final cause *for-the-sake-of-which* while simultaneously being the end *to-which* of the very same glory and entering into the constitution of the end *which*, or the adequate end, which is glorified man.²²⁹ And in the selfsame Christ, natural filiation from God was the end *for-the-sake-of-which* of predestination in respect of his humanity, or of Christ as subsisting in it, yet from this no one infers that the decree of Christ's

---

228. That is, the very person of the one who is predestined.

229. The Salmanticenses' point is subtle. The *finis cuius gratia* ("the end *for-the-sake-of-which*") can be divided into the *finis qui* ("the end *which*") and the *finis quo* ("the end *whereby*"). The *finis qui* is the thing itself (the objective end), while the *finis quo* is the possession or enjoyment of the thing (the formal end). Here, they are saying that if the thing itself intended by God's predestination is the glorified human being (the *finis qui*), then the fact that a human being enjoys glory is necessarily included. In this way, the *finis qui* could not be what it is without a given *finis cui*. To take a different example, the physician can only will health (the *finis cuius gratia*) by willing it in a patient (the *finis cui*), since health can only exist as the state of a living organism. Thus, the patient is both the *finis cui* and also part of the *finis qui*, since what is really willed is not just "health" but "this healthy person." So, the total, adequate end that the agent wills includes certain effects of the *finis cuius gratia*, if those effects are not *mere* effects but are also characterized by a share in the end. Cf. Complutenses, *Artium cursus, Liber II Physicorum*, disp. 14, q. 1, § 1, no. 1 (ed. Chevalier, 2:231–32); the Salmanticenses, *Cursus theologicus*, tract. 8, *De ultimo fine*, q. 1, praef., no. 4 (ed. Palmé, 5:3); and Reginald Garrigou-Lagrange, "Le principe de finalité," *Revue Thomiste* 26, no. 3 (1921): 420. Aquinas uses the same distinction (between *finis qui* and *finis quo*), except that what the Salmanticenses call the *finis qui*, he calls the *finis cuius*. *ST* I-II, q. 1, a. 8 (Leonine ed., 6:16); and q. 2, a. 7 (Leonine ed., 6:23).

predestination was altogether complete in the genus of final cause independently of the humanity or of Christ as man. For the humanity or the man Christ was the end *to-which* of the aforementioned natural filiation from God and pertained to the end *which*, or the adequate end, namely Christ the natural Son of God. The same, therefore, occurs in the present case. For the passive redemption of men was in this way the effect of the Incarnation in the genus of final cause *for-the-sake-of-which* while at the same time being the end *to-which* of the very same Incarnation and pertaining to the adequate end of the decree whereby God intended the Incarnation, as we have often said. And the other things touched on in this reply also had their precedences in other genera on the part of the thing willed, or at least a necessary connection to the end willed as intended by God.

35 The fourth objection: Original justice or the grace of the state of innocence was not an effect of Christ's predestination. But it would be if it regarded him as an end, for, in fact, on that supposition it would have been produced for him and dependently on him. Therefore at least the aforementioned grace did not have a dependence on Christ in the genus of final cause but was from another decree and providence. Proof of the major premise: The aforementioned grace was not redemptive, just as the grace of the angels was not. But for this reason their grace was not the effect of Christ's predestination, as St. Thomas teaches (*De Veritate*, q. 29, a. 4, ad 5, and a. 7, ad 5).[230] Therefore the same should be said of original grace or justice.

We respond by denying the major premise. Everything that God decreed and made, he ordered to Christ as to the end first and principally willed among all things, according to the testimony of the Apostle already adduced in no. 4: *Who is the image of the invisible God, the first-born of every creature: For in him were all things created in heaven and on earth, visible and invisible* (Col 1:15). And we have no reason to deny this, since it was possible, would give Christ greater dignity, and is not at all opposed to the end of redemption. Hence both the grace of our first parents in the state of innocence as well as the first men themselves were for Christ and posterior to him in the genus of final cause. As for

---

230. Aquinas (Leonine ed., 22:860, 22:867).

the proof to the contrary, we deny the minor premise: For the same should be said of the angels and of their grace. Nor does St. Thomas deny this in the places cited. For he is not dealing with influence or dependence in the genus of final cause but in the genus of meritorious efficient cause, as will be obvious by reading these passages. Now whether the grace of our first parents and of the angels was from the merits of Christ in the genus of efficient cause is another difficulty, different by far, which we will decide in its own place (tract. 21, disp. 7, dub. 4),[231] introducing something of it below (nos. 42 and 44), where this objection, differently posed, will come up again.

36 The fifth objection: Original sin was in no way the effect of Christ's predestination. Therefore, it in no way supposed Christ in the genus of final cause but instead preceded him simply by virtue of another providence distinct from Christ's predestination. The *consequentia* is plain: For one thing to be posterior to another in a certain genus of cause, it has to be its effect in the aforementioned genus. Otherwise, it will nowise be subordinated to it in that genus. Therefore if sin is in no way the effect of Christ's predestination, it follows that it is in no way posterior to it in the genus of final cause. Now the antecedent is certain. This is because for sin to be in some way the effect of Christ's predestination, it would have to be willed by God for Christ as a means leading to the end. But God in no way wills sin. Also, because Christ did not come that we might sin but because we sinned. Therefore, sin is not an effect that the Incarnation entails but something supposed for the Incarnation.

We respond that, although sin in itself and as regards its malice is not an effect of Christ's Incarnation, sin as permitted, or rather the permission itself of sin or the passive dereliction of man, may well be.[232] Supposing this, sin is infallibly entailed due to our frailty. Now God decreed the permission of sin for Christ the Redeemer and for his

---

231. Tract. 21, disp. 7, dub. 4 (ed. Palmé, 13:661–700) is on the relation of Christ's merits to the Fathers who lived prior to his Incarnation. Tract. 21, disp. 16, dub. 4 (ed. Palmé, 14:593–614), where the Salmanticenses argue that Christ was not the head of Adam in the state of innocence, is also relevant.

232. "The passive dereliction of man": man's being left without the grace actually resulting in the avoidance of sin.

greater glory. Hence the permission of sin and sin itself were not going to exist or foreseen before the decree of the Incarnation. Rather, in the same stage *in-quo*, Christ was willed as the end (and thus as prior in the genus of final cause), and the permission of sin was willed as the matter to be destroyed through Christ (and thus as prior in the genus of material cause). From these, the response to both proofs is plain. For we are not saying that sin was willed by God for Christ, but that what was willed and ordered to this end was the permission of sin. Nor are we saying that Christ came for sin, but that he came as the remedy for sin and for his own proper glory arising from this. For this, sin had to precede the Incarnation as the matter, the remedy for sin as the end effected, that of benefit, and the Incarnation itself had to come before all these as the end *for-the-sake-of-which*, as we have often said. Nor does this difficulty—if it truly is one—touch specifically on the present matter. Rather, it is common to the predestination of mere men. For all the permissions for sins, both in the elect and in the reprobate, are the effects of the predestination of the elect, as we have taught with St. Thomas and the more common opinion of theologians, and professedly so in tract. 5, disp. 6, dub. unic.,[233] to which we direct the reader, where he will find the resolution to many things that could be raised against our response.

37. But you will reply *first*: If God willed to permit sin so that man might by healed of it through Christ, he would be cruel, just as a physician would be cruel to permit a man to fall ill so that he could heal him.[234] *Second*: He who wills the end wills also the means necessary for such an end. But for man to be healed from sin, sin itself is necessary. Therefore if God first willed Christ as a remedy for sin, he willed sin itself. Similarly, because Christ willed the conversion of bread into his body, on this supposition he necessarily willed bread, such that if bread's production were not already supposed, it would happen for the aforementioned end.[235]

233. Salmanticenses (ed. Palmé, 2:360–70).
234. Cf. Suárez, *Disputationes in Tertiam partem*, disp. 5, sect. 3, no. 9 (ed. Vivès, 17:236–37); and Vásquez, *Disputationes in Tertiam partem*, q. 1, a. 3, disp. 11, chap. 4, nos. 41–43 (ed. Sanchez Crespo, 1:162).
235. In other words, if Christ willed the conversion of bread into his body, then if

To the first, we respond that, although permitting evil for the sole intention of repairing evil or for the sole intention of a good less, or at least not greater, than the evil would reveal some disorder and the appearance of cruelty, the permission of evil out of the intention of the greatest good, far surpassing and overcoming the character of the evil permitted, does not at all imply this. So too, a physician would not be cruel who permitted some sickness in a friend in order to offer him a more robust health and to show the efficacy of the medicine. And this is the case in the present matter. For God permitted the sickness of the human race, not to stop at its remedy, but for the glory of Christ the Redeemer, whose dignity far exceeds the malice of the sickness permitted, for the manifestation of divine mercy and justice, which shines forth *par excellence* in the mystery of men's redemption, and, finally, for the greater good of men themselves, who by this means have received a more abundant grace and utmost nobility from the blood of Christ. Hence there appears here no trace of cruelty, but instead the most pious and gentle providence of God, who has so wisely ordered these things to his glory and that of Christ and, at the same time, for our advantage, as St. Thomas, not to mention many of the Fathers related above, specifically teaches in the present article 3, ad 3,[236] in these words: *Nothing prevents human nature from having been brought to something greater after sin. For God permitted evils to occur that he might thereby draw out something better. Hence it is said: "Where sin abounded, grace did more abound (Rom 5:20)." And in the blessing of the paschal candle: "O happy fault, which merited for us so great, so glorious a Redeemer!"* And, as a matter of fact, since it does not pertain to the gentleness of divine providence in the governance of defectible nature to permit that such a nature would fail in all individuals, being instead enough to permit deficiency in some of them or even in many of them, it was not fitting that original sin (through which human nature falls short, not in some or in many but, with the exception of the Blessed Virgin, in all individuals) would be permitted for the sole end of showing the defectibility of human nature and the gentleness of divine providence in its governance.

---

such a thing as bread did not already exist, it would have to come into existence for the conversion to take place in the way willed by Christ.

236. Aquinas, *ST* III, q. 1, a. 3, ad 3 (Leonine ed., 11:14).

It was necessary, therefore, that so universal a deficiency be permitted out of some higher end. Now the best end was Christ the Lord himself, or the glory resulting from the reparation of the human race. Hence far from having had any appearance of cruelty, the decree of permitting the aforementioned sin for this end would not appear so pious and ordered if deprived of this motive.

The response to the second is established from what has been said in the tractate cited, no. 28,[237] that it is not necessary for one intending an end efficaciously to will everything that in some way confers or is required for such an end. Rather, it suffices for him to will those things which fall under the causality of the one providing, from which we infallibly infer other things, if required (with the infallibility of logic and of *consequentia*), for he is thereby sure of the attainment of the intended end. And this is the case when God permits sin out of the intention of Christ the Redeemer or the glory of other men. For, supposing this intention and with God affording no concurrence to the formal element of sin, it is infallible that the creature will sin, yet this will be freely or with the power for the opposite in itself, as we have clarified at length in the respective places. Hence it does not follow that God, intending antecedently and efficaciously a remedy for sin, intends, approves, or wills malice, but only that it is necessitated consequently to his permission. Nor is the example adduced to the contrary convincing. For it is not a formal proof but one based on the subject matter to which it is applied, and this falls under divine causality.[238]

---

237. Salmanticenses, *Cursus theologicus*, tract. 5, disp. 6, dub. unic., § 4, no. 28 (ed. Palmé, 2:368–69).

238. *Non probat ex vi formae, sed juxta subjectam materiam, cui applicatur* ("it is not a formal proof but one based on the subject matter to which it is applied"): That is, the argument does not have unshakable logical consequence deriving from its very structure (which would be valid for any subject) but only has inferential force with reference to the particular subject under consideration.

§ 7. The contrary opinion is related and some of its lines of reasoning overturned

38. The opinion contrary to our assertion is defended by: Bl. Albert[239] (*Commentarii in III Sententiarum*, dist. 20, a. 4); Alexander of Hales[240] (*Universae theologiae summa* III, inq. unic., tract. 1, q. 2, tit. 2); William of Paris[241] (*De universo*, II); and Scotus (*Ordinatio* III, dist. 7, q. 3; and *Lectura* III, dist. 19, q. unic.).[242] It is commonly subscribed to by his disciples: Lychetus[243] (*In tertium Sententiarum Ioannis Duns Scoti Doctoris Subtilis commentaria*, dist. 7, q. 3); Fabri[244] (*Disputationes theologicae librum tertium Sententiarum complectentes*, dist. 7, q. 3, disp. 20); Rada[245] (*Controversiarum theologicarum inter S. Thomam et Scotum super tertium librum Sententiarum Pars Tertia*, contr. 5, a. 3, op. Scot., concl. 4); Smising[246] (*Disputationes theologicae de Deo uno*, tract. 3, disp. 6, q. 12); Castillo[247] (*Subtilissimi Scoti Doctorum super tertium Sententiarum librum*, tom. 1, disp. 4, q. 1); and others. The same

---

239. St. Albert the Great, OP (ca. 1200–80), *Commentarii in III Sententiarum*, dist. 20, a. 4 (ed. Borgnet, 28:360–62).

240. Alexander of Hales, OFM (ca. 1185–1245), *Universae theologiae summa* III, inq. unic., tract. 1, q. 2, tit. 2 (Quaracchi ed., 4:41–42).

241. William of Auvergne (William of Paris) (ca. 1180–1249). The Salmanticenses refer broadly to *De universo*, II, which does not seem correct. In his *Tractatus de causis cur Deus homo* (ed. Scott, 1:555–70), William assigns many reasons for the Incarnation. In *De rhetorica divina*, chap. 18 (ed. Scott, 1:357–58), he speaks as if sin is its necessary condition.

242. Scotus (Vatican ed. 9:284–91, 21:25–38). The Latin text gives the citation as: *Scotus in 3, dist. 7, quaest. 3 et dist. 9, quaest. unica*.

243. Franceso Lychetus, OFM (1465–1520), Commentary on Scotus, *In Tertium Sententiarum*, dist. 7, q. 3 (ed. Vivès, 14:349–58). The Latin text gives the citation as: *Liquetus dist. 7, quaest. 5*.

244. Filippo Fabri, OFM Conv. (1564–1630), *Disputationes theologicae librum tertium Sententiarum complectentes*, dist. 7, q. 3, disp. 20 (ed. Ginamus, 103–12).

245. Juan de Rada, OFM Obs. (ca. 1545–1608), *Controversiae theologicae* III, contr. 5, a. 3, op. Scot., concl. 4 (ed. Ioannes Crithius, 3:164–65).

246. Theodore Smising, OFM Obs. (ca. 1580–1626), *Disputationes theologicae de Deo uno*, tract. 3, disp. 6, q. 12 (ed. Wolffchatius, 781–98).

247. Francisco del Castillo Velasco, OFM Obs. (d. 1641), *Subtilissimi Scoti Doctorum super tertium Sententiarum librum*, tom. 1, disp. 4, q. 1 (ed. Bellerus, 1:89–110).

is also defended by Catarino[248] (*De eximia praedestinatione Christi*); Galatino[249] (*De arcanis Catholicae veritatis*, I, chap. 3); Albert Pigghe[250] (*De libero hominis arbitrio*, VIII); Jaime de Valencia[251] (*In psalmos Davidicos lucubratissima expositio*, on Psalms 52 and 81); Clichtove[252] (*De necessitate peccati Adae et felicitate culpae ejusdem apologetica disceptatio*, chaps. 13–20); Cartagena[253] (*De praedestinatione et reprobatione hominum et angelorum*, disc. 11); Suárez (*Disputationes in Tertiam partem*, disp. 5, sect. 2ff.);[254] Puente Hurtado[255] (*Disputationes de Deo Homine sive de Incarnatione Filii Dei*, disp. 13, sect. 2); Pérez[256] (*Disputationes de Incarnatione divini Verbi*, disp. 15, sect. 1); Fonseca[257] (*In Metaphysicorum Aristotelis Stagiritae libros*, VI, chap. 2, q. 6, sect. 2); Spinelli[258] (*Maria Deipara Thronus Dei*, chap. 14); Perlín[259] (*Apologia scholastica sive*

248. Ambrogio Catarino, OP (1484–1553), *De eximia praedestinatione Christi* (ed. Guillard). The Latin text gives the citation as: *Catherin. lib. 2, de praedest. Christi.*

249. Pietro Colanna Galatino, OFM (1460–1540). The teaching in question appears obliquely in Galatino, *De arcanis Catholicae veritatis*, III, chap. 30 (ed. Heruagius, 128–29). I have not found the relevant doctrine in the place cited by the Salmanticenses (ed. Heruagius, 5–7).

250. Albert Pigghe (Pighius) (ca. 1490–1542), *De libero hominis arbitrio*, VIII (ed. Novesianus, 133–51).

251. Jaime Pérez de Valencia (1408–90), *In psalmos Davidicos lucubratissima expositio*, on Psalms 52 and 81 (ed. Fabius and Zopinos, 437–40 and 611–24).

252. Josse van Clichtove (Judocus Clichtoveus) (d. 1543), *De necessitate peccati Adae et felicitate culpae ejusdem apologetica disceptatio*, chaps. 13–20 (ed. Henricus Stephanus, 16–22). The Latin text gives the citation as: *Ayctoneus opusc. de necessitate, et felicitate peccati Adae a cap. 13 usque ad 20.*

253. Francisco de Cartagena, OFM (fl. 1581), *De praedestinatione et reprobatione hominum et angelorum*, disc. 11 (ed. Accoltus, 355–414).

254. Suárez (ed. Vivès, 17:216–63).

255. Pedro Hurtado de Mendoza, SJ (1578–1641), *Disputationes de Deo Homine sive de Incarnatione Filii Dei*, disp. 13, sect. 2 (ed. Nutius, 130–32). Sections 12 (ed. Nutius, 170–71) and 13 (ed. Nutius, 171–74) are more directly to the point.

256. Antonio Pérez, SJ (1599–1649). Pérez's *Disputationes de Incarnatione divini Verbi* remains unedited. It can be found in the Salamanca University library as Ms. 461.

257. Pedro da Fonseca, SJ (1528–99), *In Metaphysicorum Aristotelis Stagiritae libros*, VI, chap. 2, q. 6, sect. 2 (ed. Zetznerus, 3:186–90).

258. Pietro Antonio Spinelli, SJ (fl. 1613), *Maria Deipara Thronus Dei*, chap. 14 (ed. Gymnicus, 191–201).

259. Juan Perlín, SJ (ca. 1569–1638), *Apologia scholastica sive controversia theologica pro magnae Matris ab originali debito immunitate*, dist. 4, chap. 15 (ed. Prost, 239–50).

controversia theologica pro magnae Matris ab originali debito immunitate, dist. 4, chap. 15); and others. Granted that they explain their opinion in various ways and describe the order of the divine decrees differently, these agree on Christ's having terminated an efficacious decree regarding him independently of the remediation of sin in every genus and, consequently, that by virtue of such a decree Christ would come even if Adam had not sinned. This opinion's particular foundations consist both in the evasions whereby they meet the challenge of St. Thomas's argument, those we have already cut off in § 3 and § 4, and in the difficulty of fitting together that God intended Christ as the first willed for his excellence and that, at the same time, he intended him as a remedy for sin. We have given a harmonization of this in the preceding two §. Hence there are not many things remaining that we still need to resolve.

First, then, the argument is made from authority: St. Augustine (*On Marriage and Concupiscence*, I, chap. 21)[260] identifies three goods of marriage, namely, the work of propagating offspring, the faithfulness of modesty, and the sacrament of marriage signifying the joining of Christ with the Church.[261] And he concludes that matrimony in the state of innocence would have such goods: *And certainly*, he says, *the goodness of marriage would exist perfectly with these three goods whereby even now marriage is good.* St. Augustine supposes, therefore, that the Incarnation and joining of Christ with the Church would have been going to exist even if the state of innocence had been going to continue and there never would have been original sin. Proof of the *consequentia*: Otherwise, the signification of the sacrament would not be true on account of lack of the object, which cannot be maintained. Nor can it be said that St. Augustine is speaking of a sign and representation that are not actual but aptitudinal.[262] For, on the contrary, the Holy Doctor

260. Augustine, *De nuptiis et concupiscentia*, I, chap. 21 (CSEL 42:236).

261. The argumentation of this paragraph and the following two is from the earliest stages of the debate surrounding whether Christ would have come absent sin. The argument from the symbolism of matrimony can be found already in Robert Grosseteste (ca. 1175–1253), *De cessatione legalium*, III, cap. 1, nos. 20–21 (ed. Auctores Britannici medii aevi, 7:127).

262. An aptitudinal sign is in proximate potency to signify something, whereas an actual sign actually does signify the object. It is the difference between a sign that is fit to mean something (*significativum*) and one that actually means it (*significans*).

affirms that the three goods he enumerated befitted matrimony in the state of innocence perfectly. But as long as a sign is aptitudinal, it is not perfectly a sign, since it is lacking the actual imposition and representation through which it is formally constituted in the character of a sign.

This is confirmed, first, from St. Bernard (Advent Sermon 1),[263] where he teaches that the devil foresaw that human nature would be assumed by God into personal unity, envied this, and tempted man out of this envy. If, however, the Incarnation were not going to be except dependently on man's sin, the devil would not at all have incited man to sin, since man would thereby actually be moved closer to the good that the devil envied. The devil knew, therefore, that the Incarnation was going to be even if man were not to sin and willed that through sin man should become unworthy of so great a good.

It is confirmed, second, from St. Thomas, where he says of the first man in the state of innocence: *Now it seems that he had foreknowledge of Christ's Incarnation through the fact that he said, "Wherefore a man shall leave father and mother, and shall cleave to his wife: and they shall be two in one flesh," as is related (Gn 2:24). And the Apostle says this is a great sacrament in Christ and in the Church (Eph 5:32). And it is not credible that the first man was ignorant of this sacrament* (ST II-II, q. 2, a. 7).[264] But Adam did not know his own future sin, as St. Thomas observes in the place cited, which is also clear because by apprehending the fact that it was going to occur, he would develop a sadness incompatible with that most happy state. Therefore, he knew the future Incarnation independently of sin. And since the aforementioned knowledge was true, as proceeding from a divine revelation, it follows that the Incarnation was going to occur even if Adam were not to sin.

39 We respond to the argument that, since St. Augustine teaches our assertion, not in one place but in several, not obscurely but in clear words, as was shown in no. 10, his mind cannot be rendered

---

263. Bernard (ed. Leclercq and Rochais, 4:162–64). This argument from the authority of Bernard can be found in Alexander of Hales, *Universae theologiae summa* III, inq. unic., tract. 1, q. 2, tit. 2 (Quaracchi ed., 4:42).

264. This argument from Adam's knowledge of the Incarnation prior to the Fall appears in Robert Grosseteste, *De cessatione legalium*, III, cap. 1, no. 20 (ed. Auctores Britannici medii aevi, 7:127).

doubtful. Much less can it be drawn on for the contrary opinion from the testimony in the objection, a testimony that is applied to the contrary opinion not immediately but by way of various *consequentiae* that are easy to tear apart. And even though the response employed within the objection is probable, because our adversaries insist that the Holy Doctor is speaking about an actual sign and this makes little difference to us, we grant this to them, conceding that in the state of innocence, matrimony signified in the second act[265] the joining of Christ and the Church. But if they speak with *consequentia*, then they must concede that it signified the joining that has *de facto* existed and exists between Christ the Redeemer in passible flesh and the Church with the sacraments and redemptive grace. For it is ridiculous that the marriage of Adam and Eve should have signified actually another joining that has never existed nor will exist, such as that with Christ not the Redeemer and not in passible flesh, which neither has been nor will be, and that it should not have signified the joining that *de facto* has existed and does exist. It is about this joining that the Apostle is speaking: *This is a great sacrament: but I speak in Christ and in the Church* (Eph 5:32). This is especially since the Fathers commonly teach that the formation of Eve as Adam's bride from one of his ribs signified the building of the Church coming forth mystically from the side of Christ on the cross. St. Epiphanius, among others, speaks thus: *He took, it says, one of his ribs and built it into a wife for him. By this it shows that the Lord formed a body for himself from Mary, that from his very rib the Church was built, in that his side was pierced and opened and the mysteries of blood and water, the prices of redemption, took place* (III, haer. 78, after the middle).[266] Hence the argument formed from the testimony of St. Augustine should be turned back on our adversaries in this way: In the state of innocence, matrimony signified in the second act the joining of Christ and the Church with the circumstance of passible flesh and of redemptive grace that *de facto* exist. But such a signification could only be true if the object signified were going to exist. Therefore even

---

265. *In actu secundo*: That is, in addition to possessing the ability to express the union of Christ with the Church (the "first act"), matrimony would actually have expressed this union (the "second act").

266. Epiphanius, *Panarion*, haer. 78, no. 19 (ed. Holl, 1.3:470).

if the state of innocence had continued and Adam had not sinned, Christ would come in passible flesh and the Church would exist with redemptive grace. The consequent is altogether absurd and contrary to the very thing our adversaries suppose. Therefore they must recognize the inefficacy of the aforementioned argumentation and resolve it. We respond, therefore, that, granted that the marriage of our first parents before their sin signified perfectly that there was going to be a joining of Christ and the Church and thus that Christ would come, it did not signify that Christ would come before their sin or independently of it. For it was sufficient for the former that Christ's coming be supposed as already decreed and foreseen by God as a remedy for future sin, but the latter required its having been decreed and foreseen independently of sin, which was not the case, as we have shown above. Nor does this have to be the meaning in Augustine's words: *The goodness of marriage would exist perfectly with these three goods whereby even now marriage is good*, whereby he seems to mean that that marriage was going to have the goodness of the aforementioned representation even if the state of innocence had continued forever. For it signifies not this but instead that state's conditionally lost longer duration, which was enough for his intention of showing that marriage was not the cause or the effect of contracting sin and not to be considered reprehensible on that basis.

To the first confirmation, we respond that it will not afford the contrary opinion much support if we concede that the devil held it and, leaving aside the premises, admit the *consequentia*. For what does it matter that the devil thought this way, if he is very often mistaken when he attempts rashly to figure out God's plans? But we add that, even if the devil knew in some way that God would assume man's nature, it does not thereby follow that he knew the motives of the Incarnation. Hence he could have not known that Adam's future sin would be the occasion and matter *concerning-which* of the aforementioned mystery. Supposing this ignorance, he could also have tempted him to sin out of envy, intending to worsen his condition. This is the response of St. Thomas, where he says: *It should be said that even if we posit that the devil foresaw that a rational creature would be assumed by the Son of God, it is not necessary for him to have foreseen the things antecedent to it. So too, as Bernard says in the same place, he foresaw that he would be the prince of the wicked, which he received through his fall, and yet he did not foresee his own fall, as was said in Book II (Super III Sent., dist. 1, q. 1, a. 3, ad 7).*[267]

From this we also establish [the response] to the second confirmation. For, granted that in the state of innocence, independently of future sin and of knowledge of it, Adam knew that Christ was going to be, he did not know or positively judge that Christ would be independently of sin. Rather, he knew in an absolute way the mystery and something of its motive (the glory of God, the dignity of Christ, and the exaltation of human nature), while the other motive and the end *to-which* of the aforementioned mystery (the remediation of sin) were hidden to him, since the state [of innocence] required this. St. Thomas hands down this response in the present article 3, ad 5, in these words: *It should be said that nothing prevents the effect's being revealed to someone to whom the cause is not revealed. The mystery of the Incarnation, then, was able to be revealed to the first man without his having foreknowledge of his own fall. For not everyone who knows the effect knows the cause as well.*[268] This is especially the case when the cause is not natural and necessary but one voluntarily assumed, as was the motive for which God was able to will and did will the Incarnation. For it suffices to know a motive that is sufficient and really intended, even though not adequate and independent of others. Nor do we infer from this (to anticipate a tacit reply) that Adam's intellect remained restless and anxious from not comprehending all the motives of the aforementioned mystery. For an intellect rightly disposed, such as Adam had in that state, does not investigate God's plans and supernatural objects with curiosity but with humility and placidly rests in the knowledge that it grasps of them from divine revelation, harboring no anxiety about what lies hidden, most of all when it knows a sufficient and truly extant motive for God's works, even if it is not really adequate, as in Adam's case.

40 Second, the argument is made drawing at the same time from authority and from reason, from Our Holy Father Cyril of Al-

---

267. Aquinas (ed. Moos, 3:23–24).
268. Aquinas (Leonine ed., 11:14).

exandria (*Thesaurus*, assert. 15),²⁶⁹ that if the first decree of God concerning the Incarnation was for the Son of God to become man as a remedy for sin and not to come otherwise than dependently on this motive, it would follow that the Incarnation is an occasioned good, that Christ had to thank men for the Incarnation, that it is less perfect than the remediation of sin, and, finally, that with such an end attained it is superfluous. But all these are quite absurd, as is clear of itself. Therefore it should not be said that the Incarnation was willed as a remedy for sin but as independent of this motive. The *sequela* is shown: If the Son of God were made for the production of creatures or from this end, as some heretics thought, we would infer all the aforementioned absurdities from their position. Hence St. Cyril refutes their opinion by these unfitting conclusions in the place cited. It runs as follows: *If [God] produced him from nothing, as the heretics say, to provide for us and other creatures through the Son of God, then he will be made for us, not us for him. And thus we will be more prominent than he in creation, while he will be the instrument to create other creatures. Why, then, does he not thank us, who is for us?* And again: *If the Son was made for us, not us for the Son, we will be much more prominent than the Son, which is most absurd.* And finally: *Add that, impelled by necessity, since otherwise he could not create us, he produced the Son, whom, according to them, he would not have produced if he had not willed to create us. For this reason, with us having been created, the Son seems needless, since once creatures are produced the Father has no need of him.* Now the same arguments militate in the present matter, if Christ was intended and produced as a remedy for sin and would not come lacking that motive, as will be readily obvious to one who considers it, if he applies Cyril's

---

269. Cf. *Thesaurus de sancta et consubstantiali Trinitate* (PG 75:257–59). The Latin text gives the citation as: *P. N. S. Cyrillo Alexandrino lib. 5 Thesauri c. 3*. The Latin quotation given by the Salmanticenses differs slightly in content from Migne's Greek text. They use the Latin translation found in Georgius Trapezontius, *Divi Cyrilli patriarchae Alexandrini ... opus insigne, quod Thesaurus inscribitur* (Basileae: Apud Andream Cratandrum, 1524), 252. Both versions echo Athanasius, *Sermo II contra Arianos*, no. 30, in Kyriakos Savvidis, ed., *Athanasius Werke*, vol. 1.1.2 (Berlin: De Gruyter, 1998), 206–7. Juan de Rada employs this quotation from Cyril as an argument for the Scotistic position in *Controversiae theologicae* III, contr. 5, a. 3, obs. 4 (ed. Ioannes Crithius, 3:159).

inferences to this matter. Therefore all the unfitting conclusions related are inferred from our opinion.

We respond that this argument, if it proves anything, proves too much. This is because it succeeds not only with reference to the present providence but also with respect to absolute power. For the unfitting conclusions could be applied to the Incarnation willed as a remedy for sin on any hypothesis. But no one will deny (whatever may be the case concerning the present decree) that God, in his free power and will, was able to bind the fact that the Incarnation was going to occur to sin's remediation, decreeing [the Incarnation] in no other way than dependently on it, since no contradiction appears in this, as we have shown from the very outset of the doubt, in no. 1. Hence, on that hypothesis, everyone will have to resolve this argument. Also, because it succeeds in proving that not only was the Incarnation in itself not willed as a remedy for sin or dependently on it, but that neither was the Incarnation in passible flesh or Christ as he has *de facto* come and has lived in the world. For Christ, considered in this way, too, was not (properly speaking) an occasioned good. Nor was he less perfect than the remediation of sin. Nor did he have to thank us for the benefit of the Incarnation. Nor is he superfluous or needless with his redemption completed. These are the unfitting conclusions raised as objections to us that our Father Cyril opposes to the heretics. Therefore just as the aforementioned unfitting conclusions cannot be applied to Christ in passible flesh and as he has *de facto* come, although all admit that, considered in this way, he came as a remedy for sin and that he would not come in this way if there were no sin, so, too, they cannot be applied to Christ considered in substance or in himself, even if the substance of the Incarnation was first willed and ordered to the remediation of sin.

Hence to the aforementioned argument we respond by denying the *sequela* in all parts. The proofs of this, as much as can be founded on reason, are established from what was said in no. 2, where we anticipated them, without need of adding anything new. To the authority of St. Cyril it should be said that the Holy Doctor quite well rails against the heretics with the unfitting conclusions consequent upon their position. For they said that the Son of God is a creature and an instrument made by God for the production of other creatures. Hence the consequent was that he would yield to their perfection, regard them as the end, thank them for their production, and cease when they were created. For this is the way in which an instrument is related to the artisan's principal end. But it is apparent that this is not the case in the present matter, since we admit that Christ was the principal end *for-the-sake-of-which*, not only of this mystery but also of all the divine works, in accord with the infinite dignity of the God-man, and that he was first and chiefly willed by God and that all things were ordered to him. At the same time, it is quite coherent with this that God also first willed him to be the Redeemer of men and willed that he would assume flesh for our remedy and would regard us as the end *to-which* of his coming. Supposing this, there is a mutual dependence between the aforementioned ends, which are truly parts of one adequate and total end *which*, such that neither has existed or would have existed independently of the other in the different genera of cause, as we have declared beginning from no. 29. Hence we do not at all infer that Christ was less perfect than our remediation, but vice versa, nor that Christ had to thank us, but vice versa, and so forth for the other unfitting conclusions that are purported in the argument. Yet we recognize that the aforementioned unfitting conclusions push not lightly against the manner of speaking related in no. 25, in accord with which the order of nature and grace preceded the predestination of Christ simply and he was principally intended as a remedy for sin without the dependence of the aforementioned on Christ in the genus of final cause. For not a few of the things cited from Cyril push back against that manner of speaking. Hence a supporter of that manner of speaking needs to resolve the argument in a different way.

41 Third argument: Christ the Lord was *de facto* predestined and came into the world not only for the end of our redemption but also for other ends. Therefore, even if the end or necessity of our reparation were lacking, he would still come for the other ends for which he was predestined. The *consequentia* seems manifest: For, even if a partial end is lacking, it is not consequent that the intention had for other ends that still remain is lacking. Persuasion for the antecedent:[270]

---

270. Cf. Claude Frassen, OFM (1620–1711), *Scotus academicus*, vol. 7, *De divini Verbi Incarnatione*, tract. 1, disp. 1, a. 3, sect. 3, q. 1, n2 (ed. Sallustiana, 7:261).

Christ came to be the teacher of men, as he testifies of himself: *For this was I born, that I should give testimony to the truth* (Jn 18:37).[271] He came also to be the most perfect exemplar for our actions, as he says: *For I have given you an example, that as I have done to you, so you do also* (Jn 13:15). Hence the Apostle says: *For the grace of God our Saviour hath appeared to all men: Instructing us, that, denying ungodliness and worldly desires, we should live soberly and justly and godly in this world* (Ti 2:11–12). He came, finally (to omit the other tasks of king, shepherd, leader, and the like), for the glory and exaltation of human nature, according to the passage: *But we speak the wisdom of God in a mystery, a wisdom which is hidden, which God ordained before the world, unto our glory* (1 Cor 2:7). Therefore, Christ was predestined to come into this world for many other ends besides the remediation of sin. And St. Augustine clearly teaches thus, where he says: *There are many other things to consider in Christ's Incarnation besides absolution from sin* (*On the Trinity*, XIII, chap. 17).[272] And where he says: *Let us not say that sin is necessary for there to be a cause for God's mercy* (*On Nature and Grace*, chap. 25).[273] In fact, St. Thomas hands down this very thing in the preceding article, at the end of the body, where, having related many benefits coming from the Incarnation, he concludes: *But there are many other benefits that have resulted beyond what the human mind can apprehend.*[274] Hence without foundation and not without injury to so great a mystery do we gather that it was as a remedy for sin alone, since it had many other ends and could have taken place if these were still in place.

We respond with the Angelic Doctor in the present article, where he says: *To the first objection it should be said that all the other causes that have been assigned pertain to the remediation of sin. For if man had not sinned, he would have been thoroughly imbued in the light of divine wisdom and uprightness of justice from God for everything necessary to know and to do. But because, having abandoned God, man had fallen*

---

271. The Latin text cites this verse as Jn 8. It also omits the middle part of the verse: "and for this came I into the world."
272. Augustine, *De Trinitate*, XIII, chap. 17 (CCSL 50A:412).
273. Augustine, *De natura et gratia*, chap. 25 (CSEL 60:253).
274. Aquinas, *ST* III, q. 1, a. 2 (Leonine ed., 11:10).

into bodily things, it was fitting that God, having assumed flesh, would afford him a remedy of salvation also through bodily things. Hence Augustine says on the passage, "The Word was made flesh" (Jn 1:14): *"Flesh had blinded you, flesh heals you, since Christ came to extinguish the vices of flesh by means of flesh."*²⁷⁵ Hence, even if all the motives related in the argument were sufficient of themselves so that any one of them could be intended as adequate by itself, they were nevertheless all *de facto* willed by God for *the remediation of sin*, as St. Thomas puts it. For *de facto* God did not intend them without a dependence on the remediation of sin or at least without an order to it and a connection with it. Hence the remediation of sin has entered, at least after the manner of an inadequate motive, the adequate and total end that God intended in this mystery. And in accord with this doctrine, by distinguishing the antecedent, the *consequentia* should be denied absolutely. Nor do the proofs of the antecedent succeed in proving anything further, as will presently become more obvious.

Now that what we have said is the case and that the testimonies related in the argument prove nothing more is established from those others that we laid out in § 2, which succeed in proving that Christ came for the remediation of sin as for a very chief motive by virtue of the first decree that God had concerning the Incarnation and, consequently, that the aforementioned motive was at least a quasi-part of the end principally intended by God. Also, because the testimonies related in the argument proceed *de facto* and are applied to Christ as he has *de facto* come in passible flesh, and they predicate that he came to be the teacher and exemplar of men and to further God's glory,²⁷⁶ and yet there is no one among our adversaries who would contend that, lacking the motive of the remediation of sin, Christ would be going to come in mortal flesh for other ends different from that remediation. And finally, because in the testimonies themselves it is signified expressly enough that the other motives were subordinate to the remediation of sin or at least connected to it by God's will (which is St. Thomas's response).

---

275. Aquinas (Leonine ed., 11:14), referring to Augustine, *In Iohannis Evangelium Tractatus*, tract. 2, no. 16 (CCSL 36:19).

276. Where the Latin text has *venerit, et esset doctor et exemplar*, I have read *venerit, ut esset doctor et exemplar*.

Hence, granted that Christ came as teacher, as shepherd, as exemplar, and to further God's glory, he regarded all these as to be carried out as a means of redemption or in an order to the remediation of sin, as we are taught from the same testimonies and others. For, speaking of the role of exemplar, the Apostle adds: *That, denying ungodliness and worldly desires*, etc., which only have a ground on the supposition of sin. On the office of shepherd, the Lord himself says that he was sent *to seek and save the sheep that had been lost* (Lk 15).[277] On the office of king it is said: *The Lord is our king: he will save us* (Is 33:22), surely supposing our ruin and captivity. On the office of teacher it is said in the same book: *The spirit of the Lord is upon me, because the Lord hath anointed me: he hath sent me to preach to the meek, to heal the contrite of heart, and to preach a release to the captives, and deliverance to them that are shut up* (Is 61:1). Finally, our glory and exaltation, which the Apostle indicated in the place cited, were meant to be held up for comparison by the mediation of redemption. Hence after the words related he immediately added: *Which none of the princes of this world knew. For if they had known it, they would never have crucified the Lord of glory* (1 Cor 2:8). And in the preceding chapter he had said: *Who of God is made unto us wisdom and justice and sanctification and redemption* (1 Cor 1:30). These are quite clearly persuasive that the rest of the motives were intended by God in the mystery of the Incarnation, by his decree, either as subordinate or as connected to the remediation of sin.

§ 8. The challenge of two other arguments for the same opinion is met

42 Fourth argument: If the predestination or first intention of the fact that Christ was going to exist was as a remedy for sin and dependently on it, it would follow that the reprobation of men was from foreseen demerits. The consequent is contrary to the Apostle, where he says: *When the children were not yet born, nor had done any*

---

277. This is not a quotation but a paraphrase of the sense of the parable of the lost sheep in Lk 15 conflated with Lk 19:10: "For the Son of man is come to seek and to save that which was lost."

good or evil [...], not of works, but of him that calleth, it was said to her: [...] Jacob I have loved: but Esau I have hated (Rom 9:11–13).²⁷⁸ Therefore the predestination or first intention of the fact that Christ was going to exist was not as a remedy for sin or dependently on it. Proof of the *sequela*: The predestination of Christ is the cause and exemplar of our predestination, as is established from the Apostle (Eph 1) and as we will declare in its own place. And thus it is prior to the predestination of the elect and, consequently, the reprobation of the rest. Therefore, whatever is presupposed for Christ's predestination is also presupposed for the predestination or reprobation of others. But if Christ had been predestined as a remedy for sin, the latter would have been foreseen antecedently to Christ's predestination. Therefore, it would precede the reprobation of the wicked, and, consequently, this would occur from foreseen demerits. So too, if merits were foreseen as going to be antecedently to the predestination of the elect, it would be impossible for this predestination not to occur from foreseen merits and for the selection of the elect not to be founded on them.

Confirmation from another unfitting conclusion: From our opinion it follows that the angels were not predestined or glorified except dependently on Adam's sin. The consequent is false and unbelievable. For who would believe that if Adam had not sinned the angels were not to be glorified? Therefore, etc. Proof of the *sequela*: Christ's predestination was the exemplar cause of the predestination of the angels because the natural filiation from God to which Christ was predestined, as the Apostle teaches (Rom 1:4), has the character of the exemplar cause of adoptive filiation, whether found in angels or in men.²⁷⁹ Hence he is the first of all the predestined, in accord with the passage from the same Apostle: *He hath made him head over all the church* (Eph 1:22). And, consequently, the angels' predestination had a dependence on Christ's

---

278. The Salmanticenses do not note the omissions.

279. Romans 1:4 in the Vulgate runs: *qui praedestinatus est Filius Dei in virtute secundum Spiritum sanctificationis ex resurrectione mortuorum Iesu Christi Domini nostri*. In the Greek New Testament, the word rendered in Latin as *praedestinatus* is universally attested to be ὁρισθέντος ("designated") and not προορισθέντος ("predestined"). Aquinas acknowledges this discrepancy when commenting on the passage. *Super Rom.*, chap. 1, lect. 3 (ed. Cai, 1:11.49–50).

predestination. But this, as we say, had a dependence on Adam's sin such that, lacking it, this man, Christ, would not be assumed to natural filiation from God. Therefore by the chain rule[280] it follows that the predestination of the angels depended on Adam's sin.

To the argument, in which Master Medina is entangled to no small extent,[281] we respond that it consists for the most part of confusion that we will avoid by distinguishing. For if we are speaking of reprobation taken in the most proper sense as consisting in the act of command pertaining to execution, then there is nothing unfitting in its supposing foreseen and future demerits, at least inadequately. And the Apostle is not dealing with this in the passage cited. If, however, we are speaking of the will of excluding some from glory, then again we must distinguish. For, when speaking of the aforementioned exclusion as having the character of a punishment, it is not absurd, and, in fact, is necessary, that it presuppose the fault for which it is inflicted. And the Apostle is not denying this. Still, when speaking of the aforementioned exclusion as indicating the mere denial of an undue benefit, it does not presuppose future or foreseen merits, as the Apostle hands down and we have established in tract. 5, disp. 8, dub. 1, § 5.[282] And in this sense we deny the *sequela*, whose proof is not compelling. For (taking 'reprobation' in the aforementioned way), reprobation's being from foreseen demerits required the latter to exist and to be foreseen as going to exist antecedently to the reprobation itself. This is not the case here. Rather, demerits are logically inferred from the very same reprobation. And the process[283] purported in the proof of the *sequela* is vicious because it passes from one genus of cause to another. For Christ's predestination is prior in the genus of final cause in respect of both the reprobation and the

---

280. *De primo ad ultimum* (lit. "from the first to the last"): In logic, hypothetical syllogism, also called the chain rule, is a rule of inference of the form: If p, then q; and if q, then r; therefore if p, then r.

281. See Medina, *Expositio in Tertiam D. Thomae partem*, q. 1, a. 3 (ed. Gastius, 80–81). Medina goes through five possible responses to this argument, complaining that none of them is truly sufficient. He ends up preferring the solution that Christ's predestination presupposes foreknowledge of *future* sin, but reprobation is only for committed sins, not future ones.

282. Salmanticenses (ed. Palmé, 2:388–89).

283. I.e., the logical procedure.

predestination of men, and God chose some and excluded others from the kingdom for the greater glory of Christ. Now sin, as whose remedy Christ was intended, preceded his passive predestination not in the genus of final cause but in the genus of material cause after the manner of the matter to be destroyed. And only in this genus was it foreseen prior to Christ. Hence it does not follow that it was foreseen as going to exist prior to reprobation. For it did not precede [reprobation] in any genus, but rather is inferred, since it logically followed on reprobation carried out for the glory of Christ. Recall what was said above in nos. 31 and 35 and what we said in the tractate cited, dub. 3, no. 99.[284]—The authors related in no. 25 will not disencumber themselves from this argument so easily, since they affirm that the foreseeing of sins went before Christ's predestination simply. But perhaps they will say that they were antecedent as the sufficient matter of reprobation, though God did not thereby will to be moved efficaciously to exclude any from the kingdom. Still, they will be overcome by the example of merits. If merits are supposed as going to be and foreseen prior to the predestination of the elect, they could not help moving God connaturally to the election and, consequently, election would occur from merits. Why, then, should the same not be said proportionately of demerits in the order toward reprobation, if they are presupposed to it as going to be and foreseen? Hence [these authors] will have to see what response to make in accord with their principles.

As regards the confirmation, we concede the *sequela* understood by virtue of the present providence and with reference to a mediated or indirect dependence. In this sense it is successfully proved by the proof adduced, so that we do not know how to deny it and see nothing unfitting in it. Instead, we see its consonance with the truth and its *consequentia* in relation to what has been said up to this point. For the angels were predestined for Christ's glory such that they had the property of being created, adorned with grace, and attaining beatitude in an order to him as to the end *for-the-sake-of-which*, as is established from what was said in no. 5 and no. 26. Hence by virtue of the present prov-

---

284. Salmanticenses, *Cursus theologicus*, tract. 5, disp. 8, dub. 3, § 4, no. 99 (ed. Palmé, 2:410–11).

idence, they would have none of these if Christ were not going to be. But Christ was predestined as going to be as a remedy for Adam's sin or with an order to our salvation as the end effected, the end *to-which*. And thus if Adam had not sinned, he would not come by virtue of the present decree. Therefore, the consequent is that the predestination and glorification of the angels had a dependence on Adam's sin, at least a mediate and indirect one. Nor is this false or unbelievable, since the aforementioned dependence was not from the nature of the thing but from the free will of God connecting objects not of themselves connected. For if he established this connection between Adam's sin and Christ, whose dignity far surpasses that of the angels, is it any wonder that he established it mediately between the aforementioned sin and the passive predestination of the angels, who are elect in Christ and for Christ?—We said *at least a mediate and indirect one* because the grace and glory of the angels was not willed as a remedy for sin and does not in this way depend on it. Rather, it was willed for Christ, who depended on it in a given genus of cause. We said, too, *by virtue of the present providence* because if Adam had not sinned and Christ had not come, it would pertain to another providence of God to order some angels efficaciously to eternal life. For it pertains to the aforementioned providence to permit sins in defectible natures in such a way that, although certain individuals fall short of their end, not all of them do. And the same should be said of men on the supposition that Adam had not sinned. For, with some sinning, others would attain glory by virtue of another decree different from the one that there *de facto* has been, as Álvarez has rightly observed (*De Incarnatione divini Verbi disputationes*, q. 1, a. 3, disp. 9, concl. 1),[285] and which is not obscurely established from what we have said in tract. 14, disp. 1, dub. 2, no. 40.[286]

43 Fifth argument: Even if Adam had not sinned, he would have had the original justice in which he was created. Hence the grace of such a state had no dependence on Adam's future sin. But the aforementioned grace was the effect of Christ's predestination. Therefore, even if Adam were not to sin, Christ would come by virtue of the

---

285. Álvarez (ed. Facciottus, 73–74).
286. Salmanticenses (ed. Palmé, 9:19).

present decree.²⁸⁷ The *consequentia* is plain and the major premise is certain. Proof of the minor: Every effect of Adam's predestination is an effect of Christ's predestination and depends on his merits. But the grace that Adam had in the state of innocence was an effect of Adam's same predestination, both because a given grade of glory corresponds to it and because he elicited certain praiseworthy acts by which he merited grades of the glory that he *de facto* has. Therefore the grace that Adam had in the state of innocence was an effect of Christ's predestination and dependent on his merits.

The force of this argument, which usually stirs up trouble, for the most part falls apart if we presuppose (as is most certain) that Christ only had merit in the state of passible flesh and by means of the acts ordered to our redemption. For he did not merit through what he was able to have or in accord with a state that he was able to have. Rather, he merited really in that state and through those things that he *de facto* did have. And it would be altogether absurd to imagine something else. Supposing this, the argument can be turned back the other way. For the grace that Adam had in the state of innocence did not depend on his future sin. And yet it was the effect of Christ's predestination and dependent on his future merits in the state of passible flesh, for Christ had no other merits, as we just observed. Therefore, even if Adam were not to sin, Christ would come and would have merits in passible flesh. Since, then, our adversaries would hardly concede this, they must recognize that their argument is blunted and instruct us further or else choose a way to solve it together with us. And, leaving aside others, the way that seems more probable and more coherent with what has been said up to this point is the one we have proposed in tract. 5, disp. 4, dub. 2, nos. 25 and 54.²⁸⁸ In accord with it, as far as the argument goes, omitting the major, we deny the minor. For the grace possessed in the state of innocence, precisely as such, was not the effect of Christ's predestination and not dependent on his merits. Rather, it pertained to another providence that ordered the aforementioned grace—only ac-

---

287. Cf. Rada, *Controversiae theologicae* III, contr. 5, a. 3, op. Scot., concl. 1 (ed. Ioannes Crithius, 3:160–61).

288. Salmanticenses, *Cursus theologicus*, tract. 5, disp. 4, dub. 2, § 2, no. 25 (ed. Palmé, 2:328–29); and dub. 3, § 5, no. 54 (ed. Palmé, 2:336).

cording to a kind of general notion, one common also to other things of the natural order—to Christ's glory as to the most remote end, as can be said of all individuals of the natural order. In this sense, they would all be lacking if Christ were not going to come, since all things were willed for him, as we were saying in the preceding number in response to the confirmation. And under this consideration there is nothing unfitting about saying that original justice had a mediate or indirect dependence on Adam's sin, as whose remedy Christ was predestined as the end of all things. But we are not speaking in such a general way of taking [the term "dependence"], but instead speaking of a more proper and immediate dependence, one in the genus of meritorious cause. And in this sense we deny the minor, at least as regards its second part. For the grace or original justice that Adam had in the state of innocence was not an effect of Christ's merits and did not pertain to redemption. For Christ did not merit or suffer and die so that Adam would possess original justice but so that he would rise from sin.

Now as to the proof to the contrary, the minor premise should be denied. For Adam's grace, as it constituted the state of original justice and pertained to him, was not the effect of Adam's predestination. For taken in this way it did not lead effectually to eternal beatitude and proceeded not from the efficacious will of bestowing glory but from another effect and providence. For, granted that the aforementioned grace, as long as it existed, founded the right to glory as an inheritance, and granted that the upright acts then proceeding from that same grace gave also the right to the same glory or its increase as a crown, both the aforementioned grace and the merits were extinguished through Adam's intervening sin in such a way that, by virtue of the first will whereby they were conferred, they neither preserved any right or life in the divine acceptation from that point on. Instead, they were totally lost and thus were related to obtaining glory in the order to the effect as if they had never existed. In this way, the matter is plain enough as regards both proofs given for the minor. Now as to the fact that such grace was restored through subsequent penitence and conferred the right to glory, this was not by virtue of the first will whereby it was given (which its being the effect of Adam's predestination required) but took its origin by virtue of a new will or decree of redemption, not only as from a cause removing a prohibition but as from a new and *per se* cause of the aforementioned right. And in this way and no other it was an effect of Adam's predestination. But taken in this way, it supposes his sin, as is clear of itself. Hence the revival of the stated grace and the merits proceeding from it in the state of original justice differed greatly from the revival of our merits that have been interrupted through a subsequent sin. For when grace in us is destroyed through sin, there still remains one principle of the works whereby we merited something before God, namely Christ the Lord. Just as he is the cause of all our merit, so also does he preserve it before God so that, once the obstacle of sin is removed, it may be again imputed to us and profit us. But in respect of the works that Adam elicited in the state of original justice, Christ did not have an influence after the manner of a meritorious or redemptive moral cause. Rather, such merit depended on the grace of that state alone. Thus when it was destroyed, the merit was thoroughly destroyed so that it not only was rendered as dead but died.[289] And thus it did not return to life through subsequent penitence. And this is the response that the authors related in no. 25 chiefly have to use, since they teach that the fact that both original justice and original sin were going to exist and foreknowledge of them preceded Christ's predestination simply. What we said in the tractate cited, disp. 5, dub. unic., no. 26, can be added as confirmation of this.[290]

44 But because in the same passages from the aforementioned tractate, we said that another response is probable and deferred its explanation to this place, and because in reality it is greatly coherent with the manner of speaking that we have chosen and explained (beginning from no. 26), we meet the challenge of the argument in another way by conceding that the grace that Adam had in the state of innocence and the merits then elicited were from the merits of Christ, were an effect both of Christ's predestination and of Adam's, and, consequently, that the aforementioned merits, when Adam sinned, did not die but were rendered as dead and revived through subsequent peni-

---

289. *Ut non solum mortificatum, sed mortuum fuerit.*
290. Salmanticenses, *Cursus theologicus*, tract. 5, disp. 5, dub. unic., § 3, no. 26 (ed. Palmé, 2:353–54).

tence, in accord with the common opinion of Thomists together with the Holy Doctor (*ST* III, q. 89, a. 5),[291] which we explained in tract. 16, disp. 5, dub. unic.[292] For this we should recall what we said above (no. 5 and elsewhere), namely, that we should distinguish only two stages *in-quo* for this matter and the difficulties that occur in it: one in which God knew all possible things and their possible combinations and mutual dependencies, and the other in which he chose from the foreknown those things he willed, by constituting them and knowing them as going to be. For this one single act on the part of God touching on and connecting the objects that he pleased was sufficient. Therefore, God knew that it was possible for him to become man, for Christ to be the end *for-the-sake-of-which* of all things, for him to be the Redeemer, and for him to have an influence by his merit or by efficient or final cause on the effects that God willed. He knew it was possible for man to be created in original justice and for him, once fallen from it, to be repaired through grace, and for some men to be chosen for glory. He knew that it was possible for the aforementioned effects, namely grace, first given and later repaired, to be ordered to the glory of the elect, and chiefly to Christ, and for them to depend on him in the genus of final cause. He knew that it was possible for the aforementioned grace, first given and later repaired, to be conferred from the merits of Christ, at least in the genus of final cause, and, thus, for it to depend not only on Christ but also on his merits. He knew that it was possible for there to be established such a connection and mutual dependence among all the aforementioned things that Christ and his merit would be the end of all things, while, conversely, all grace, whether first given to Adam or later conferred to repair his fall, would be the end of benefit, the end *to-which*, in an order to which Christ would be predestined. God knew all these possible things because they are truly possible, since no contradiction occurs in them either in themselves or considered with reference to their dependencies and causalities just explained.

Now just as he knew the aforementioned as possible in the first stage, so also in the second stage he decreed and foresaw them as going

---

291. Aquinas (Leonine ed., 12:331–32).
292. Salmanticenses (ed. Palmé, 10:778–88).

to be. And in accord with the efficacy of this sort of decree, the objects had the mutual dependencies just as God willed. Hence Christ had a dependence on the grace given to fallen men as the end effected and on the Fall or sin itself as the matter *concerning-which*, the matter to be destroyed. And in the same genus he had a dependence, at least a mediate and indirect one, on original justice to be destroyed through the first sin. For all these things are desired and come together, though in different ways, for the end intended by God, which was Christ as the universal Redeemer. But contrariwise, both original justice and original sin as well as the reparation of grace and all the others had a dependence on Christ as on the end *for-the-sake-of-which*, and in this they all agreed. And moreover, both original justice and its reparation as well as every grace given to men had a dependence on Christ's merits. For God willed all the aforementioned not only for Christ's glory but also on account of Christ's merits. And, consequently, they were effects of the predestination of Christ and the elect because they proceeded from the efficacious intention of their glory and led efficaciously to it. Hence the original justice given to Adam, even though it was destroyed through sin, came to life again through subsequent penitence, as is the case in the grace of the other predestined, as we said in the place cited from tract. 5.[293] And thus the same is the case in the merits that Adam had in the state of innocence. For even if the grace that was their principle was destroyed through intervening sin, their other principle, namely Christ the Lord, continued, by virtue of which they possessed being in the divine acceptation. And thus they did not die through sin but were rendered as dead or impeded, and when this obstacle was taken away, they enjoyed their proper effect, as is the case in the merits of others.

Therefore, in accord with this doctrine, which is for the most part established from what was said above in the doubt, and particularly in no. 26 with the following, we respond to the argument by denying the major premise. For original justice truly had a mediate and indirect

---

293. Salmanticenses, *Cursus theologicus*, tract. 5, disp. 5, dub. unic., § 3, no. 26 (ed. Palmé, 2:353–54). In this passage, however, the Salmanticenses deny that Christ is directly the meritorious cause of original justice. They may mean to refer instead to tract. 16, disp. 5 (ed. Palmé, 10:778–88), which they cited above and which is more to the point.

dependence on Adam's future sin, such that by virtue of the present decree Adam would not be going to receive this justice if he were not going to sin. And the reason is established from what has been said: For Adam received that justice dependently on Christ in the genus of final cause and likewise on his merits and as an effect of Christ's predestination as well as Adam's own predestination. But Christ was predestined with a dependence on the permission of Adam's sin, such that lacking the sin he would not come. Therefore just as all other effects of the predestination of Christ and the elect had a dependence on the permission of Adam's sin by virtue of the present decree and, lacking it, would not exist by virtue of such a decree, the same must be said of the grace or justice and of the merits that Adam had in the state of innocence. And it is no obstacle to this that Adam had this grace before sin because he received it dependently on sin. So too, in the opinion of all he received many things after sin and before Christ dependently on the future Christ that he would hardly have had by virtue of the present decree if Christ were not going to be. Therefore the same should be said proportionately of the dependence of original justice on future sin, as whose remedy Christ was predestined.

45 Nor does it matter if you offer the opposition that *first* these things are said arbitrarily. For, granted that they are possible or not logically incompatible on the basis of their terms, nevertheless there is no foundation for us to affirm that they were *de facto* arranged this way by God. *Second*, it is certain that if Adam had not sinned he would have preserved original justice perpetually. For grace is only destroyed through sin. Therefore, it is false that he had this original justice dependently on future sin and that if he had not been going to sin he would not have had it. For the aforementioned propositions are opposed by contradiction. *Third*, every grace given from the merits of Christ is redemptive and healing and consummated through his death. But original justice was not of this sort, both because it supposed no sin from which to heal and because Christ did not die so that Adam would have original justice but so that men would be freed from original sin and other sins. *Fourth*, the grace given to the Fathers who preceded Christ, although it was an effect of him in the genus of final cause, was

not in the genus of meritorious cause as distinguished from final cause, as we established in tract. 16, disp. 6, dub. 5, no. 104.²⁹⁴ Therefore, even if Adam's original justice depended on Christ as on the end, it did not depend on him as on a meritorious cause. Therefore we do not consequently say that this justice was given from Christ's merits.

These objections, I say, do not matter. To the *first*, we respond that the aforementioned doctrine is founded on all the principles that we have established in this doubt and in all the testimonies of Scripture that we have laid out in it. For they are more easily understood and reconciled in accord with what was said before, as we have already said above (no. 30). This is especially because if this was possible, as the objection supposes, there is no reason why we should not extend Christ's final and meritorious influence to original justice, since this pertains to his greater glory. To the *second*, we deny the antecedent and its supposition as regards the present decree. For, although grace once possessed is only destroyed through sin, God gave Adam the first grace out of the intention of Christ the Redeemer and, consequently, dependently on Adam's future sin. He thus would not receive the grace if he were not going to sin. And thus, absent this condition, the grace that would be preserved or destroyed would not be by virtue of the present decree. To the *third*, we should say that, granted that every grace from the merits of Christ is healing or redemptive on the part of the principle, it is not necessary for every aforementioned grace in actual exercise to heal or redeem from sin. Rather, it suffices that it heal, would heal, or, in the end, that it preserve, as is piously believed of the Blessed Virgin's grace. And granted that the particular motive on our part that Christ would die was liberation from sin contracted, supposing this, the merit of Christ's death extends to many other goods. Hence we do not affirm that Christ died so that Adam would have original justice. For this denotes the motive of the death. Rather, we affirm that, dying, he embraced that grace as well with his merit. Now as to whether the same ought to be said of the grace of the angels we will see in its own place.²⁹⁵ To the *fourth*, it should be said that we have never denied that

---

294. Salmanticenses (ed. Palmé, 10:861).
295. See Salmanticenses, *Cursus theologicus*, tract. 21, disp. 16, dub. 5 (ed. Palmé, 14:614–30); and disp. 28, dub. 10 (ed. Palmé, 16:230–60).

the grace given to the Fathers of old was an effect of Christ's merits, as the objection falsely supposes. Rather, we doubted as to the quality and mode of the influence that the aforementioned merits had. This is a far different difficulty, one that we will decide with a solution in its own place (disp. 7, dub. 4).²⁹⁶ For now, however, it is enough to say in the present matter that Adam had original justice from the merits of Christ in that proportional or lower mode whereby the Fathers of the Old Testament had justice,²⁹⁷ granted that these latter had the further property of being redeemed through Christ. But which of these two responses we have employed should be preferred absolutely will be established in disp. 16, dub. 4.²⁹⁸

296. Salmanticenses, *Cursus theologicus*, tract. 21, disp. 7, dub. 4 (ed. Palmé, 13:661–700).

297. The Latin text has: *satis sit dicere, quod Adamus habuerit justitiam originalem ex meritis Christi eo proportionali, aut inferiori modo, quo illam habuerunt Patres veteris testamenti*. The word *illam*, whose antecedent is grammatically *justitiam*, evidently does not mean that the Fathers had original justice but simply that they had justice or grace.

298. Salmanticenses, *Cursus theologicus*, tract. 21, disp. 16, dub. 4 (ed. Palmé, 14:593–614).

Doubt II

Whether, if Adam had not sinned, Christ would come by virtue of another decree that God would have?

The actuality and perfection of the divine will is such that, concerning all and every one of the possible objects proposed [to it], whether absolutely or conditionally, and under every possible condition, it has positively exercised itself by determining their being or nonbeing in such a way that it has not been able to remain indeterminate and suspended concerning anything presented [to it] in any way, as we have shown (tract. 3, disp. 9, no. 63, and tract. 4, disp. 5, no. 73).[1] This doctrine precludes nearly any ground for the present difficulty, supposing the resolution of the preceding doubt. For from this [doctrine], it is established that God did not have an absolute decree of the Incarnation independently of Adam's sin, since he had the opposite decree. It is established, too, that he did not have an objectively conditioned decree[2] whereby he willed the Incarnation if Adam were not to sin. For if he had had a decree of this sort, then by virtue of it Christ would come if Adam had not sinned, the contrary of which is established from what has been said. Hence Christ would not at all come if Adam did not sin by virtue of any decree, either absolute or conditioned, that God has *de*

---

1. Salmanticenses, *Cursus theologicus*, tract. 3, disp. 9, dub. 5, § 2, no. 63 (ed. Palmé, 1:594), and tract. 4, disp. 5, dub. 3, § 2, no. 73 (ed. Palmé, 2:89).

2. I.e., a decree in which one object has a conditional relation to another.

facto had. But, to grant a ground to the present difficulty, let us entertain the contrary supposition and imagine that God exercised his freedom concerning the Incarnation precisively in a way dependent on the objective condition of Adam's sin, which he foresaw absolutely as going to be, yet decreed nothing dependently on the opposite condition that this sin were not going to be. And our inquiry is: Whether, supposing that he had not foreseen that Adam would sin, God would have had another decree whereby he would will the Incarnation? In this difficulty all readily agree that Christ would not come in passible flesh, for the reason for suffering would be lacking. Hence the difficulty is reduced to the Incarnation absolutely. Nor should we make our decision only by focusing on the object's possibility or only from the elements of appropriateness we imagine. Rather, [we should decide] through reasonable foundations that positively determine our understanding at least with probability to one side. For knowledge that does not reach at least this point hardly pertains to theology and should be spurned by a theologian.

§ 1. The true opinion is clarified by some assertions

46 First, it should be said that on the aforementioned supposition it cannot be determinately affirmed that Christ would be going to come. All the authors to be related below agree in this conclusion, except those we will give in no. 50. It is proved by the argument of St. Thomas in the present third article,[3] since the decree concerning whether Christ would exist depends only on the free will of God, which is made manifest to us through Scripture and the teaching of the Church. But from these we do not at all have knowledge of things that God would be going to do in another series of affairs. For they only instruct us concerning the things that God *de facto* has arranged. Therefore, on the aforementioned supposition, it cannot be determinately affirmed that Christ would be going to come.

First confirmation: It could be determinately affirmed that, in that event, God would have a decree whereby he would will that Christ

---

3. Aquinas, *ST* III, q. 1, a. 3 (Leonine ed., 11:13–14).

would come absolutely for the reason that Christ is the most excellent object, bringing an excellent dignity to the whole created nature and greatest glory to God. But this does not suffice for us determinately to affirm that Christ would come in that case. Therefore, etc. Proof of the minor premise: This is because *de facto* the same motive presented itself to the divine intellect, and yet *de facto* God did not decree the mystery of the Incarnation for this reason by itself. Otherwise, *de facto* Christ would come for it even if there were no sin, the opposite of which is established from what was said in the preceding doubt. Therefore, although such a motive would present itself to the divine intellect in this event, it hardly offers a foundation for us determinately to affirm that God would be going to decree the Incarnation. Also, because even if such an object with all its perfection and all its effects strikes the divine intellect, it does not at all necessitate God but leaves him most free in the first act to choose the side that he prefers, namely, whether it is going to exist or whether it is not going to exist. But by virtue of a free and indeterminate principle (even if it were comprehended) one side of the aforementioned indifference cannot determinately be gathered (this line of reasoning is commonly and effectively used to overturn middle knowledge).[4] Therefore, the dignity of the mystery and the elements of appropriateness that follow on it are not at all sufficient for us to affirm determinately that God would be going to decree it.

Second confirmation: Leaving aside the fact that sin was going to exist and focusing on another possible series of affairs, there would be no reason for the person of the Son to assume flesh rather than the person of the Father or the person of the Holy Spirit. Nor would there be a reason why he would assume this humanity numerically rather than that or another. In fact, there would be no reason why he would assume human nature rather than angelic nature. But we cannot determinately affirm a decree of God concerning the other objects, as for example,

---

4. I.e., even comprehensive knowledge of a free principle does not yield determinate knowledge about which of two possibilities that principle will choose. As the Salmanticenses remark, this is an argument against the legitimacy of middle knowledge as a conceptual category of divine knowledge. The implication here is that prior to his own choice, even God himself does not know whether he would decree Christ's coming or his noncoming.

that God would be going to decree the Incarnation of the Father or the assumption of angelic nature or of a humanity other than that which was in Christ. For one who would determinately affirm these things would be proceeding altogether rashly and by divination. Therefore, one who determinately affirms that Christ would come on this hypothesis proceeds in the same fashion. The *consequentia* is plain from parity.[5] And the major premise is established: The dignity of the mystery, the elevation of created nature, and the glory of God would be preserved in the same way in a hypostatic union of any divine person, of any created nature, and of any given humanity. For [the dignity, the elevation, and the glory] consist most especially and principally in the fact of a created nature's being assumed to divine being in unity of person.

47 Nor is it any use if, based on the doctrine of some more recent thinkers, we say that, in the aforementioned event, the mystery would be constituted by the person of the Son and this nature numerically rather than by the person of the Father or the Holy Spirit and another created nature because the habitual grace *de facto* existing is connected *per se* radically with the mystery of the Incarnation that *de facto* exists by the fact that it inclines as a root to specific acts concerning this sort of object.[6] And since in the aforementioned event the same grace would remain, it would call for the selfsame object.[7] And thus, from this perspective at least, a reason could be given both for the fact that the Incarnation would occur and for its being constituted by the person of the Son and this humanity numerically rather than other terminations.[8]—This, I say, is no use because it is bereft of any solid foun-

---

5. *A paritate* ("from parity"): the logical ground for an argument from the equality of cases.

6. Cf. Godoy, *Disputationes theologicae in Tertiam partem Divi Thomae*, tract. 1, disp. 8, § 1, no. 3 (ed. Hertz, 1:113).

7. In other words, the grace that is in the actually existing world leads to faith in the Incarnation of the Son in a given human nature numerically. But, the grace that would exist in a different hypothetical series of events would be radically the same as it is in the actually existing series of events. Therefore, it would lead to faith in the Incarnation of the same person in the same humanity.

8. *Extrema*: the two sides of a relation, in this case the relation connecting the individual human nature to the divine person.

dation and manifestly begs the question. This is because grace *de facto* inclines as a root to assent concerning the mystery of the Incarnation from the fact that the aforementioned mystery is revealed by God, faith (and it is by the mediation of faith as a proximate virtue that grace has its influence) tending as it does to its object dependently on divine revelation as on the aspect *under-which*, as we have said (tract. 17, disp. 1, no. 89).[9] But what God has revealed is the mystery of the Incarnation that *de facto* exists with reference to the present providence, not the mystery of the Incarnation that would exist in another state and with reference to another providence, as is clear of itself. Therefore, even if the grace that *de facto* exists *de facto* inclines as a root to the present mystery of the Incarnation as an object and is connected with it in the aforementioned way, it is not connected with the mystery of the Incarnation that would exist with reference to another providence that is not actually carried out. Also, because faith does not tend to an object that has not been revealed by God, and God cannot reveal what he has not decreed about this mystery. But *de facto* God did not decree that the Incarnation would occur in that event, as we supposed at the outset of the doubt. Hence we are not dealing with a decree that God has but one that he would have. Therefore, faith (and the same goes for grace as a root) does not tend to the mystery of the Incarnation that would exist in that event and is not connected with it. And finally, because if the opposite line of reasoning were at all valid, it would also succeed in proving that in such an event the mystery of the Incarnation would occur in passible flesh and with the circumstances of death and the Passion, which no one would say. For the grace that *de facto* exists is *de facto* connected with the aforementioned mystery in this way, since, in fact, faith touches on it with all the aforementioned circumstances. From these, the aforementioned response's line of reasoning is overturned without need to add anything else. See Godoy (*Disputationes theologicae in Tertiam partem Divi Thomae*, tract. 1, disp. 8, § 1, beginning from no. 3),[10] where he refutes it at greater length.

Again, it does not successfully address [our challenge] if one says

---

9. Salmanticenses, *Cursus theologicus*, tract. 17, disp. 1, dub. 3, § 2, no. 89 (ed. Palmé, 11:41–42).

10. Godoy (ed. Hertz, 1:113).

that the opposite opinion's understanding does not require that, on the aforementioned hypothesis, the determinate person of the Son would assume this determinate human nature numerically but instead that it suffices that the mystery of the Incarnation would be going to exist absolutely, abstracting from the modes and terminations whereby it would be accomplished. This, I say, does not successfully address [our challenge]. For, even granted that in a way it meets the challenge of the last confirmation, it does not meet the challenge of the first nor of the principal rationale for the assertion. Besides, it abandons the proper subject of the present difficulty, namely Christ. For it is with respect to the same subject whose coming we deny by virtue of the present decree if Adam were not to sin, that we are asking whether he would come by virtue of another decree that God would have. It is the case, too, that in this difficulty nothing can be said determinately except from some revelation or some trace of one concerning God's will, to whom alone it belongs to determine whether this will occur. For the opposite manner of proceeding in a similar matter is neither theological nor probable, since it has no foundation on which it determinately relies but is mere arbitrary divination. Now if any revelation or if any trace of revelation concerning the present difficulty presents itself, it is assuredly directed to the mystery of the Incarnation of the person of the Son and this humanity numerically. For it is certain that there exists nothing revealed about the assumption of other natures to the person of the Father or the Holy Spirit. Since, then, it cannot be determinately affirmed that, on this hypothesis, the Incarnation would be going to be from the person of the Son and this humanity numerically, as the second confirmation proves and this response supposes, it follows that it cannot be determinately affirmed that the Incarnation would be going to be absolutely or prescinding from the person assuming and the nature assumed.

48 Second, it should be said that on the aforementioned supposition it cannot be determinately denied that Christ would be going to come. Thus speak all the authors to be related below, except for some, whom we will give in no. 51. And this is proved by the same foundations that we used for the first conclusion. This is because whether the aforementioned mystery would exist or whether it would not exist

depends on God's free will, which, in his good pleasure and within the bounds of his wisdom, could decree the fact that [the mystery] would be going to exist just as it could decree the fact that it would not be going to exist. Therefore, just as this rationale does not allow us to assert determinately that he would decree that it was going to exist, so also we cannot determinately deny that he would decree it. Also, because effects depending on God's will alone only become known to us through his revelation, as St. Thomas declares quite well in this third article. But just as there is no revelation from which to gather that, on this hypothesis, this mystery would be going to exist, neither is there a revelation allowing us to gather the opposite. Therefore, we cannot determinately deny that on the aforementioned hypothesis such a mystery would be going to exist. And finally, because even absent the fact that sin was going to exist and the fittingness of redeeming the human race from it, there remain other objectively possible elements of fittingness for which God could will such a mystery and decree that it would be. Hence no one denies the possibility while, from the other angle, no compelling reason presents itself for us to deny determinately that it would be. Therefore, one who would determinately deny that the aforementioned mystery would not be going to exist in such an event would be proceeding without foundation.

You will say that out of two propositions opposed by contradiction one is determinately true and the other determinately false and that it cannot be the case that both are false. But these propositions, *If Adam had not sinned, Christ would come by virtue of another decree that God would then have* and *If Adam had not sinned, Christ would not come by virtue of another decree that God would then have*, are opposed by contradiction. Therefore, since the former is determinately false, as we established in the first conclusion, it follows that the latter is determinately true, and we fail in *consequentia* when we deny it in this second assertion.

We respond that in the first conclusion we are not asserting that the aforementioned proposition is false nor in the second denying that it is true. Rather, we are only saying that neither side can be determined by us. These two things are vastly different. For, over and above the first, this latter adds reasonable rationales and foundations for our affirmation or denial of the aforementioned object. Yet we are bereft of these, since nothing solid presents itself that would allow us to be determined to one side, at least with probability. And there is no doubt that this is frequently the case. For it is certainly obvious that there are many future contingents, not only conditioned ones but also absolute ones, that lie hidden to us, and so it would be rash for us to proceed either by affirming or denying them. It is also the case that propositions about a future contingent prior to the determination of the divine will, which is the primal root of the fact that something is going to exist,[11] have no objective truth or falsity but instead have nontruth and nonfalsity, being, in fact, propositions only materially. Hence from the fact that one is not true or (to speak properly) is not-true, we do not infer that the other, opposed to it by contradiction, is true. Rather, at most we infer that it is not false or that it is not-false, as we explained at length when resolving a similar argument (tract. 3, disp. 7, dub. 6, § 8),[12] where we employed other responses. Since, then, for the present we are considering the conditioned fact of existence[13] antecedently to God's decree, which (while we are inquiring whether, in that event, it would be going to exist) is supposed not to exist actually, it follows that the aforementioned propositions do not determinately have any truth or falsity due to lack of an object. For subjectively it is actually nothing, as it also is objectively under the aspect of being something that is going to exist.[14] This line of reasoning is so effective that it plainly succeeds in proving that it is logically impossible even for God himself, antecedently to the decree of his will, to know future contingents, not only conditioned ones but even absolute ones, as we declared with the common opinion of Thomists and other theologians (tract. 3, disp. 7, no. 96).[15] If, then, prior to his own determination, God does not know what he would be going to decree on this or that hypothesis if it were to occur—for this is not determinately knowable on a given side prior to such a determi-

---

11. *Prima radix futuritionis.*
12. Salmanticenses (ed. Palmé, 1:518–24).
13. *Futuritionem conditionatam.*
14. *Actu nihil est subjective, et objective etiam in ratione futuri.*
15. Salmanticenses, *Cursus theologicus*, tract. 3, disp. 7, dub. 6, § 2, no. 96 (ed. Palmé, 1:502–3).

nation, since it is objectively free and indifferent to either one—much less will we be able to indicate determinately what God would be going to decree if he had not permitted and foreseen that Adam's sin was going to exist.

49 Third, it should be said that it is uncertain whether, if Adam had not sinned, Christ would come by virtue of another decree that God would then have and that this question cannot be determined by us. This is what St. Thomas teaches, as we will see shortly. To it subscribe: Godoy (*Disputationes theologicae in Tertiam partem Divi Thomae*, tract. 1, disp. 8, § 1, no. 2);[16] Lorca (*Commentarii ac disputationes in Tertiam partem D. Thomae*, q. 1, a. 3, disp. 10, memb. 1);[17] Vásquez (*Commentarii ac disputationes in Tertiam partem S. Thomae*, q. 1, a. 3, disp. 10, chap. 1);[18] Ragusa (*Commentarii ac disputationes in Tertiam partem D. Thomae*, disp. 28, § 20);[19] Bernal (*Disputationes de divini Verbi Incarnatione*, disp. 17, sect. 2, no. 22);[20] and others. It is proved from what has been said up to this point. For we cannot define that in such an event Christ would be going to come by virtue of another decree that God would have, as was said in the first conclusion. Nor can we define that he would not be going to come, as we established in the second. Therefore, it remains that this matter is altogether uncertain to us and cannot be determined by us.—Confirmation and clarification: *De facto* we can resolve with probability that Christ would not come if Adam were not to sin, since *de facto* we have the testimonies of Scripture manifesting God's providence and decrees concerning this mystery. From these we gather the aforementioned resolution with great probability, as established from what was said in the preceding doubt. In contrast, *de facto* we have no testimonies of Scripture that in any way reveal to us the providence and decrees of God concerning another series of affairs conditionally proposed. For it would be ridiculous to understand Scripture in such a way. Therefore, *de facto* we do not have the

16. Godoy (ed. Hertz, 1:113).
17. Lorca (ed. Sanchez de Ezpleta, 1:64–65).
18. Vásquez (ed. Sanchez Crespo, 1:128–29).
19. Ragusa (ed. Cardon, 246–48). The Latin text gives the citation as *Ragusa disput. 28, § 29*.
20. Bernal (ed. Nosocomius, 128).

principles through which to be determined to one side in this question.

All these things are drawn from the Angelic Doctor in his commentary on 1 Timothy, lect. 4, at the words *To save sinners.* He explains them in the following way: *That is, for the salvation of peoples:* "For God sent not his Son into the world, to judge the world: but that the world may be saved by him" (Jn 3:17). "I came not to judge the world, but to save the world" (Jn 12:47). *But if no one had been a sinner, would he have been incarnate? It seems that he would not because he came to save sinners. Therefore the Incarnation would not have been necessary. Again, a Gloss says: "Take way the sick and the medicine will not be necessary." I respond: It should be said that this is plain enough from the words of the saints. But this question does not enjoy great authority. For God has ordained what must happen insofar as certain affairs were going to occur. And we do not know what he would have ordained if he had not foreseen sin. Yet even so, the authorities seem expressly to sound as if he would not have been incarnate if man had not sinned. I am personally more inclined to this side.*[21] And granted that St. Thomas in this testimony is embracing the difficulty that we examined in the preceding doubt, he also touches on what we are treating of in the present and resolves it in these words: *For God ordained what would happen insofar as certain affairs were going to occur. And we do not know what he would have ordained if he had not foreseen sin.* Nor do the final words *I am personally more inclined to this side* (namely the negative) pose an obstacle to our assertion. This is because they should be referred to the difficulty according to the present providence, as is clear from the fact that he confirms that side by the testimonies of the saints, which proceed *de facto* and with reference to God's decree revealed in the Scriptures. Also, because, even if we refer them to another providence, they do not indicate a determinate judgment but only an inclination within the bounds of what is uncertain simply, as is obvious from these words: *We do not know what he would have ordained if he had not foreseen sin.*

---

21. Aquinas, *Super I Tim.*, chap. 1, lect. 4 (ed. Cai, 2:219.40).

§ 2. The foundations of the adverse opinions are demolished

50. Against the first and the last assertion are the opinions of: Suárez (*Disputationes in Tertiam partem*, disp. 5, sect. 1);[22] Granado (*In Tertiam Partem S. Thomae Aquinatis commentarii*, tract. 3, disp. 3);[23] and others who affirm that if Adam had not sinned or been foreseen to sin, Christ would come by virtue of another decree that God would then have. They usually prove this opinion by the rationales related beginning from no. 38, which we have already addressed. Further proof: Leaving aside the fact that sin was going to exist and the necessity of a remedy for it, it would be very much in harmony with God's goodness that he should decree the Incarnation. Therefore, it should be said that in such an event he would have a decree of this sort. The *consequentia* is plain. For we should hold the opinion of God that fits most with his goodness. Persuasion for the antecedent: For God to communicate himself *ad extra* in the supreme manner, as occurs in the Incarnation, is an act most befitting his goodness, as St. Thomas gives in the solution to article 1 and as we have explained in our commentary.[24] This fittingness would be preserved independently of sin and its remediation, as is clear of itself.

First confirmation: In whatever series of affairs and concurrence of circumstances, God always wills that which is best in those circumstances. But if Adam had not sinned, it would be better simply for God to become incarnate than the opposite of this. Therefore, in such a case God would assume flesh by virtue of another decree that he would then have. Proof of the minor premise: That is better simply which is more glorious for God, more beneficial for the world, and better for the thing being brought about.[25] But this is how the Incarnation would be on this

---

22. Suárez (ed. Vivès, 17:197–215).

23. Granado (ed. de Lazcano, 4:80–81).

24. Aquinas, *ST* III, q. 1, a. 1 (Leonine ed., 11:6–7); and Salmanticenses, *Cursus theologicus*, tract. 21, commentary on *ST* III, q. 1, a. 1 (ed. Palmé, 13:5–9).

25. Where the Latin text has *rei faciendo magis bonum* ("better in the doing of the thing"), I have read *rei faciendae magis bonum*, which better parallels the rest of the sentence and fits better with the explanation that follows, though both readings are plausible.

hypothesis. For Christ would offer works of infinite value to God that would yield him the greatest glory, he would be the visible head of all the world's creatures, upon which he would bestow the greatest nobility by agreeing with them in a grade of being, and finally, the humanity assumed by the Word would be promoted to the greatest dignity, and that man would truly be God.—Second confirmation: It is apparent that it is thoroughly unbelievable that on the hypothesis that sin would not be going to exist, the world and other works of God would be going to exist and yet that God's most noble and perfect work, namely the Incarnation, would not be. Therefore, we ought to concede determinately that it would be going to exist by virtue of another decree that God would then have.

We respond that this argument and its confirmations, if they have any force, prove that God *de facto* decreed the mystery of the Incarnation for himself and other elements of fittingness independently of the remediation of sin, since the same elements of fittingness presented for another series of affairs have also *de facto* presented themselves. And yet this has not been the case, as is established from the preceding doubt. Therefore, the preceding elements of fittingness are not sufficient for us to make a determinate judgment by virtue of them that Christ would be going to come by virtue of another decree that God would have on account of these elements of fittingness. Hence as regards the argument, we concede that the Incarnation is a work very fitting to the nature of the highest good. But such a fittingness is not predicated of the divine goodness as a property of it but instead only as an exercise of its communicability. Hence just as communicating himself hypostatically could be fitting to God, focusing on the nature of the good inclining to its communication, so also not communicating himself hypostatically could be fitting to God in an order to other ends, most lofty and hidden to us, such as he could think up in his wisdom. And thus we do not have an effective reason for having the determinate opinion that God would assume flesh on this hypothesis. Recall what we said in our commentary on a. 1, no. 6.[26]

Hence [the response] to the first confirmation is also plain. This is

---

26. Salmanticenses, *Cursus theologicus*, tract. 21, commentary on *ST* III, q. 1, a. 1, no. 6 (ed. Palmé, 13:8–9).

because it is false that God always decrees or does what is better. Otherwise, he could not make better things,[27] which is absurd and contrary to St. Thomas (*ST* I, q. 19; and q. 105, a. 6).[28] Also, because, even granted that on this hypothesis the Incarnation would be something better than its opposite, this would not determine the divine will necessarily to pursue it. Rather, it would leave it altogether free to decree the Incarnation and to decree the opposite. And just as the former would be contingent, so also would the latter. Hence its accomplishment (even conceding that this would be the greater good) does not afford a sufficient foundation for us to judge determinately that on this hypothesis God would decree the Incarnation. And finally, because we speak of the notion of 'better' in an order to an end preconceived and intended by the agent. Now just as in the order to the ends mentioned in this confirmation, the Incarnation appears as something better than its opposite, so it could also be the case that, in an order to other ends appointed from the divine wisdom and intended by God, the negation of the Incarnation would be something better than it. This would be the case *de facto* if Adam were not to sin, as Granado, who is opposed to these [arguments], concedes.[29]—[The response] to the second confirmation is also plain. For whether God would be going to create the world by virtue of another decree related to another series of affairs that he does not now have and then would have suffers from the same incertitude and cannot be resolved by us. For, in fact, it cannot be resolved by God himself prior to his decree, whether absolute or objectively conditioned, as we said above (no. 48). But even given that the world would then be going to exist, it could not at all thereby be determinately inferred that the mystery of the Incarnation would exist. For the former antecedent has no connection with this latter consequent, since the Incarnation, being the highest grace, is above the whole of nature and depends on the free will of God alone, and there is no determinate means whereby we can investigate concerning this will what it would decree in another series of affairs.

27. Or: "could not do better things [than he does]."
28. Aquinas (Leonine ed., 4:231–51 and 5:477–78).
29. Granado, *In Tertiam Partem S. Thomae Aquinatis commentarii*, tract. 3, disp. 3, nos. 3–4 (ed. de Lazcano, 4:80).

51 The opinion contrary to the second and final conclusion is held by Álvarez (*De Incarnatione divini Verbi disputationes*, disp. 9, concl. 3)[30] and Araújo (*In Tertiam partem Divi Thomae commentarii*, q. 1, a. 3, dub. unic., concl. 2),[31] who make the determination that if Adam had not sinned, Christ would not be going to come by virtue of another decree that God would then have, although in the proofs they use their understanding seems only to be that this matter is uncertain, as we have established in the last assertion. But whatever may be the case concerning their meaning, this opinion is proved *first* because the Fathers adduced (no. 10) openly deny that Christ would come if Adam were not to sin. To omit others, St. Augustine says: *There was no cause of the coming of Christ the Lord except to save sinners*. And St. Leo the Great says: *If man had remained in his honor, the creator of the world would not become a creature*. These utterances become false if Christ were going to come by virtue of another decree. *Second*, because Christ was only decreed *de facto* dependently on the fact that sin was going to exist, as is established from what was said in the preceding doubt. Therefore, neither would he be decreed as going to exist in another series of affairs in which sin were not going to exist. Proof of the *consequentia*: If on that hypothesis he were decreed as going to exist, this would be most of all on account of the dignity and excellence of the mystery. But this *de facto* presented itself to the divine intellect, and yet he was not decreed as going to exist on this account, except dependently on the fact that sin was going to exist and in a way connected to its remediation. Therefore, the same would be the case on another hypothesis. *Third*, since the fact of whether the Incarnation is going to occur depends on God's decree, it cannot stand without it. But God does not have a decree that the Incarnation is going to occur on this hypothesis, seeing as every decree *de facto* existing in God is connected on the part of the object with the permission of sin and the fact that it would exist, as we established in the preceding doubt. Therefore, on another hypothesis or in another series of affairs, Christ would not be going to come.

30. Álvarez (ed. Facciottus, 76–77).
31. Araújo (1636 ed., 98). The Latin text gives the citation as: *Arauxo, dub. unico, conclus. 1*.

But these are easily overturned by what has been said. To the *first*, we respond that the Fathers are speaking with reference to the present providence and focusing on the decree that God has *de facto* had and that is revealed to us in Scripture, as we have said (no. 11). But they are not defining what God would do or would decree in another order of affairs. Hence their solution is true, even if God would be going to have another decree on another hypothesis. To the *second*, conceding the antecedent, we deny the *consequentia*. In proof of this it should be said that the Incarnation's dignity and excellence is a sufficient motive on whose account it can be intended. And, there is no doubt that God, for the aforementioned motive, was able to decree the mystery of the Incarnation. Now, that he *de facto* only decreed it dependently on the remediation of sin is established for us from no other source than divine revelation in the testimonies adduced in no. 9. But since we have no testimony in Scripture whereby it becomes known to us that in another series of affairs and apart from the fact that sin was going to exist, God would not have a decree concerning whether Christ would be going to exist, we cannot determinately deny this. Rather, we suffer uncertainty and have to suspend determinate judgment concerning these matters. Hence the response is plain as regards the *third*. From these premises we only infer that, if Adam were not to sin, Christ would not be going to come by virtue of the decree that [God] actually has. But we do not gather whether he would be going to come or not by virtue of another decree that God would then have. For, in his freedom and given the fittingness of the ends, he could choose either side, and it lies hidden to us what he would decree.

Doubt III

Whether, by virtue of the present decree, Christ would come if only original sin existed and actual sins did not exist?

Even though it is established from what was said in doubt 1 that Christ was predestined as a remedy for sin, we must go further by examining more specifically for which sin he was primarily or principally decreed as a remedy. For the legitimate sense of St. Thomas when he asserted that *Christ more principally came to take away original sin* (*ST* III, q. 1, a. 4)[1] will thereby be further established. We will take care to put this forward in this doubt and the following one. But for the easier resolution of both it is expedient to note briefly a few things up front.

§ 1. The certain is separated from the uncertain

52. The sins for whose remediation one could conceive of Christ's having come are different in angels and in men. And again, the sins of men are divided into original and actual. Finally, these latter are divided into grave and light, or mortal and venial. We need not explain, but rather presuppose, the proper notions of these here because we do this broadly in the whole of tract. 13, and chiefly in disp. 16, dub. 5,

---

1. Aquinas (Leonine ed., 11:17).

and disp. 19, dub. 1.² Now we suppose that Christ was not predestined and did not come to provide a remedy for the angels' sin or to save the angels from sin, as Origen falsely thought, whose opinion St. Augustine relates and calls heretical (*On Heresies*, chap. 43).³ Hence whatever we say in this part refers only to a consideration of the sins of men.

And we suppose as altogether certain that Christ the Lord came as the remedy for all sins. For whatsoever is forgiven men is forgiven through Christ's satisfaction. Hence it is said: *And he is the propitiation for our sins: and not for ours only, but also for those of the whole world* (1 Jn 2:2). And it is said that Christ appeared *that he might destroy the works of the devil* (1 Jn 3:8), and in a certain true sense all sins are the works of the devil. *He was wounded for our iniquities* (Is 53:5), without any exception. *Whom God hath proposed to be a propitiation, through faith in his blood, to the shewing of his justice, for the remission of former sins* (Rom 3:25), concerning which there was greater possibility of doubt. On the basis of these and other passages, the Council of Trent (Session 6, *On Justification*, chap. 2)⁴ hands down this truth. And St. Thomas openly supposes it in this fourth article, when he inquires: *Whether Christ's Incarnation took place more principally to take away original sin than actual sin?* For, as Cajetan has observed quite well, a question using the comparative supposes as certain both parts of the comparison, namely, that Christ came to take away original sin and also came to take away actual sin.⁵ And this, as we have already said, is clear from the effect, since the remission of each and every sin happens because of Christ's satisfaction.

53 Next, it should be observed that Christ came more principally to take away original sin than actual sin. This is sufficiently gathered from all the testimonies of the saints adduced in no. 9, for many are expressly speaking of original sin. Hence, as we related in that place, St. Leo says: *Because by the envy of the devil death entered into the world and human captivity could be loosed in no other way*

---

2. Salmanticenses (ed. Palmé, 8:273–98 and 451–66).
3. Augustine, *De haeresibus*, chap. 43 (CCSL 46:310–11).
4. Council of Trent, Session 6, chap. 2 (ed. Tanner, 2:671).
5. Cajetan, Commentary on *ST* III, q. 1, a. 4, no. 1 (Leonine ed., 11:18).

than that he would take up our cause who, without loss to his majesty, would become true man and alone would not have the contagion of sin* (Tractate 77, Sermon 3 on Pentecost, chap. 2).[6] And, as we related in no. 10, St. Gregory says: *And indeed if Adam were not to sin, it would not be necessary for our Redeemer to take on our flesh* (Commentary on 1 Sm 8:8).[7] Hence in St. Leo's Letter 165 to Leo Augustus, chap. 4,[8] in the Sixth Council of Toledo, chap. 2,[9] and in the Eleventh Council of Toledo,[10] at the beginning, the Fall of men in Adam is proposed precisively or at least in the first place alone as the occasion or motive of the Incarnation. The Council of Trent (in the place cited) was the same, for in chap. 1 it proposes the doctrine of original sin and the miseries consequent on it, and the following chapter begins immediately with these words: *Whereby it happened that the heavenly Father of mercies and God of all consolation has had mercy, sent Christ Jesus his Son, etc.* In this place the Council openly signifies that the Incarnation was chiefly willed and decreed as a remedy for original sin. But lest anyone think that Christ came only as the remedy for original sin, the Council added that Christ is the propitiation for our sins and those of the whole world. And St. Thomas proves the same supposition quite well in article 4, in these words: *The greater a sin is, the more principally Christ came for the destruction of that sin. Now something is said to be greater in two ways. In one way, intensively, as whiteness that is more intense is greater. And in this way actual sin is greater than original sin because it is more characterized by voluntariness, as related in the Second Part. In the other way, something is said to be greater extensively, as whiteness that exists on a larger surface is called greater. And in this way original sin (through which the whole human race is infected) is greater than any actual sin, which is proper to an individual person. And in this regard Christ more*

---

6. Leo the Great, *Tractatus LXXVII: Item alius de Pentecosten* (CCSL 138A:488).

7. Gregory the Great, *Expositio in librum primum Regum* (CCSL 144:300–301).

8. Leo the Great, *Epistola CLXV ad Leonem Augustum*, chap. 4 (PL 54:1161). The Latin text gives the citation as: *Epist. 97 S. Leonis ad Leonem Augustum capit. 2.*

9. *Concilium Toletanum VI*, chap. 1, related in *Collectio canonum S. Isidoro Hispalensi ascripta* (PL 84:394–95).

10. *Concilium Toletanum XI*, related in *Collectio canonum S. Isidoro Hispalensi ascripta* (PL 84:455–57).

principally came to take away original sin, inasmuch as the good of the race is more divine and eminent than the good of one, as it says at the beginning of the Ethics.[11]

54 Nor does it matter if you say *first* that St. Thomas does not teach that Christ came absolutely more principally as a remedy for original sin. For when he distinguishes two ways of being greater, to wit, the intensive and extensive, he concludes: *And in this regard* (namely as regards extension, about which he was just speaking) *Christ more principally came to take away original sin.* This does not exclude that as regards intensity he more principally came to take away actual sin. *Second* (whereby the preceding objection is strengthened), when making the comparison between being greater intensively and being greater extensively, the former is greater simply, as is clear in the example adduced by St. Thomas. For whiteness is not called greater simply because it extends to a larger subject but from the fact that it has in itself more degrees of intensity or perfection. Therefore, if actual sin is greater than original sin intensively, it follows that it is the greater evil simply and, consequently, that Christ more principally came as a remedy for actual sin. But even granting that we should focus on being greater extensively as more principal, we would not infer from this that Christ more principally came as a remedy for original sin. For actual sin is not less extended than it. For if we focus on them in terms of numbers, there are more actual sins than original sins by far. If, on the other hand, we focus on them in terms of subjects, they are nearly equal to one another, for indeed every subject having original sin is also capable of actual sin and *de facto* contracts it when he reaches adulthood. Therefore, we gather no greater principalness in original sin than in actual sins from St. Thomas's discussion.

These things, I say, do not matter. For to the first we respond that the words *and in this regard* do not limit St. Thomas's solution but rather denote its cause, so that the sense is: *And on this account Christ came more principally to take away original sin,* as Suárez has rightly observed

---

11. Aquinas, *ST* III, q. 1, a. 4 (Leonine ed., 11:17), referring at the end to Aristotle, *Nichomachean Ethics*, 1.2.1094b10–11.

in his commentary on this article.¹² And that this is the legitimate understanding of it is established because from the opposite perspective it would be the case that St. Thomas did not resolve the question he had proposed: *Whether Christ's Incarnation took place more principally to take away original sin than actual sin?*, which is absurd and unworthy of so great a Doctor. Also, because it is so established from the response to objection 3, where without any restriction or limitation he affirms: *And thus it is not excluded that he more principally came to wipe away the sin of the whole nature than the sin of one person.* And finally, because that this is the manifest opinion of St. Thomas is clear from his other writings where he confronts the same difficulty, and specifically *Responsio de 36 articulis*, a. 23, where he says: *Just as the common good is better than the particular good of one man, so also the common evil of many is worse. Hence Christ more principally came to take away original sin, which had infected the whole human nature, than the particular sins of individuals. Hence on the passage "Behold him who taketh away the sins of the world" (Jn 1:29), a Gloss says: "Original sin is called 'the sin of the world' as being common to the whole world," and later on: "Christ looses original sin and the super-added sins of individuals as well."* Therefore it seems better to answer in the affirmative, that Christ came more principally to take away original sin than the others, than to answer in the negative, as if positing that Christ principally came to take away original sin alone. For to take away actual sins also pertains to the principal intention of Christ, whereby he came to save the world, according to the passage: *"I came not to call the just, but sinners to repentance"* (Lk 5:32).¹³ And *Responsio de 43 articulis*, a. 29,¹⁴ has nearly the same. From these we clearly have it that Christ principally came to take away all sins, both original and actual, as we suppose in the title of the present article and as we observed in the preceding number. Yet, we also have it that *Christ came more principally to take away original sin than actual sins.* Now that it was perchance more than equal (despite being sufficiently

---

12. Suárez, *Disputationes in Tertiam partem*, commentary on *ST* III, q. 1, a. 4, no. 2 (ed. Vivès, 17:495).

13. Aquinas (Leonine ed., 42:343).

14. Aquinas, *Responsio de 43 articulis*, a. 29 (Leonine ed., 42:332). The Latin text gives the citation as: *opusc. 10, art. 28.*

established from the text) we will now demonstrate for the sake of some whom, though they are disciples of the Holy Doctor, we must impugn below.

To the second, we respond that the antecedent only becomes true when making a comparison of being greater intensively and extensively in an order to a good or evil of the same order. For then what is greater intensively is greater simply, but the case is otherwise if the comparison is made to an evil or good of a different order. For then what is greater extensively of a higher order is greater simply than what is greater intensively of a lower order. And this is the case in the present matter. For actual sin, though intensively greater, is a particular evil or the evil of a person, whereas original sin is greater extensively, not in just any way but as a common evil, one of the whole nature. Hence just as the common good, the good of the whole race, is something more divine and eminent than the particular good, as Aristotle hands down (*Ethics* 1, chap. 2),[15] so must original sin be an evil of a higher order than the sin of particular persons.—Through this the response to what is added in this objection is clear. For we note the greater extension that we attribute to original sin not on the basis of an order to a multitude but by way of a habitude to the objects.[16] For original sin is *per se* the sin of nature derived from Adam through seminal propagation. Hence, speaking *per se*, it is common to all individuals to whom human nature is communicated through the aforementioned propagation. Actual sin, on the other hand, is the proper sin of only one person, and it is accidental to him that the same or a similar actual sin be found in another person. There is not, speaking *per se*, anything common concerning it, and it does not have the extension in which original sin shares. This is especially since [original sin] concurs with all actual sins as a root or as removing a restraint. For this reason it is customarily called "all sins" in accord with the passage: *For behold I was conceived in iniquities; and in sins did my mother conceive me* (Ps 50:7). This passage is commonly

---

15. Aristotle, *Nichomachean Ethics*, 1.2.1094b10–11.
16. In other words, we evaluate how extended original sin is not by counting the number of people who actually contract original sin but by considering that original sin is related to all Adam's descendants as that which they are liable to contract by that very fact.

understood by the Fathers as meaning original sin, which, even though it is one, is called "all" virtually and causally, as we observed in tract. 13, disp. 14, no. 5.[17] Since, then, original sin is an evil so grave and common, divine providence was warranted in regarding it more principally than actual sins when it decreed the provision of the medicine of the Incarnation for the human race, as is St. Thomas's solution.

55 From these testimonies just related the calumny of a certain follower of the Reformation found in Gregorio de Valencia (*Commentarii theologici*, vol. 4, disp. 1, q. 1, pt. 6)[18] is excluded, this person asserting that the Angelic Doctor was of the opinion that Christ did not satisfy for actual sins but only for original sin. He gathered this from the doctrine of this article and the *Opusculum on the Sacrament of the Altar*, chap. 1,[19] where St. Thomas established as the difference between the sacrifice of the cross and that of the altar that the former was more principally for original sin while the latter is for actual sins.

But as we have said, the aforementioned calumny is refuted and proven guilty of falsity. For it is patently established from the aforementioned passages that Christ principally came as a remedy for all sins, and it is only the subject of this question for which sin he came more principally as the remedy. This truth (plainly a Catholic truth)[20] comes across more clearly from what St. Thomas hands down below, where he says: *But there are two sins impeding from entry to the kingdom of heaven. One is common to the whole human nature, which is the sin of our first parent. And through this sin man was cut off from access to the kingdom of heaven. Hence we read (Gn 3:24) that after the sin of our first parent God placed Cherubim and a rotating sword of flame*

---

17. Salmanticenses, *Cursus theologicus*, tract. 13, disp. 14, dub. 1, § 1, no. 5 (ed. Palmé, 8:15–16). The Salmanticenses repeat this argument in part in no. 56 of the present disputation. The point is that Scripture sometimes speaks of original sin in the plural, as in the example of the verse quoted, because it is the source of all other sins.

18. Gregorio de Valencia (ed. Cardon, 4:59–61). The person in question is the Lutheran theologian Jacob Heerbrand (1521–1600). The Salmanticenses call him a *novator* (lit. "innovator"), meaning a follower of the Reformation.

19. *Opusculum de venerabili sacramento altaris*, chap. 1 (ed. Fiaccadorus, 17:135–36). A work of unknown authorship.

20. A "Catholic truth": a proposition definitively taught by the Church.

to guard the way to the tree of life. The other is the specific sin of each person, which is committed through each man's proper act. Now through Christ's Passion we have been freed not only from the sin common to the whole human nature, both as regards fault and as regards the guilt liable to punishment, but also from the proper sins of individuals, who share in his Passion through faith, charity, and the sacraments of faith (ST III, q. 49, a. 4).[21] This is totally in harmony with what St. Thomas has in the present article 4, where he says: *It is certain that Christ came into this world not only to wipe out that sin that has been passed on by origin to offspring but also for the wiping out of all sins that have afterwards been added over and above it.* Hence we do not know by what impression anyone could have imagined the opposite from this passage. Now in the *Opusculum* cited, he only teaches that the sacrifice of the cross was more principally offered for original sin, just as he so frequently finds that Christ came more principally as a remedy for original sin. But he does not at all exclude that he principally came and offered himself on the cross for actual sins. The sacrifice of the altar, however, was more principally instituted for actual sins. For it was instituted for the faithful, in whom, speaking as a rule, original sin is no longer found. From this root it arises that the sacrifice of the cross is not repeated, whereas the sacrifice of the altar is found to be most frequent.

Now having examined beforehand what pertains to the manner whereby God willed the remediation of original sin and actual sins through Christ, it must be seen whether he so principally intended redemption from original sin that, if it existed, Christ would come, even lacking all actual sins. And the question proceeds *de facto* and with reference to the present decree whereby God established that the Incarnation would be, whatever may be the case with what he would arrange through other decrees in another series of affairs.

---

21. Aquinas (Leonine ed., 11:474–75).

§ 2. The affirmative opinion is preferred

56 It should be said that, if original sin existed and actual sins did not exist, Christ would come by virtue of the present decree. This is what Thomists and other theologians, with the exception of just a few authors, commonly teach: Juan Vicente (*Relectio de habituali Christi Salvatoris nostri sanctificante gratia*, sol. q. 6, concl. 4, around the end);[22] Medina (*Expositio in Tertiam D. Thomae partem*, q. 1, a. 4);[23] Álvarez (*De Incarnatione divini Verbi disputationes*, q. 1, a. 4, disp. 9, no. 2);[24] Cippullo (*Commentariorum scholasticorum in Tertiam Partem Summae Theologiae Doctoris Angelici*, q. 1, a. 4, dub. unic., concl. 1);[25] our Cornejo (*Tractatus primus de Incarnatione Verbi divini*, q. 1, a. 4, dub. 1);[26] Araújo (*In Tertiam partem Divi Thomae commentarii*, q. 1, a. 4, dub. unic., concl. 1, speaking of the decree of intention);[27] our Philippe (*Disputationes theologicae in Tertiam partem Divi Thomae*, disp. 1, dub. 6, at the end);[28] Gonet (*Clypeus theologiae Thomisticae*, part 3, tract. 1, disp. 5, a. 2, concl. 1);[29] Parra (*Incarnationis arcanum scholastice disputationibus et quaestionibus reseratum*, tract. 1, disp. 1, q. 7, a. 5);[30] Suárez (*Disputationes in Tertiam partem*, disp. 5, sect. 6);[31] Vásquez (*Commentarii ac disputationes in Tertiam partem S. Thomae*, q. 1, a. 4, disp. 13);[32] Valencia (*Commentarii theologici*, vol. 4, disp. 1, q. 1, pt. 6);[33] Becanus (*Theologiae scholasticae pars tertia*, tract. 1, chap. 1,

---

22. Vicente (ed. Dianus, 694–97).
23. Medina (ed. Gastius, 107–13).
24. Álvarez (ed. Facciottus, 77–78).
25. Cippullo (ed. Manelphius, 1:141–46).
26. Cornejo de Pedrosa (ed. Varesius, 2:116–18).
27. Araújo, *In Tertiam partem Divi Thomae commentarii*, q. 1, a. 4, dub. unic., concl. 1, no. 63 (1636 ed., 112–13).
28. Philippe de la Trinité (ed. Iullieron, 16).
29. Gonet, *Clypeus theologiae Thomisticae*, part 3, tract. 1, disp. 5, a. 2, § 1, no. 71 (ed. Vivès, 5:486).
30. De la Parra y Arteaga (ed. Sanchez, 105–108).
31. Suárez (ed. Vivès, 17:263–66).
32. Vásquez (ed. Sanchez Crespo, 1:173–79).
33. Gregorio de Valencia (ed. Cardon, 4:59–61).

q. 9);[34] Granado (*In Tertiam Partem S. Thomae Aquinatis commentarii*, tract. 3, contr. 1, disp. 2, no. 2);[35] and many others.

It is proved first by the argument drawn from St. Thomas in the testimonies related in the preceding §, since if original sin existed and actual sins did not exist, the same decree formally whereby God intended the Incarnation would remain. Therefore, in such a case the Incarnation would take place by virtue of the same decree. The *consequentia* is plain. Persuasion for the antecedent: The same decree formally continues for as long as its primary occasion, after the manner of a primary object and motive, remains. But, making the comparison between original sin and actual sins, the former was [the Incarnation's] primary occasion, after the manner of its primary object and motive. Therefore, if original sin existed, even if there were no actual sins, the same decree formally whereby God intended the Incarnation would continue. The minor premise, in which lies the difficulty, is proved from the certain and common doctrine of St. Thomas and theologians that Christ was more principally decreed and came as a remedy for original sin than as a remedy for actual sins, as is established from what was said in no. 53. This doctrine can only become true if original sin was the primary occasion and the primary quasi-object and motive of the decree of the Incarnation.

Further confirmation and explanation: Since what God has decreed is hidden to us except from God's own revelation manifested in Scripture and the Church's teaching, that sin should be regarded as having been the primary occasion and motive of the Incarnation which is signified in this way in Scripture and the Church's teaching. But this is how it is with original sin. Therefore, it was the occasion or primary motive for the decree of the Incarnation. And thus if it existed, then even if actual sins were lacking, Christ would come by virtue of the present decree. Proof of the minor premise: This is because, when the archangel Gabriel put forward the future Incarnation, he makes mention of original sin alone: *That transgression may be finished, and sin may have an end, and iniquity may be abolished; and everlasting justice*

34. Becanus (ed. Pillehotte and Cassin, 49–54).
35. Granado (ed. de Lazcano, 4:76–77).

may be brought; and vision and prophecy may be fulfilled; and the Saint of saints may be anointed (Dn 9:24). Here the expositors of the aforementioned passage commonly teach that original sin is understood by the term "transgression," "sin," and "iniquity" by way of antonomasia.[36] Also, because it is said of Christ: *Behold him who taketh away the sin of the world* (Jn 1:29), as it reads in the Bible of the Complutenses[37] and in the Vatican edition at the time of Clement VIII.[38] And this is how it was read by Pope St. Caius (*Epistle to the Bishop Felix*);[39] St. Leo (Letter 16, chap. 6; and Letter 124, chap. 5);[40] St. Cyprian (*De duplici martyrio*);[41] St. Augustine (*Contra Faustum*, XII, chap. 30);[42] Venerable Bede (adduced by St. Thomas in the argument On the Contrary);[43] and other Fathers. They commonly observe that "the sin of the world," which the Lamb of God most specifically came to take away, means original sin, which was the chief cause of the aforementioned coming. And this pas-

---

36. A rhetorical device whereby one substitutes a title or description for a proper name.

37. The Complutensian Polyglot Bible was the first polyglot Bible produced on the printing press. It issued from Alcalá de Henares (whose Latin name is Complutum), near Madrid.

38. I.e., the Clementine Vulgate of 1592.

39. Pope St. Caius (d. 296). *Epistola Caii papae ad Felicem episcopum*, no. 4 (PL 5:186–87).

40. Leo the Great, *Epistola XVI ad universos episcopos per Siciliam constitutos*, chap. 6 (PL 54:702); and *Epistola CXXIV ad monachos Palestinos*, chap. 5 (PL 54:1065). The Latin text gives the citation as: *S. Leo epist. 47, cap. 2 et epist. 82, cap. 3*. It is unclear whether the two epistles I have cited are those the Salmanticenses mean to reference. In *Epistola CXXIV*, Migne's Latin text gives *peccata* instead of *peccatum* (contrary to the point the Salmanticenses are making). However, Migne's Greek version of *Epistola CLXV ad Leonem Augustum*, chap. 6 (PL 54:1164), to which the Salmanticenses referred above, has the singular τὴν ἁμαρτίαν.

41. A work falsely ascribed to Cyprian, possibly composed by Desiderius Erasmus (1466–1536). See *De duplici martyrio ad Fortunatum*, chaps. 7–8 (CSEL 3.3:225–26).

42. Augustine, *Contra Faustum*, XII, no. 30 (CSEL 25:358). The Latin text gives the citation as: *Augustinus lib. 2, contra Faustum cap. 3*.

43. St. Bede the Venerable (ca. 673–735). There is a textual variant in Aquinas's, *ST* III, q. 1, a. 4, *Sed contra* (Leonine ed., 11:17). Some manuscripts omit the reference to Bede. The quotation ascribed to Bede, "The 'sin of the world' means original sin," is found in the *Glossa ordinaria* on John 1:29 (ed. Fevardentius, Dadraeus, and Cuilly, 5:1042).

sage has the same meaning when following the Vulgate translation (by which we must always stand): *who taketh away the sins of the world*. For original sin is in a certain way all sins, as we have already said (no. 54). Furthermore, because the Councils and Fathers signify the same, as we have pondered (no. 53). And finally, because for this reason the universal Church, well learned in the sense of Scripture, sings as a blessing for the Paschal candle: *O truly necessary sin of Adam, destroyed completely by the death of Christ! O happy fault, which merited for us so great, so glorious a Redeemer!* Therefore, it was original sin under the aspect of the evil to be taken away that was the primary occasion or motive of the decree of the Incarnation.

57 Our adversaries respond by conceding that original sin pertained to the primary occasion or motive of the aforementioned decree not adequately but inadequately. For the adequate primary object or quasi-object, or the evil for the remediation of which God ordained the Incarnation, is constituted by original sin and actual sins. Hence it is the case that, lacking actual sins, Christ would not come as a remedy for original sin alone by virtue of the present decree because if part of the adequate object is lacking, the consequent is that the object itself and the decree primarily concerned with it is lacking.

But this response does not successfully address [our assertion]. *First*, because in accord with it we do not at all preserve Christ's coming more principally as a remedy for original sin than to take away actual sins. The consequent is openly against the express solution of St. Thomas in article 4 and against the common opinion of the Fathers and theologians, as is established from what was said above. Therefore, the aforementioned response cannot be maintained. Proof of the *sequela*: Supposing that God regarded the remediation of original sin and the remediation of actual sin with equal primacy as inadequate parts of the same primary object, no greater principalness appears in the remediation of original sin than in the remediation of actual sin, but rather an equality and subordination between them in an order to the constitution of one total motive. And this is what our adversaries affirm—or it is clear from it—that, just as lacking original sin Christ would not come to take away actual sins, so also lacking the latter he would not come to wipe away original sin. Hence they philosophize in the same way about the same matters, both in the order to constituting the primary adequate motive of the Incarnation and in the order to mutual dependence or connection in the order to whether Christ is going to be.[44] Therefore, according to the doctrine of our adversaries, it cannot at all be preserved that Christ more principally came as a remedy for original sin than to take away actual sins. Or else let them say in what else this greater principalness consists. Concerning this we have no doubt that their opinion (and they are Thomists) is contrary to St. Thomas. *Second*, because on the supposition that Christ was predestined as a remedy for sins, as is established from what was said in doubt 1, the consequent is that the aforementioned decree regarded these sins according to the order that they have among themselves. For, supposing the revelation of a divine decree concerning a given object, we ought to understand in the mode and circumstances that which is more in harmony with the natures of things, even if this is not so clearly established by virtue of such a revelation. But making a comparison between original sin and actual sins, the former is prior simply and independent of actual sins, since it could be found without them and not vice versa. Again, the former is far greater in the order to nature, since it extends (as far as it is concerned) to all individuals of human nature proceeding from Adam through seminal propagation, which is not the case in actual sins. Therefore, granted that God decreed that Christ would be as a remedy for all sins, he nevertheless willed that the aforementioned remedy would be primarily to take away original sin and secondarily to wipe away actual sins. And, consequently, even if the latter did not exist, such a decree would still be preserved in the order to its primary object. And thus Christ would come by virtue of the present decree.

44. *Unde eodem modo de eisdem philosophantur tam in ordine ad constituendum motivum primarium adaequatum Incarnationis, quam in ordine ad mutuam dependentiam, sive connexionem in ordine ad futuritionem Christi.* In other words, the Salmanticenses' opponents argue that original sin and actual sins are parts of a larger adequate object 1) in terms of making up the primary motive of the Incarnation and 2) in terms of how they are related to the question of whether Christ is actually going to come or not. The Salmanticenses object that this leaves no way in which Christ's coming could be "more principally" as a remedy for original sin than actual sins.

To these [we add]: When God decrees Christ, what he intends primarily (from the perspective of the remediation of the human race and the Incarnation's matter *concerning-which*) is that the human race not be impeded from attaining the last end and entrance into the kingdom of heaven. But if there were original sin, even if there were no actual sins, the human race would be impeded from the aforementioned end and glory. For, in fact, original sin (as far as it is concerned) infects all individuals of human nature that descend from Adam through seminal propagation, excludes them from the kingdom of heaven, and impedes them from attainment of the last end. Therefore, if original sin existed, even if there were no actual sins, the Incarnation would still be necessary for what God primarily intends when he decrees Christ. And thus the primary object or quasi-object of the aforementioned intention and the decree would be preserved.

58 But you will object that God could not have decreed that Christ would be as a remedy for original sin without at the same time seeing certain actual sins. Therefore, he primarily predestined Christ as the remedy for the latter as well. And, consequently, their remediation also pertains to the primary object or quasi-object of the stated intention. This second *consequentia* is plain from the first, which is rightly inferred from the antecedent. For if original sin and actual sins were compared after the manner of primary and secondary objects, they would not be touched on and foreseen at the same time. Instead, original sin would be first and then actual sins. Persuasion for the antecedent: This is because God could not have seen original sin unless he saw the actual or personal sin of Adam, which introduced original sin, and at the same time the sin of Eve, who was the occasion of sinning for her husband. And, consequently, he not only saw but foresaw at least these two actual sins prior to original sin. Also, because God decreed Christ as a remedy for original sin, not in any way whatsoever, but as Redeemer through his death and Passion. But by this very fact he saw the sins of those who slew Christ. Therefore, in the same indivisible stage in which he decreed Christ as a remedy for original sin, he also saw actual sins.

Whatever may be the case concerning the truth of the antecedent, we respond by denying both *consequentiae*. For we do not doubt that God knew all things that were going to be in the same stage *in-quo*, without needing to multiply others, as we observed above (no. 6). But it is inappropriate to gather from this that he saw all things as primary objects of his decree. For it may quite well be the case that he willed some things primarily and others secondarily or by consequence. For, to omit other examples that easily present themselves, in this same matter it is certain that in the same stage in which he saw all future sins, both mortal and venial, God also willed the remediation of them all through Christ, and yet he did not equally will the aforementioned remediation for them all. For the remediation of venial sins, which are a light evil, he willed only secondarily and by consequence. Otherwise, if all mortal sins, original and actual, remained and venial sins were lacking, Christ would not come by virtue of the present decree, which is absurd and contrary to the common opinion. Therefore, just as in this example it is rightly coherent that God by a single decree willed to permit all future sins, that in the same stage *in-quo* he foresaw that they would be, that he ordained Christ as the remedy for them all as the most perfect and universal Redeemer, and that he nevertheless decreed the aforementioned remediation primarily in an order to grave sins and secondarily in an order to light ones, so also it fits together quite well that in the same stage *in-quo* God foresaw both original and actual sin and that he prepared the remedy for both through Christ. But he did this in a different way in either case by decreeing in a single act the aforementioned remedy primarily in an order to original sin and secondarily in an order to actual sins. For what God primarily willed in this line was a remedy for the whole human nature fallen in Adam and for all men, insofar as all have sinned. Now other sins are particular losses and do not carry with them so grave a detriment. Hence it was enough that God willed their remediation secondarily and by consequence, just as he proportionately willed the remediation of venial sins.

Now the examples that are introduced as persuasion for the antecedent are not opposed to this doctrine. For we easily concede that more than one and, in fact, all sins were foreseen in the same stage *in-quo*. But we do not gather from this that their remediation was willed in the same way, as we have just explained. And indeed as regards the first example of the first sins of Adam and Eve, it can be said that, as far as the present consideration is concerned, they do not add anything numerically to the original sin of the whole nature but rather pertain to it after the manner of its cause or occasion. If, on the other hand, we were to consider them as merely personal, then we should have the same judgment of these sins as of others. And granted that they preceded original sin in execution, nevertheless, just as God willed the remediation of original sin more principally than these personal sins, so also he willed it prior on the part of the thing willed. To the second, some learned theologians respond that, intending Christ as Redeemer of the human race through his death and Passion, God did not see by virtue of this the particular mode of the [death and Passion] nor the sins that would intervene in them, but that he saw this in specific by virtue of another decree pertaining to execution, one that determined the means. Supposing this doctrine, the example has no ground. But we judge it false on account of what we said above (no. 28). Hence, consequently, we respond to what was just handed down by conceding that by virtue of the first decree concerning the existence of Christ and in the same stage *in-quo* God would see these and all other actual sins and that he preordained Christ as their remedy. It does not follow from this, however, that he willed it primarily, but instead that he willed it either in this way or secondarily and by consequence.

59 Second, the same assertion is proved from the unfitting conclusion inferred from the opposite opinion. For it follows that, lacking any mortal sin in particular, the object or matter *concerning-which* of the decree of the Incarnation is taken away and, consequently, that, lacking any actual mortal sin in particular, Christ would not come by virtue of the present decree. But this is quite absurd. This is because it is opposed to the common sense of theologians, with whom it has never been the object of controversy or even heard of that just as Christ would not come if Adam had not sinned, so also he would not come if Luther or Nero had not sinned. Also, because it is unbelievable that a benefit so great and universal as was prepared for the human race through Christ would have been bound to one sin of Nero in such a way that if he did not sin it would cease and human nature would be

left in all the miseries it suffers. And, although this was not logically impossible absolutely, this logical nonimpossibility can be conducive to metaphysical consideration but has no ground in moral matters such as we are treating of. For in these we ought to attend not only to absolute possibility but to what, supposing knowledge of the divine decree, is more becoming of divine providence and has greater harmony with right reason. But who could persuade himself that the holiness and glory of the Blessed Virgin and all the blessed and, in fact, the renewal of the whole world and the utmost exaltation of human nature in Christ were arranged by God with a binding to a single sin of Luther's such that if he had not sinned none of them would follow? Proof of the *sequela*: If by virtue of the present decree Christ had been ordered to the remediation of actual sins primarily, as to the object or the matter *concerning-which*, this would not be in an order to them confusedly but in particular, in accord with the mode of divine knowing. And thus the adequate primary object of the aforementioned intention or ordering would be composed of each and every actual sin as the parts *per se* constituting it. Now it is obvious that a corresponding decree regarding the object is lacking not only when the total object is lacking but also when any part of it is. For by this very fact the object is formally deficient in the aspect of "total" and "adequate." Therefore, we infer from the aforementioned opinion that lacking any grave actual sin, Christ would not come by virtue of the present decree.

60 Godoy meets this argument's challenge (disp. 8, no. 266)[45] by conceding the *sequela* and not regarding it as unfitting. And to its first proof (not touching on the second, which is more important for us), he responds that, even though theologians have commonly disputed about this difficulty by way of the order to Adam's sin (original sin) because in the opinion of St. Thomas (a. 4) this was the principal motive of the Incarnation, this does not prevent the possibility also of treating it in the order to any particular sin by defending the same solution.

But this is unsatisfactory. And indeed the most learned Thomist repeats without warrant that St. Thomas said that original sin was the

---

45. Godoy, *Disputationes theologicae in Tertiam partem Divi Thomae*, tract. 1, disp. 8, § 11, no. 266 (ed. Hertz, 1:141).

principal motive of the Incarnation. For the Angelic Doctor does not speak in this way, as if putting original sin and actual sins on equal footing. Rather, he affirms that Christ came *more principally* as a remedy for original sin, placing it before actual sins by great measure. From this there is sufficient success in proving effectively that in his opinion (which on this point is the common one) original sin was the primary matter *concerning-which* of the Incarnation, while other sins pertained to the secondary matter by consequence, as we laid out above (beginning from no. 56). But, leaving this aside, let us come to the impugnment of the given solution. And we readily recognize that it is difficult to convince someone willing to swallow unfitting conclusions but that it is necessary for the arguer either to stop at the unfitting conclusion that he admits (and it truly is unfitting) or, from what was admitted, to lead the respondent into even greater unfitting conclusions, in which the absurdity becomes even more evident. And, following this approach, let us shore up the argument made above. For it follows that lacking any venial sin, Christ would not come by virtue of the present decree, which is absurd and unbelievable. Proof of the *sequela*: Since he was predestined the most perfect Redeemer of men from all sins, Christ was ordained by God as the remedy not only for original sin and grave actual sins, but also as the remedy for light ones or for all [sins] absolutely. But for this reason, if original sin existed and there were no grave actual sins, Christ would not come in virtue of the present decree, as the aforementioned author affirms. Therefore, granted the existence of original sin and all mortal actual sins, it is equally the case that if there were not each and every light sin, Christ would not come by virtue of the present decree. Hence lacking any, even the least venial sin, the world's remedy would be impeded. And the same argument can be made for any degree of grace and for any other reward that Christ has *de facto* merited for us. For he was predestined for all these, and thus lacking any of them, he would not come by virtue of the present decree.

61 The aforementioned author responds by denying the *sequela*.[46] In proof of this he says that Christ was ordained as a remedy for all

---

46. Godoy, *Disputationes theologicae in Tertiam partem Divi Thomae*, tract. 1, disp. 8, § 11, no. 269 (ed. Hertz, 1:142).

sins, but differently in different cases: primarily as the remedy for grave sins and secondarily as the remedy for light sins. This is because not to redeem from the former would be a substantial defect in the character of redemption, since through these sins man is constituted as under the power of the devil, whereas not to redeem from the latter would be not a substantial but a light and accidental defect in the Redeemer's role, since due to venial sin man does not become the slave of the devil but is still under the amicable dominion of God. Now lacking the primary object, God's decree concerning it is lacking, whereas the case is otherwise if only the secondary object is lacking. And thus, lacking any grave sin, Christ would not come by virtue of the present decree, but he would come by virtue of it even if venial sins were lacking.

Still, this response strengthens our opinion by teaching the way to resolve all the counterarguments. For just as it is compatible with the most perfect office of the Redeemer from all sins that Christ would come primarily as a remedy for grave sins and secondarily as a remedy for light sins, as in the aforementioned author's discussion, so also it would be coherent that he came primarily as a remedy for original sin and secondarily as a remedy for actual sins. For what God primarily intended in providing the remedy of the Redeemer was to heal human nature from its general corruption, which was the most grave evil, whereas he secondarily and by consequence intended to heal it from other personal or actual sins, which are found in the individuals of this same nature. For this reason, St. Thomas repeats so often that Christ came *more principally* to take away original sin. Hence as regards this type of subordination actual sins are related to original sin in the same proportional way as light sins are to grave sins. Now what is added in this response about the substantial defect in the role of the Redeemer is of no importance. For we admit that there is an argument for such a defect if the office of Redeemer and the decree predestining him did not extend to the remediation of grave sins. But for this it is not at all required that they regard the latter primarily. Rather, it suffices that their causality and efficacy extend to it, even if secondarily, by consequence, and with a subordination to the remediation of original sin as to the primary motive in this genus. So too, an argument could be made for substantial defect and lack of power in an agent if its causality did not extend to what follows on the form, yet it does not follow from this that the agent regards or touches on these primarily. Rather, it suffices that it does so secondarily and by consequence, as sufficiently expressed in the common maxim: *One who gives the form gives also what follows on the form.* This can also be confirmed by other examples.

Nor can we infer from this that Christ did not more principally come as a remedy for grave actual sins than as a remedy for light ones, if, in fact, as we say, he only came secondarily and by consequence as a remedy for all these. Now this appears false even from the fact that grave sins more than light ones impede from the attainment of the last end.—This, I say, is not inferred from what was said. For, granted that all the aforementioned sins are regarded secondarily and by consequence, within the breadth of the secondary object there is still a variance on account of greater or lesser approximation to the primary object. This also appears within the breadth of the object or term of a natural agent, for although it regards all the accidents of the composite to be generated secondarily and by consequence, it nevertheless regards proper accidents more than common ones because the former are more connected with the primary term. And this is the case in the present matter. For the primary object or quasi-object of the divine intention decreeing Christ was to heal human nature from the general languor that it had contracted through Adam's sin, while that which was secondary and by consequence was to heal from all infirmities or miseries. And because mortal actual sin is a greater misery than light sin, comes nearer to original sin, and in it the defect of the principle vitiated through original sin comes across more clearly within the breadth of the secondary object, God more willed the remediation of grave actual sins than light ones, even though the remediation of all sins with the inequality or gradation so explained pertained to the role of the perfect Redeemer and the principal intention of God, as St. Thomas plainly supposes in this fourth article, identifying no difference as regards principalness between grave and light sins but including them all under the name "actual sin."

62 But you will object: The same unfitting conclusion that we opposed to the contrary opinion militates against ours as well.

Therefore, it is either null or we ought to resolve it. Proof of the antecedent: Since we say that original sin was the motive and primary quasi-object of the decree of the Incarnation, it follows that, lacking original sin in any individual, the object of the aforementioned decree would be taken away and, consequently, if Luther were not conceived in original sin, Christ would not come by virtue of the present decree and the universal remedy of the redemption of the human race through Christ would be impeded, which is the unfitting conclusion that was objected against the adverse opinion.

We respond by denying the antecedent. In proof of this, leaving aside the opinion of those who say that the original sin for whose remediation God provided the benefit of the Incarnation was not original sin as contracted by each individual but original sin as originating and impending against them,[47] we respond by admitting that original sin was foreseen in all those individuals by whom it is *de facto* contracted. Yet we do not infer from this that if original sin were lacking in a given individual (either because [the individual] we presuppose is going to exist would not be going to exist, or else because [the individual] would exist but would be preserved from original sin in another way), then the primary motive of the decree of the Incarnation would by this very fact be lacking. And the reason is: The primary motive of the Incarnation was the remediation of original sin as the evil common to human nature, not as the evil of this or that individual taken determinately. For it is rightly coherent that a given individual should be preserved from the aforementioned evil and that nevertheless we truly and properly say that the whole community of the human race bears it, as is *de facto* the case, notwithstanding the preservation of the Blessed Virgin from this sin, as we piously believe. Hence from the lack of original sin in

---

47. *Non fuisse peccatum originale ut ad singula individua contractum, sed ut originans, et illis imminens*. The Scholastics distinguish between *peccatum originale originatum* ("originated original sin"), which is the state of original sin contracted by each individual, and *peccatum originale originans* ("originating original sin"), which is Adam's personal sin that gives rise to that state. Here the Salmanticenses are referring to the view that the Incarnation is primarily a remedy for Adam's personal sin (which, considered in itself as a personal act, merely forebodes loss to his posterity) instead of being directly a remedy for the actually deficient state of Adam's posterity resulting from his sin.

a given individual in whom it had been foreseen as going to exist by virtue of originating original sin, whether because of the nonexistence of the subject or because of some preservation (which, even so, would not occur without remediation through Christ) the adequate or inadequate primary object of the decree of the Incarnation would not at all be taken away. For it is not the sin of this or that particular [individual] taken in isolation and separately (the way in which it implies a particular evil) but is the evil of this individual and that one and all the rest, as the community of the whole nature arises from the collection of them. For this is how it has the character of the common and most grave evil as whose remedy Christ was primarily ordained. Now concerning original sin as contracted by the particular individual and taken separately we should have the same judgment as in the case of actual sins. For taken in this way, they are all particular evils and pertain secondarily to the object of the aforementioned decree. Hence just as if actual sins were lacking, so also lacking this or that original sin in this or that individual taken in isolation, Christ would still come by virtue of the present decree, whereby he primarily willed to provide a remedy for the whole community of human nature concerning the general evil that it bore and then secondarily and by consequence willed to provide the remedy for determinate individuals, that concerning specific evils as their particular losses. For this is the way in which it was appropriate for divine providence to provide for evils so different or considered in such different ways, as we were saying (no. 57).

This different consideration of original sin also as contracted by individuals can be explained further by the example of the providence of a prince who intends primarily the common good, for example, that of the city. For the aforementioned common good is not a logical universal or a Platonic idea separate from individuals. Rather, it is something existing in them and contracted by them. And yet, from the fact that this or that individual is lacking or from the fact that the common good is not preserved in this or that individual, the primary object of the aforementioned providence is not therefore lacking. Otherwise, the providence itself would be lacking, which is contrary to experience, as is clear of itself. The reason for this is that even though providence regards the common good existing in particular individuals and contracted by them, it does not primarily regard particulars considered in isolation and separately. Hence even if, so taken, it is lacking, the primary object of providence is not thereby lacking. Instead, it regards the aforementioned particulars in an order to the common good and as constituting a community. In this way, they are not lacking, since the community of them is always preserved, even if this or that one is not there. And thus, if certain individuals are changed or varied, there still remains the providence's primary object and, consequently, the same providence. In this way, therefore, God preordained and provided Christ primarily as a remedy for original sin, which we admit was not only originating and impending but contracted by individuals. Still, it did not regard, at least primarily, the individuals contracting it taken in isolation and considered separately *per se* but rather as constituting the community of the human race, such that the primary motive of the aforementioned remedy was the good of the community. Hence where this is preserved, the primary object of such an ordination is also preserved. And since the former would be preserved even if this or that individual were not there or would not actually contract original sin due to another kind of remedy, the consequent is that the primary object of the present decree would be preserved and thus that Christ would come by virtue of it.—We can also add another example in the doctrine that we regarded as probable in tract. 6, disp. 12, no. 107,[48] that the *per se* material object or virtual specifying object of the divine omnipotence is not the accumulation of these possible creatures numerically but the accumulation of possible creatures, whatever they may be and in whatever number, and, consequently, that omnipotence would still not be varied *a posteriori* from the variation of an object that is not a given kind *per se* but only from the variation of one that is *per se* a given kind.[49] Therefore, the same should be said in the case of the objection, as one will easily be able to apply.

---

48. Salmanticenses, *Cursus theologicus*, tract. 6, disp. 12, dub. 2, § 10, no. 107 (ed. Palmé, 3:525).

49. *Omnipotentia non variaretur adhuc a posteriori ex variatione objecti, quod non est tale per se sed solum ex variatione ejus, quod est per se tale.*

§ 3. The rationales for the contrary opinion are addressed

63. The opposing opinion is defended by: Cabrera (*In Tertiam partem Sancti Thomae Aquinatis commentarii et disputationes*, q. 1, a. 4, disp. unic., no. 10),[50] even though this author does not sufficiently explain himself by distinguishing between the primary and secondary object or motive but instead says that all grave sins pertained to the adequate object of the decree of the Incarnation; Nazario (*Commentaria et controversiae in Tertiam partem Summae Divi Thomae Aquinatis*, q. 1, a. 4, contr. unic., concl. 1);[51] and Godoy (*Disputationes theologicae in Tertiam partem Divi Thomae*, tract. 1, disp. 8, § 11, no. 241),[52] adducing several more recent thinkers, without mentioning their names, whom we have not seen. The argument for this opinion is made first from St. Thomas (in the present fourth article, *Responsio de 43 articulus*, a. 29, and *Responsio de 36 articulis*, a. 23).[53] In these places, he affirms that Christ principally came as a remedy for actual sins, which we confirmed with other testimonies in no. 52. Now that which was the principal motive of Christ's coming pertained at least inadequately to the primary object of the decree of the Incarnation. Therefore, lacking actual sins, even if original sin remained, the primary object of the aforementioned decree would be taken away. And thus Christ would not come by virtue of it.

We respond, conceding the major premise, by denying the minor. This is because in the same passages St. Thomas affirms that Christ *more principally* came as a remedy for original sin than for actual sins, identifying a wide discrepancy between them both. This [affirmation] would not become true if he identified them equally as parts of a single primary adequate object, as we pondered in no. 57. Also, because in the

---

50. Cabrera (ed. Barrera, 336).
51. Nazario (ed. Rossius, 4:155).
52. Godoy (ed. Hertz, 1:139).
53. Aquinas, *ST* III, q. 1, a. 4 (Leonine ed., 11:17); *Responsio de 43 articulis*, a. 29 (Leonine ed., 42:332); and *Responsio de 36 articulis*, a. 23 (Leonine ed., 42:343). The Latin text again cites the *Responsio de 43 articulis* as: *opusc. 10, art. 28*.

aforementioned passages he identified no difference between grave and light personal sins but included them all under the name "actual sins." And yet, we do not gather from this that in the Holy Doctor's opinion venial sins pertained to the primary object of the Incarnation. Therefore, just as our adversaries exclude the remediation of venial sins from the aforementioned primary object or motive, so also we, with greater right, exclude actual sins, since St. Thomas plainly affirms that Christ came *more principally* as a remedy for original sin. Nor can there be force in the fact he said that [Christ] came *principally* as a remedy for actual sins because it is certain that something can pertain principally to a given line even if it does so not primarily but instead secondarily and by consequence. So too, not only the common good but also the good of particular individuals pertains to the governor's providence principally, and yet only the common good constitutes the primary object of such providence, while other goods regard it secondarily, by consequence, and as integrated into it, as we explained in the preceding number. Likewise, enjoyment pertains to beatitude principally, and other acts of the will following on the vision of God in himself pertain to it, and yet they do not pertain primarily so as to constitute essential beatitude after the manner of a part but instead regard it secondarily and in a completing way. Hence formal beatitude would be preserved absolutely without these. In this way, therefore, even though actual sins, at least grave ones, pertained principally to the motive of Christ's coming in a way soon to be clarified more fully, it does not follow from this that they pertained as parts of a primary adequate object.

64. Second, an argument is made by impugning the doctrine just handed down. For the adequate motive of the decree of the Incarnation was not the remediation only of original sins but also of mortal actual sins. But lacking the adequate motive of a decree or part of it, the decree cannot continue. Therefore, lacking actual sins, the aforementioned decree would be lacking and, consequently, by virtue of it Christ would not come as a remedy for original sin. The minor premise and both *consequentiae* are established. As for the major, in which there could have been a difficulty, we offer persuasion for it in this way: The end of Christ's coming was perfect redemption from captivity to the

devil. But it would not be perfect redemption if it had brought a remedy for original sin in a precisive way and not for actual sins. Therefore, the adequate motive of the decree of the Incarnation was not the remediation of original sin alone but also of all grave actual sins.

We respond by denying the major premise understood of the primary adequate object. In proof of this, admitting the major, the minor must be distinguished: That redemption would not be perfect if it had in no way brought a remedy for existing mortal actual sins, this we concede. That it would not be so if it had not brought a remedy for the aforementioned sins primarily, this we deny. And next we deny the *consequentia* understood absolutely of the primary adequate motive. Hence we admit that it pertains to the role of the perfect Redeemer that he should bring a remedy for all grave sins, but it does not at all pertain [to this role] that he should regard the aforementioned sins in the same way or with equal primacy, nor that he should exist as their remedy [in the same way or with equal primacy]. Rather, it suffices that he heal from them all, from some primarily and from others secondarily and by consequence. For in this way passive liberation, which is the perfect Redeemer's end, is sufficiently brought to perfection. And thus Christ would not be the perfect Redeemer if he did not free man from preexisting grave actual sins, but he would be if he freed from them, despite doing so secondarily. And likewise, (staying with this providence) God would not perfectly provide the human race a remedy if, having foreseen original sin and grave actual sins, he did not decree Christ as a remedy for them all but instead for no more than original sin. But, he did provide perfectly by decreeing Christ primarily as a remedy for original sin and secondarily as a remedy for grave actual sins. For in this way no sin is left without a remedy. And the force of the aforementioned syllogism that Godoy uses can easily be turned around by the example of venial sins, if we turn it back in this manner: Christ was predestined not only as a perfect Redeemer but as the most perfect and came into the world to bring not only perfect redemption but also most perfect redemption from captivity to sin. But he would not be the most perfect Redeemer and would not have brought the most perfect redemption if he conferred a remedy for mortal sins alone and not for venial ones. For most perfect freedom and redemption demands liberation from any bond, even a light one. And thus one who is subject to venial sins is not most perfectly free from the misery of fault and is not most perfectly unfettered for entrance into glory. Therefore, the adequate motive of the Incarnation was the remediation not only of grave sins but of all sins, however light. And, consequently, lacking any light sin, Christ would not come by virtue of the present decree. Yet the aforementioned author (no. 268)[54] does not dare to concede this. Therefore, he must respond that it does pertain to the most perfect Redeemer to bring a remedy for all sins as far as sufficiency goes, though not with equal primacy for all sins, and that, instead, he brings it primarily for some and secondarily for others, as is really the case. And this is what we respond to his argument, without needing to address the reply that he proposes in no. 243.[55] For it contains the same difficulty, though proposed in a different way, and is resolved in the same way. We can also recall and apply the example posed above of providence that would not be perfect unless it regarded more than one thing and bore upon many, while from this we do not infer that it touches on them all equally. Rather, it touches on some primarily and some secondarily, as the affairs themselves and their greater and lesser gravity demands, or at least as the will of the provider himself, if he is the supreme governor, decrees.

65. Third argument: The decree of the Incarnation would have ordained it primarily as a remedy for original sin and then as a remedy for actual sins because original sin would have been foreseen before the latter, as their root and cause. But this account is null. Therefore, etc. Proof of the minor premise: This is because the first sins of Adam and Eve were prior to original sin, since it was introduced through them. Also, because many are conceived from illegitimate concourse, where it is necessary that an actual sin precede the original sin contracted by the aforementioned [offspring]. Therefore, this account of precedence and foresight cannot stand in general.

Confirmation: If there were some reason for Christ not to be pre-

---

54. Godoy, *Disputationes theologicae in Tertiam partem Divi Thomae*, tract. 1, disp. 8, § 11, no. 268 (ed. Hertz, 1:142).

55. Godoy, *Disputationes theologicae in Tertiam partem Divi Thomae*, tract. 1, disp. 8, § 11, no. 243 (ed. Hertz, 1:139).

destined primarily as a remedy for actual sins, it would be most of all because we are able to avoid actual sins through the grace of Christ. And thus they suppose the grace of Christ as given and so also [suppose] his predestination. It is not coherent with this that these things were foreseen absolutely in respect of the decree of the fact that Christ would exist. But this account, too, has no strength. Therefore, etc. Proof of the minor premise: In our opinion original sin, even contracted by individuals, is supposed for the Incarnation, for, in fact, Christ was predestined as its remedy. And yet its actual contraction can be avoided through Christ's grace and merits, as is piously believed to have been the case in the Blessed Virgin. Therefore, the fact that actual sins can be avoided through the grace of Christ does not at all prove that they could not have been foreseen absolutely in respect of the decree of the fact that Christ would exist.

We respond that this argument and the confirmation contain two foundations, which the author cited establishes in a second and third place and lays out at greater length.[56] But they do not directly impugn our assertion or touch on its lines of reasoning, which are very different from the former, as is obvious from what has been said. But perhaps they are directed to other authors who use them. Hence it is not necessary for us to confront them. We add, however, that all sins were foreseen in the same stage *in-quo*. We concede, too, that all sins can be avoided and sometimes actually are avoided through Christ and thus that no difference is taken from these roots as to why the remediation of original sin should have been willed primarily while that of others was willed secondarily. Rather, the aforementioned difference is taken *a priori* both from God's will, which is made known to us through the testimonies adduced in nos. 53 and 56, and from the magnitude of the evil of original sin (for by so decreeing, God made provision for this quite well and in a way that harmonizes with its condition), which is the evil of the whole community of the human race and which far surpasses actual sins in the harm it does to nature. *A posteriori*, however, the same difference is taken from the unfitting conclusion that we infer

---

56. Cf. Godoy, *Disputationes theologicae in Tertiam partem Divi Thomae*, tract. 1, disp. 8, § 11, nos. 245–73 (ed. Hertz, 1:139–42).

from the opposite opinion, namely, that Christ would not come as a remedy for the whole human race if one sin of Luther's were lacking. This consequent cannot be avoided and is absurd to admit. Our opinion relies on these latter lines of reasoning, not the former impugned by the arguer, as is obvious from what was said above.

66 Fourth argument: The mode and circumstances in which the Incarnation was put into execution were determined by God by virtue of the present decree, whereby God ordained Christ as a remedy for sin, but if actual sins did not exist, the Incarnation would be put into execution with a different mode and circumstances than it has *de facto* been put into execution. Therefore, a different decree prescribing these would be necessary. And thus, lacking actual sins, Christ would not come by virtue of the present decree. This second *consequentia* is plain from the first. For if by virtue of the present decree he were going to come, another decree would not be required. And, the first *consequentia* is legitimately inferred from the premises because for new and distinct circumstances, a new and distinct decree is required. Now, the major premise is certain because nothing is put into execution that was not previously preordained by God. Otherwise, something would occur in execution without falling under the divine intention, which cannot be said. Finally, for the minor, in which lies the difficulty, we can easily offer a persuasion. This is because if actual sins did not exist, Christ would not institute the sacraments he has instituted as a remedy for them. Also, because in that event all men would be preserved from actual sins through the grace of Christ. Yet in all of these redemption patently occurs with a different mode and circumstances than it now exists.

Araújo is convinced by this argument in the following way:[57] He concedes that if original sin existed and actual sins did not exist, Christ would come by virtue of the present decree of intention. In this he agrees with the common opinion. Yet, he thinks that in that case [Christ] would not be going to come by virtue of the same present decree of execution but instead by virtue of another, in accord with a different execution of the Incarnation as regards mode and circumstance. For the aforemen-

---

57. Araújo, *In Tertiam partem Divi Thomae commentarii*, q. 1, a. 4, dub. unic., concl. 1, nos. 63–64 (1636 ed., 112–15).

tioned author thinks that two decrees intervened in preordaining this mystery: one of intention, whereby God willed Christ in passible flesh and as a remedy for the human race, and the other of execution, whereby he willed all the means, modes, and circumstances pertaining to its execution. Among these latter were *de facto* the sacraments and other things pertaining to the remediation of personal sins. And because these would be varied if the aforementioned sins did not exist, he infers that the Incarnation would not be going to be committed to execution by virtue of the present decree of execution but instead by virtue of the decree of intention that God *de facto* has and by virtue of another decree of execution that on this hypothesis he would have. Hence he follows a sort of middle way between our opinion and the opposite.

But, although this opinion does not give much prejudice to our assertion, since it preserves that Christ would come by virtue of the present decree of intention and preserves that the adequate primary motive of [the decree] was the remediation of original sin, which is the particular scope of this controversy, its way of explaining itself and of meeting, or rather succumbing to, the argument does not please us. This is because it identifies in God a kind of confused and potential intention not reaching to all the modes and means that occur in execution, which thereby come about apart from the intention, despite later being chosen by God. Also, because it multiplies decrees in God without necessity. For, granted that God has acts in execution that are different from first intention, such as command and use, he needs no other act to choose the means because through the first act he wills the end through the determinate means. For these and other reasons, we have already rejected a like manner of speaking above (beginning from no. 28), so that we need not spend any more time on this matter. Hence to the argument we respond by conceding the premises and by distinguishing the first consequent: That a new decree would be necessary with a substantial innovation and as regards the adequate primary object or motive, this we deny; as regards a certain extension or contraction of it, this we concede. And then the second *consequentia* must be denied absolutely.

Explanation of the solution: In the present difficulty everyone supposes that, given the hypothesis conditionally proposed in it, an argument would be made for some variation in God's decree or decrees. For now personal sins are supposed as absolutely going to exist and, on that hypothesis, they would not be going to exist; now there is a specific remedy for these sins that then would not be necessary. Hence the consequent is that God would have decreed and foreseen otherwise than he has *de facto* foreseen and decreed. But the difficulty is whether the variation on the part of the object or motive would be so great as to render the primary and adequate object different or whether it would only vary it in extension or as being integrated in an order to certain secondary objects willed under it. For if we assert the first, as the authors contrary to us affirm, consequently it must be said that God's decree is varied substantially or specifically and thus that Christ would not be going to come by virtue of the present decree. If, on the other hand, we only admit the second, as our opinion holds, God's decree is consequently said not to be varied substantially or specifically. And thus we say that Christ would have been going to come by virtue of the present decree, granted that such a decree would undergo some variation in the order to secondary objects and to the modes or circumstances of its execution. Since, then, the primary object or motive of the decree of the Incarnation was the remedy of the whole nature or the human race from original sin, as Araújo thinks with us, and such an object would be preserved even if actual sins were lacking, Christ would therefore come on this hypothesis by virtue of the same decree substantially or specifically. But because such a decree regarded original sin in such a way that it extended secondarily and by consequence to the remediation of personal sins and to the modes appropriate to such a remediation, and because this extension would be lacking on the aforementioned hypothesis, the decree would be different in extension and mode, and Christ would then come by virtue of a decree that would be the same substantially and specifically and different only in extension and mode, without need to think up other decrees. This doctrine can also be explained further by the example of venial sins, to whose remediation the decree of the Incarnation extends. If these did not exist, such a decree would lack this extension and yet no one denies that, lacking venial sins, Christ would come by virtue of the same decree absolutely as that whereby he has *de facto* come.

Doubt IV

Whether, by virtue of the present decree, Christ would come if actual sins existed, even if original sin did not exist?

Supposing the preceding decision, the resolution of this difficulty takes little trouble and thus should be dealt with in only a few words, even though discussing it separately has been necessary for the sake of greater clarity. Now it should be observed that, lacking original sin, we can conceive of there being actual sins in three ways: First, in all or in most men. Second, in only one or very few. Third, as the middle way, in a considerable multitude. Now as to which would be the case, the only one who knows is God, who,[1] on such a hypothesis, decreed to permit this by a decree subjectively absolute and objectively conditioned. We grant that St. Gregory (*Moralia*, IV, chap. 36)[2] and St. Anselm (*Cur Deus homo?*, II, chap. 18)[3] mean that if Adam had not sinned, sins would be in the minority, and St. Thomas seems to have the same opinion (*ST* I, q. 100, a. 2, and *Super II Sent.*, dist. 20, q. 2, a. 3).[4] There is no need to examine this further, since it makes little or no difference for the resolution of the proposed difficulty.

---

1. Where the Latin text has *quid*, I have read *qui* in accord with the 1687 edition.
2. Gregory the Great, *Moralia in Iob*, IV, chap. 36 (CCSL 143:214–17).
3. Anselm (ed. Schmitt, 2:126–29).
4. Aquinas (Leonine ed., 4:444, and ed. Moos, 2:515–19). The Latin text gives the citations as: *1 p. quest. 10, art. 2 et in 2 sent. dist. 20, quaest. 2, art. 4.*

§ 1. The negative opinion is preferred and contrary lines of reasoning are torn apart

67 It should be said that, if original sin were lacking and actual sins existed, whether few, many, or all of them, Christ would not come by virtue of the present decree. This is what is taught by Cabrera, Nazario, and Godoy (related in no. 63); Juan Vicente (In *Relectio de gratia Christi*, q. 6, p. 695);[5] Our Cornejo (*Tractatus primus de Incarnatione Verbi divini*, q. 1, a. 4, dub. 2);[6] Cippullo (*Commentariorum scholasticorum in Tertiam Partem Summae Theologiae Doctoris Angelici*, q. 1, a. 4, dub. unic., concl. 2);[7] Juan Prudencio (*Commentarii in Tertiam partem Sanctissimi Thomae*, tract. 2, disp. 1, dub. 3, sect. unic., concl. 4);[8] Gonet (*Clypeus theologiae Thomisticae*, part 3, tract. 1, disp. 5, a. 2, concl. 2);[9] Lorca (*Commentarii ac disputationes in Tertiam partem D. Thomae*, q. 1, a. 4, disp. 10, memb. 4, beginning from no. 59);[10] Vásquez (*Commentarii ac disputationes in Tertiam partem S. Thomae*, q. 1, a. 4, disp. 13, chap. 1);[11] Ragusa (*Commentarii ac disputationes in Tertiam partem D. Thomae*, disp. 33);[12] Pérez (*Disputationes de Incarnatione divini Verbi*, disp. 15, sect. 3, concl. 2); and quite a few others. And it is proved in the first place from St. Thomas, who expressly resolves it in this way. This is in article 3, where, although he only inquires, *Whether, if man had not sinned, God would have been incarnate?* (words wherein he seems to prescind from original and actual sin), his intention and resolution are nevertheless directed toward original sin. This is clear from the responses to objections 1, 3, and 5,

---

5. Vicente, *Relectio de habituali Christi Salvatoris nostri sanctificante gratia*, sol. q. 6, p. 695 (ed. Dianus, 695).

6. Cornejo de Pedrosa (ed. Varesius, 2:118–19).

7. Cippullo (ed. Manelphius, 1:145).

8. Prudencio (ed. Anisson, 1:309).

9. Gonet (ed. Vivès, 5:487).

10. Lorca (ed. Sanchez de Ezpleta, 1:87–88).

11. The Salmanticenses cite chap. 1 (ed. Sanchez Crespo, 1:174–75), which is a summary of various opinions. It is, properly speaking, chap. 2 (ed. Sanchez Crespo, 1:175–78) where Vásquez explains his own position (that Christ would not have come by virtue of the present decree if there had been only actual sins).

12. Ragusa (ed. Cardon, 278–82).

and it is far clearer from the body of the article itself, where he says: *Hence, since in sacred Scripture the reason for the Incarnation is everywhere assigned from the sin of the first man, it is more fittingly said that the work of the Incarnation was ordained by God as a remedy against sin such that if sin did not exist, the Incarnation would not have been.*[13] And this is the sense theologians commonly draw from the aforementioned passage, which is why in their inquiries on this passage and on the occasion afforded by it, they ask whether if Adam had not sinned God would have been incarnate. And also, in article 4,[14] where the Holy Doctor expressly gives the solution that Christ more principally came as a remedy for original sin than as a remedy for actual sins. From this it is the case that, lacking original sin, the principal motive of the present decree would be lacking and that by virtue of it Christ would not come, as we have already laid out. Recall what we have said about the aforementioned principalness (no. 53).

Next, it is proved by an argument drawn from the same testimonies: If the adequate primary object or motive of a given decree is destroyed, the decree itself cannot continue. But, with original sin taken away, the adequate primary object or motive of Christ's Incarnation is taken away, as is established from what was said in the preceding doubt. Therefore, with original sin taken away, the adequate primary motive or object of the decree of Christ's Incarnation is taken away. Therefore, Christ would not come by virtue of the present decree, even if actual sins existed. The rest is established, and the final *consequentia* is legitimately inferred from the first. For, on a given supposition, Christ would not come by virtue of a decree that is taken away by that very supposition.

Confirmation: Even freely granting that the remediation of original sin was not the adequate primary motive of the present decree, it cannot be denied that it entered into its constitution after the manner of a principal part—indeed the more principal part—as theologians commonly teach with St. Thomas (a. 4). But the decree is taken away not only through the complete removal of its adequate object but also through an inadequate removal, or the removal of a part from which

---

13. Aquinas, *ST* III, q. 1, a. 3 (Leonine ed., 11:14).
14. Aquinas, *ST* III, q. 1, a. 4 (Leonine ed., 11:17).

the adequate object comes together. For, in fact, the object itself is also destroyed when this or that part by which it is principally constituted is taken away. Therefore, with original sin taken away, the decree of the Incarnation that has *de facto* existed would be taken away, and by virtue of it Christ would not come, even if other sins were to occur.

68 Nor is it any use to say that, in that case, even though there would not be original sin formally, there would still be an evil equivalent to it if we make the supposition that all individuals would sin actually. For they would be excluded from the kingdom in the same way as they are *de facto* excluded because of original sin.—This, I say, does not matter. This is because what *de facto* constituted adequately, or at least inadequately but principally, the primary motive of the present decree was not an equivalent to original sin but original sin taken formally and as the evil both of the whole nature and of all the individuals it has *de facto* infected. Therefore, with this taken away, the motive of the aforementioned decree is taken away. Also, because it is false to say that on that hypothesis there would be an equivalence. For on account of original sin all men proceeding from Adam through seminal propagation would be damned, whether they were little children or adults, unless a remedy had been provided them through Christ. But this cannot be admitted or supposed on the aforementioned hypothesis, since it is certain that actual sin can only be committed by adults. Hence there would be numerous infants without any sin or need of a remedy. And finally, because, granted that there would be innumerable sins, they would nowise constitute a general evil of the nature. Nor would they affect persons by the mediation of this nature's propagation. Rather, vice versa, they would infect the nature by the mediation of the persons, not the nature absolutely but the nature as in them. These are very different notions, implying a concept of voluntary evil in different ways. Therefore, in no way can it be said that, in that case, there would be the equivalence of actual sins for original sin, in such a way that the same decree as now exists would continue.

Again, it does not matter if you say that St. Thomas (*ST* III, a. 1, a. 2)[15] proved the necessity of the Incarnation and of the coming of

---

15. Aquinas (Leonine ed., 11:9–11).

Christ on the supposition of sin for two reasons, as is clear from the response to objection 2: *This is because the whole human nature was corrupted through sin. And also, because sin committed against God possesses a kind of infinity from the infinity of the divine majesty.* These reasons, since they are different, should be effective taken separately. But, even though on the hypothesis of no original sin the first would cease, the second would still have force. For any actual mortal sin would possess gravity infinite simply, as is clear from what was said in disp. 1, dub. 4.[16] The consequent would therefore be that the Incarnation would still be necessary on this hypothesis. This line of reasoning has seemed so effective to Antonio Parra that he accuses the supporters of our opinion of lack of *consequentia*.[17]

But he should be accused of lacking comprehension [of our opinion]. For we do not doubt that the satisfaction of a divine person is necessary on whatever hypothesis for any grave sin, if expiation is to be made by way of equal satisfaction and rigorous justice or if [the sin] is supposed as to be wiped away in this manner due to God's decree. For condign or equal satisfaction can only be offered for grave fault by a person of simply infinite dignity, as we suppose from the preceding disputation, dub. 5.[18] And this, precisively, is what St. Thomas proves by these arguments, prescinding from whether or not the Incarnation is actually going to occur[19] and instead investigating only whether it is necessary for the end of equal satisfaction, as is obvious from the title of the article and from what he teaches at the beginning of the body. And there is no difficulty with us concerning this, not only in a collection of actual sins but even in a single grave sin. For the equal satisfaction (if there is going to be equal satisfaction) of any sin requires the Incarnation of a divine person. Rather, the doubt hinges on this: Whether by virtue of the present decree, lacking original sin, actual sins would be going to be expiated by means of equal satisfaction through Christ

---

16. Salmanticenses, *Cursus theologicus*, tract. 21, disp. 1, dub. 4 (ed. Palmé, 13:32–72).

17. De la Parra y Arteaga, *Incarnationis arcanum scholastice disputationibus et quaestionibus reseratum*, tract. 1, disp. 1, q. 7, a. 5 (ed. Sanchez, 105–108).

18. Salmanticenses, *Cursus theologicus*, tract. 21, disp. 1, dub. 5 (ed. Palmé, 13:72–108).

19. *Praescindendo a futuritione, vel non futuritione Incarnationis.*

the Redeemer? For the reasons given above, we respond to this that the aforementioned decree only extends to the remediation of these sins by the mediation of the remedy for original sin, or at least dependently on it as on the primary inadequate object. Hence, without the continuation of original sin, these sins would not have a remedy by virtue of the present decree. Instead, they would either be absolutely bereft of a remedy, or they would have it by virtue of another providence that would then decree either condign satisfaction through Christ or another, inferior compensation. But these [remedies], as we have said, would not be by virtue of the present decree whereby Christ was predestined, but would be (if they were going to be) by virtue of another decree that God would have. Which, then, among these assertions common to Thomists lacks *consequentia*?

69 The opposite opinion is defended by Suárez (*Disputationes in Tertiam partem*, disp. 5, sect. 6, second-to-last number);[20] Valencia (*Commentarii theologici*, vol. 4, disp. 1, q. 1, pt. 6);[21] and Granado (*In Tertiam Partem S. Thomae Aquinatis commentarii*, tract. 3, disp. 2, concl. 3),[22] at least in the case where there would not be one or the other grave actual sin precisively but would be many of them. Álvarez calls this manner of speaking probable and is inclined to it (*De Incarnatione divini Verbi disputationes*, q. 1, a. 4, at the end of the exposition).[23] First proof: What chiefly moved God to the remediation of original sin in decreeing the remedy of the Incarnation was the great need of human nature, which fell in it. But a similar loss would be suffered from the multiplication of grave actual sins. For any of them destroys grace and turns man away from the supernatural last end. Therefore, just as Christ would come by virtue of the present decree as a remedy for original sin, even if there were no actual sins, as we established (no. 56), so, too, he would come as a remedy for many actual sins, even if there were no original sin.

20. Suárez, *Disputationes in Tertiam partem*, disp. 5, sect. 6, no. 7 (ed. Vivès, 17:265–66).
21. Gregorio de Valencia (ed. Cardon, 4:59–61).
22. Granado (ed. de Lazcano, 4:76–79).
23. Álvarez (ed. Facciottus, 81).

We respond by denying the *consequentia*. And the disparity is established from what was said. For if the primary object of a given decree is destroyed or does not exist, it cannot continue, but the case is otherwise if only the secondary object is destroyed or lacking. Now the remediation of original sin and the remediation of actual sins are *de facto* compared to the present decree of the Incarnation in such a way that the former is primary while the latter is secondary, as we have shown at length in the preceding doubt. And thus, granted that by virtue of the present decree Christ would come as a remedy for original sin, even if actual sins were lacking, he would not come by virtue of the present decree as a remedy for actual sins lacking original sin, seeing as, by this very fact, such a decree would be taken away due to lack of the primary object or motive.—And the same must be said even if we admit for the sake of disputation that the remediation of actual sins pertained inadequately to the primary motive of the Incarnation together with original sin. For just as the authors related in no. 63, who are of the opinion that original sin only inadequately pertained to the primary object or motive of the Incarnation, consequently strongly deny that Christ would come by virtue of the present decree as a remedy for original sin if there were no actual sins, so too it would have to be denied that he would come as a remedy for actual sins if original sin were lacking. For the primary object is always destroyed by lack of any part of it.

70. Second, and *a fortiori*, the argument is made: Christ the Lord himself (Mt 18:12–14 and Lk 15:4–10) compares himself to the watchful and loving shepherd who, if he loses one out of a hundred sheep, seeks it, leaving the ninety-nine behind, until he finds it. This parable, as not a few explain it, signifies that Christ's charity is so great that if even only one man were lost, he would hasten to provide him a remedy. How much more would he come, then, if the great multitude of men were fallen in actual sins, whatever might be the case with original sin?—This is confirmed first from the Apostle (Heb 6:6), where he teaches that sinners crucify Christ again. There is no more apt explanation of this than that by sinning, men give the occasion for Christ's coming and death, if his coming and Passion for the sins of

all men were not [already] supposed. But this would be false if Christ, by virtue of the present decree, were not going to come as a remedy for any actual sins, even lacking others.—Second, it is confirmed from St. John Chrysostom, who seems to be plainly of this opinion in two places. For, explaining the words *And they gave them lot* (Acts 1:26), he says, *The loss of one soul is such a waste as to be inestimable by all reckoning. For if the salvation of one soul is so great that for it the Son of God would become man and suffer so much*, etc. (Homily 3 on Acts of the Apostles),[24] supposing that Christ would come and would suffer death for the salvation of one soul, even if there were not other sins. And he explains what the Apostle says at the end of Galatians 2 in the same sense, and when he mulls over the Apostle's words *Who loved me and delivered himself for me* (Gal 2:20), he says, *It is fair that each of us thank Christ no less than if he had come for him alone, for he was not going to refuse, even for only one, to offer forgiveness from God* (Commentary on Galatians, chap. 2).[25]

To the argument, we respond that there is nothing in this parable to favor the contrary opinion. For "one sheep" does not signify one sinful man in comparison to all the other just men. Rather, the one sheep signifies the human race and the ninety-nine sheep represent the nine choirs of angels, as if being left by the heavenly shepherd when he came to seek out human nature. And this is the more frequent explanation of the Fathers: Ambrose (*Exposition of the Gospel according to Luke*, VII, chaps. 207–10; and *Apology for David*, chap. 5);[26] Irenaeus (*Against Heresies*, III, chap. 23);[27] Origen (Homily 2 on Genesis; and Homily 17 on John);[28] Hilary, Gregory, Theophylact, and others in Maldonado (on

---

24. John Chrysostom, *In Acta Apostolorum homilia III*, no. 4 (PG 60:40).

25. John Chrysostom, *In Epistolam ad Galatas commentarius*, chap. 2, no. 8 (PG 61:645–48).

26. Ambrose, *Expositio Evangelii secundum Lucam*, VII, chaps. 207–10 (CCSL 14:286–87); and *Apologia David*, chap. 5, no. 20 (SC 239:311). The Latin text gives the citation as: *Ambros. lib. in Lucam cap. 27 et in Apologia David c. 5.*

27. Irenaeus, *Irenaeus Lugdunensis secundum translationem Latinam – Adversus haereses seu Detectio et eversio falso cognominatae Gnoseos*, III, chap. 19, no. 3 (SC 211:378–80). Cf. III, chap. 23, nos. 1–2 (SC 211:444–50). The Latin text gives the citation as: *Irenaei lib. 3, cap. 2.*

28. Origen, *In Genesim homilia II*, no. 5 (PG 12:171). I have not been able to locate

Matthew 18:12).²⁹ St. Thomas also hands this down on the aforementioned passage.³⁰ Supposing this, there is nothing in this passage that would lead us to gather that Christ would come by virtue of the present decree as a remedy for one or more actual sins even if there were no original sin.—Even granting, however, that the passage is speaking about men alone and by "one sheep" it means one man, as some expound it in their public preaching, this would not succeed in proving anything against our assertion. For, as Cornejo has rightly observed, the sense would be that Christ, the true shepherd of souls, who has already come for the salvation of all men sufficiently, would not suffer, as far as he himself is concerned, that even one or even the least sheep of his flock should perish, but instead would seek them all by offering the helps of his grace.³¹ This has nothing in common with the motive of the decree of the Incarnation, which is what we are dealing with. Nor does it prove that Christ would come for one or many sheep lacking the motive of original sin.

To the first confirmation, we respond that the Apostle in this passage is not speaking generally about all sinners but is giving a treatment specifically against certain men wishing to introduce a second baptism, against whom he is warranted in directing this opinion. For, since baptism represents the death and burial of Christ, one who wishes to introduce a second baptism wishes a second crucifixion of Christ by virtue of which the second baptism would have efficacy, as if he values the Passion represented in the first at nothing. And this is the more literal sense of this passage. We concede, however, that some Fathers, and among them the Angelic Doctor on this same passage, interpret it in such a way that it signifies that those who sin after baptism, as far as they themselves are concerned, crucify Christ again. For Christ died

---

the other passage referenced, but the same point is made in Origen's *In Numeros homilia XIX*, no. 4 (PG 12:725–26). Cf. his Commentary on Matthew (PG 13:1173), where he refers to (no longer available) homilies on Luke.

29. Maldonado, *Commentarii in Matthaeum*, chap. 18, vers. 12 (ed. Cardon, 380–81).
30. Aquinas, *Super Matt.*, chap. 18, lect. 2 (ed. Cai, 231.1511).
31. Cornejo de Pedrosa, *Tractatus primus de Incarnatione Verbi divini*, q. 1, a. 4, dub. 2 (ed. Varesius, 2:119). In other words, even if the parable refers only to human beings (the sheep), it is speaking of Christ as he has already come and his offer of sufficient grace to all.

for our sins once, as it is said (1 Pt 3:18), and we participate in the vital efficacy of his death in baptism, when we are incorporated into Christ. Therefore, one who sins after baptism, as far as he himself is concerned, crucifies the Son of God again, for of himself he gives an occasion for him to be crucified again. It is not that God decreed to send the Son to be slain for the sin of this or another person even if Adam's sin did not exist, but that the sins of this or another person give him sufficient occasion or matter for sending the Son, if he willed, though he *de facto* does not have the decree whereby he wills or has willed it.

To the second, we respond that St. John Chrysostom, in both passages, intended to signify Christ's most ardent charity toward us, whereby he was ready, as far as the aforementioned affect was concerned, to die for each man alone if God had so decreed. But God *de facto* did not decree it. And the words of Christ the Lord to that most holy man, Carpus, that St. Dionysius the Areopagite relates, have the same sense: *And yet [I am] ready even to suffer again for the salvation of men, as is welcome to me, should other men not sin* (Letter to Demophilus).[32] By all these we are invited to hold the affect of Christ the Lord in highest esteem and not to underestimate the Incarnation's benefit, as if it had been decreed and accomplished for any one of us alone. This is Chrysostom's intention in these passages, as St. Thomas observes (a. 4, ad 3),[33] and as is clear from the same Chrysostom when he says: *This is the affect of a faithful servant: that he regard the benefits of his Lord given to all in common as if they had been offered to him alone and as if he were a debtor to him for them all, he himself alone considered as liable for them all. This is also what Paul did, who says that the death of our Lord and Savior, which is for the whole world, was offered for him alone. For, as if speaking of himself alone, he writes: "that I live now in the flesh: I live in the faith of the Son of God, who loved me and delivered himself for me."* (Gal 2:20) Now he said this, not wishing to narrow Christ's gifts, which are most abundant and spread throughout the world, but as one who, as we have said, judges himself as liable alone for them all. And in reality, what does it matter if he has offered them to others as well, when what has been offered to you is as whole and perfect as if none of it had

---

32. Pseudo-Dionysius, *Epstola VIII Demophilo monacho*, sect. 6 (PG 3:1100).
33. Aquinas, *ST* III, q. 1, a. 4, ad 3 (Leonine ed., 11:17).

been offered to anyone else? And so, too, in the parable of the good shepherd it is not said that he came to seek many sheep but one. For it is "one" because divine benefits are conferred on all as if they were one (*On the Compunction of the Heart*, II, at the end).[34]

71 But you will inquire as to whether on the hypothesis of this doubt, although Christ would not be going to come from the decree that God *de facto* has, he would still come in virtue of another decree that God would then have? Some respond in the affirmative, most of all if there had been many actual sins. Others deny it. And Parra, who appeared to himself to have thought up something unique, stands on the side of the first on the supposition that God willed the remission of actual sins by way of equal satisfaction.[35]—But, beginning from this latter, it suffers from the same difficulty and adds nothing over and above the previous hypothesis. For it is also hidden whether God would then will the remission of actual sins in this way or in another, since many ways for wiping away sins present themselves to the divine wisdom, as St. Thomas has observed quite well (a. 2, at the beginning of the body).[36] But, even given that God would will sins to be remitted through condign or equal satisfaction, whence will we conjecture that he would be going to decree the Incarnation in the person of the Son rather than in the person of the Father or the Holy Spirit? For this reason, when all the aforementioned ways [of speaking] determinately affirm or deny that the Incarnation would exist on that hypothesis, we think that they are false and proceed rashly, that is, without a determinate foundation for assent or judgment, and we respond to the question only that the matter is completely uncertain to us as depending on God's will alone, which is revealed in Scripture in the order to what he does and is going to do. But, the case is otherwise in regard to what he would do in another order of affairs that will never exist. This we professedly showed (dub. 2), so that it is not necessary to add anything

---

34. John Chrysostom, *Ad Stelechium et de compunctione*, II, no. 6 (PG 47:419–20).

35. De la Parra y Arteaga, *Incarnationis arcanum scholastice disputationibus et quaestionibus reseratum*, tract. 1, disp. 1, q. 7, a. 5, res. 2 (ed. Sanchez, 106). There Parra remarks that he has not found his explanation explicitly stated in the work of any other theologian.

36. Aquinas, *ST* III, q. 1, a. 2 (Leonine ed., 11:10).

else in the present doubt. Even so, we should presume of the divine piety that it would not leave men fallen in actual sins bereft of every remedy, even lacking original sin. But as to what sort of remedy this would be, since there can be many, this is hidden to us in such a way that we cannot determine a certain one.

BIBLIOGRAPHY

Original Text

Salmanticenses. *De motivo Incarnationis*. In *Collegii Salmanticensis Fr. Discalceatorum B. Mariae de Monte Carmeli Parenti suo Eliae consecrati, Cursus theologicus Summam theologicam Angelici Doctoris D. Thomae complectens*, editio nova correcta, 13:263–332. Parisiis: Apud Victorem Palmé; Bruxellis: Apud J. Albanel, 1878. Previously published in *Collegii Salmanticensis Fr. Discalceatorum B. Mariae de Monte Carmeli primitivae observantiae, Cursus theologicus juxta miram Divi Thomae, Praeceptoris Angelici doctrinam*, 9:182–227. Lugduni: Sumpt. Joannis Henrici Huguetan, & soc., 1687.

Ancient, Medieval, and Early Modern Sources

Acta Synodi nationalis in nomine Domini nostri Iesu Christi auctoritate d. d. ordinum generalium foederati Belgii provinciarum Dordrechti habitae. Dordrechti: Typis Isaaci Ioannidis Canini, 1620.

Albert the Great. *Commentarii in III Sententiarum*. In *B. Alberti Magni Ratisbonensis Episcopi, Ordinis Praedicatorum, opera omnia, ex editione Lugdunensi religiose castigata et pro auctoritatibus ad fidem Vulgatae versionis accuratiorumque patrologi textuum revocata, auctaque B. Alberti vita ac bibliographia operum a P. P. Quétif et Echard exaratis, etiam revisa et locupletata, cura ac labore Augusti Borgnet*, vol. 28. Parisiis: Apud Ludovicum Vivès, 1894.

Alexander of Hales. *Doctoris Irrefragabilis Alexandri de Hales Ordinis Minorum Summa theologica seu sic ab origine dicta 'Summa Fratris Alexandri.'* 4 vols. Ad Claras Aquas (Quaracchi): Collegium S. Bonaventurae, 1924–48.

———. *Glossa in tertium librum Sententiarum*. Vol. 3 of *Magistri Alexandri de Hales Glossa in quattuor libros Sententiarum Petri Lombardi, nunc demum reperta atque primum edita, studio et cura PP. Collegii S. Bonaventurae*. Bibliotheca Franciscana scholastica medii aevi 14. Ad Claras Aquas (Quaracchi): Ex typographia Collegii S. Bonaventurae, 1954.

———. *Quaestiones disputatae 'antequam esset frater'*. Bibliotheca Franciscana scholastica medii aevi 19. Quaracchi: Ex typographia Collegii S. Bonaventurae, 1960.

Alonso Tostado (Abulensis). *Alphonsi Tostati Hispani, Episcopi Abulensis, philosophi, theologi, ac pontificii juris, Caesareique consultissimi, necnon linguae Graece, & Hebraicae peritissimi, commentaria in primam partem Mat-*

thaei, cum indicibus copiosissimis. Operum tomus decimusoctavus. Venetiis: Ex typographia Balleoniana, 1728.

Álvarez, Diego. *De Incarnatione divini Verbi disputationes LXXX in quibus explicantur, et defenduntur, quae in tertia parte Summae Theologicae docet S. Tho. a Quaest. 1. usque ad 24.* Romae: Apud Guilielmum Facciottum, 1613.

Anselm of Canterbury. *Cur Deus homo?* In *S. Anselmi Cantuariensis Archiepiscopi opera omnia,* edited by Franciscus Salesius Schmitt, 2:39–133. Edinburgh: Apud Thomam Nelson, 1946.

Aristotle. *Physica.* Edited by W. D. Ross. Reprinted with corrections. Scriptorum classicorum bibliotheca Oxoniensis. Oxford: Clarendon Press, 1966.

———. *Physica (translatio vetus).* Edited by Fernand Bossier and Jozef Brams. Aristoteles Latinus 7.1. Leiden: Brill, 1990.

Francisco de Araújo. *Fratris Francisci de Arauio sacrae theologiae magistri ex Ordine Praedicatorum et in Salmantina accademia primaria cathedra moderatoris in tertiam partem Divi Thomae commentarii.* Vol 1. Salmanticae: Apud Sanctum Stephanum Ordinis Praedicatorum, 1636.

Becanus, Martin. *R. P. Martini Becani, Societatis Iesu theologi, Theologiae scholasticae pars tertia. Tractatus primus de Mysterio Incarnationis Christi Domini.* Lugduni: Sumptibus Antonii Pillehotte & Ioannis Caffin, sub signo SS. Trinitatis, 1625.

Belluto, Bonaventura. *Disputationes de Incarnatione dominica ad mentem doctoris subtilis.* Catanae: Apud Ioannem Rossi, 1645.

Bernal, Augustín. *R.P. Augustini Bernal Magallonensis e Societate Iesu in eiusdem collegio Caesaraugustano sacrae theologiae professoris disputationes de divini Verbi Incarnatione.* Caesaraugustae: Typis et sumptibus Regii Nosocomii, 1639.

Bernard of Clairvaux. *Sancti Bernardi opera.* Vol. 4. Edited by J. Leclercq and H. M. Rochais. Rome: Ed. Cistercienses, 1966.

Biblia sacra cum Glossa ordinaria, novisque additionibus. 6 vols. Edited by Franciscus Fevardentius, Ioannes Dadraeus, and Iacobus Cuilly. Venetiis: Apud Iuntas, 1603.

Biel, Gabriel. *Collectorium circa quattour libros Sententiarum.* Edited by Wilfrid Werbeck and Udo Hofmann. Vol. 3. Tübingen: J. C. B. Mohr (Paul Siebeck), 1979.

Billuart, Charles-René. *Summa Sancti Thomae hodiernis academiarum moribus accommodata.* Editio nova. Vol. 5. Parisiis: Apud Victorem Palmé, 1900.

Bonaventure. *Breviloquium.* In *Doctoris Seraphici S. Bonaventurae S.R.E. Episcopi Cardinalis opera omnia iussu et auctoritate R.P. Bernardini a Portu Romatino,* 5:199–291. Ad Claras Aquas (Quaracchi): Ex typographia Collegii S. Bonaventurae, 1891.

———. *Collationes in hexaemeron: Redactio B.* In *Doctoris Seraphici S. Bonaventurae S.R.E. Episcopi Cardinalis opera omnia iussu et auctoritate R.P. Bernardini a Portu Romatino,* 5:327–454. Ad Claras Aquas (Quaracchi): Ex typographia Collegii S. Bonaventurae, 1891.

———. *De reductione artium ad theologiam.* In *Doctoris Seraphici S. Bonaventu-*

rae S.R.E. Episcopi Cardinalis opera omnia iussu et auctoritate R.P. Bernardini a Portu Romatino, 5:317–325. Ad Claras Aquas (Quaracchi): Ex typographia Collegii S. Bonaventurae, 1891.

———. *In tertium librum Sententiarum*. Vol. 3 of *Doctoris Seraphici S. Bonaventurae S.R.E. Episcopi Cardinalis opera omnia iussu et auctoritate R.P. Bernardini a Portu Romatino*. Ad Claras Aquas (Quaracchi): Collegii S. Bonaventurae, 1887.

de Cabrera, Pedro. *Fratris Petri de Cabrera Cordubensis sacrae theologiae Magistri, ex Ordine Divi Hieronymi, in Tertiam Partem Sancti Thomae commentariorum et disputationum, tomus primus*. Cordubae: Apud Sanctum Hieronymum per Andream Barrera, 1602.

Cajetan, Tommaso de Vio. Commentary on the *Summa theologiae*. In Thomas Aquinas, *Opera omnia iussu impensaque Leonis XIII. P. M. edita*, vol. 11. Romae: Ex typographia polyglotta S. C. de propaganda fide, 1903.

Capréolus, Jean. *Johannis Capreoli Tholosani Ordinis Praedicatoru, Thomistarum principis defensiones theologiae Divi Thomae Aquinatis de novo editae cura et studio RR. PP. Celsai Paban et Thomae Pègues ejusdem Ordinis olim in conventu Tholosano professorum*. Vol. 5. Turonibus: Sumptibus Alfred Cattier, bibliopolae editoris, 1904.

de Cartagena, Francisco. *Doctoris Francisci Carthagenae sacrae theologiae professoris de praedestinatione et reprobatione angelorum & hominum tractatus in discursus duodecim divisus*. Romae: Apud Vincentium Accoltum, 1581.

del Castillo Velasco, Francisco. *Subtilissimi Scoti doctorum super 3. Sententiarum librum, tomus primus, de Incarnatione Verbi divini, et praeservatione Virgin. Mariae ab originali*. Antuerpiae: Apud Petrum Bellerum, 1641.

Catarino, Ambrogio. *F. Ambrosii Catharini politi Senensis de praescientia, providentia, & praedestinatione Dei, libri duo. Eiusdem de eximia praedestinatione Christi, tractatus. Item, de statu futuro puerorum, qui sine sacramento, & in antiquo peccato defuncti sunt, tractatus*. Parisiis: Ex officina Carolae Guillard, sub Sole aureo, via ad divum Iacobum, 1541.

Cippullo, Gregorio. *Commentariorum scholasticorum in Tertiam Partem Summae theologiae Doctoris Angelici S. Thomae Aquinatis tomus primus complectens XIX priores quaestiones*. Romae: Ex typographia Manelphi Manelphii, 1646.

van Clichtove, Josse (Judocus Clichtoveus). *De necessitate peccati Adae & foelicitate culpae eiusdem: apologetica disceptatio*. Parisiis: Apud Henricum Stephanum, 1519.

Complutenses. *Collegii Complutensis Fr. Discalceatorum B. M. de Monte Carmeli, artium cursus, ad breviorem formam collectus, et novo ordine, atque faciliori stylo dispositus*. 5 vols. Lugduni: Sumptibus Petri Chevalier, in via Mercatoria, 1670.

Cornejo de Pedrosa, Pedro. *Operum R.P.M.F. Petri Cornejo Carmelitae theologi praestatissimi ac publici Salmanticensis academiae cathedrarii cum indice copiosissimo tomus alter*. Excudit Ioannes Baptista Varesius Typographus in Carmelo Pinciano, 1629.

Denis the Carthusian. *Commentaria in tertium librum Sententiarum.* In *Doctoris Ecstatici D. Dionysi Cartusiani opera omnia*, vol. 23. Tornaci: Typis Cartusiae S. M. de Pratis, 1904.

Duns Scotus, John. *Lectura in librum tertium Sententiarum.* Vols. 20–21 of *Doctoris subtilis et Mariani Ioannis Duns Scoti Ordinis Fratrum Minorum opera omnia iussu et auctoritate Rmi P. Iosephi Rodriguez Carballo totius Ordinis Fratrum Minorum ministri generalis, studio et cura Commissionis Scotisticae ad fidem codicum edita.* Vatican City: Typis Vaticanis, 2003–2004.

———. *Ordinatio: liber tertius.* Vols. 9–10 of *Doctoris subtilis et Mariani Ioannis Duns Scoti Ordinis Fratrum Minorum opera omnia iussu et auctoritate Rmi P. Iosephi Rodriguez Carballo totius Ordinis Fratrum Minorum ministri generalis, studio et cura Commissionis Scotisticae ad fidem codicum edita.* Vatican City: Typis Vaticanis, 2006–2007.

———. *Quaestiones in librum tertium Sententiarum.* Vols. 14–15 of *Joannis Duns Scoti doctoris subtilis, Ordinis minorum, opera omnia.* Editio nova juxta editionem Waddingi XII tomos continentem a patribus Franciscanis de observantia accurate recognita. Parisiis: Apud Ludovicum Vivès, bibliopolam editorem, 1894.

———. *Reportata Parisiensia: liber tertius, dist. I–XXXV.* In *Joannis Duns Scoti doctoris subtilis, Ordinis minorum, opera omnia*, editio nova juxta editionem Waddingi XII tomos continentem a patribus Franciscanis de observantia accurate recognita, 23:234–530. Parisiis: Apud Ludovicum Vivès, bibliopolam editorem, 1894.

Fabri, Filippo. *F. Philippi Fabbri Faventini Ordinis minorum conventualium. In Universitate Patavina sacrae theologiae professoris. Disputationes theologicae in tertium Sententiarum, complectentes materiam de Incarnatione.* Venetiis: Ex officina Bartholomaei Ginami, sive de Albertis, ad Signum Spei, 1613.

de Ferrara, Francesco Silvestri. Commentary on the *Summa contra gentiles IV*. In Thomas Aquinas, *Opera omnia iussu impensaque Leonis XIII. P. M. edita*, vol. 15. Romae: Apud sedem Commissionis Leoninae, 1930.

da Fonseca, Pedro. *Commentariorum Petri Fonsecae Lusitani, doctoris theologi Societatis Iesu, in Metaphysicorum Aristotelis Stagiritae libros, tomus tertius.* Coloniae: Impensis Lazari Zetzneri Bibliopolae, 1604.

Frassen, Claude. *Scotus academicus seu universa Doctoris subtilis theologica dogmata.* Editio nova. Vol. 7. Romae: Ex typographia Sallustiana, 1901.

Galatino, Pietro Colonna. *Petri Galatini opus de arcanis Catholicae veritatis.* Basileae: Per Ioannem Heruagium, 1661.

de Godoy, Pedro. *Illustrissimi, ac Reverendissimi D. D. Fr. Petri de Godoy Ordinis Praedicatorum: Salmanticensis academiae in sacra theologia Magistri: eiusdemque universitatis quondam cancellarii: diu vespertina, & primaria cathedra moderatoris: concionatoris regii: & nunc Episcopi Oxomensis disputationes theologicae in Tertiam Partem Divi Thomae.* Tomus primus. Venetiis: Apud Ioannem Iacobum Hertz, 1696.

Gonet, Jean-Bapiste. *Clypeus theologiae Thomisticae contra novos eius impugnatores.* Vol. 5. Parisiis: Apud Ludovicum Vivès, 1876.

Gotti, Vincenzo Lodovico. *Theologia scholastico-dogmatica juxta mentem D. Thomae Aquinatis ad usum discipulorum ejusdem Angelici Praeceptoris accommodata ... Tomus I in Tertiam partem*. Vol. 12. Bononiae: Ex typographia Bononiensi Sancti Thomae Aquinatis, 1732.

Granado, Diego. *R. P. Iacobi Granado Gaditani e Societate Iesu in Tertiam Partem S. Thomae Aquinatis commentarii in duos tomos distincti, quartum, scilicet, & quintum, a quaestione prima usque ad ultimam: et ex additionibus, a q. 1 ad 20. & a 25. usque ad 40.& a 69. usque ad ultimam*. Granatae: Typis Antonii Rene de Lazcano, 1633.

Gregorio de Valencia. *Gregorii de Valentia, e Societate Iesu, sacrae theologiae in academia Ingolstadiensi professoris commentariorum theologicorum tomus quartus complectens materias Tertiae Partis, ac Supplementi, D. Thomae. Editio postrema: ab auctore nunc ultimum diligentissime accuratissimeque emendata, multisque in locis locupletata: & ultra praecedentes editiones, nitori suo reddita*. Lugduni: Sumptibus Horatii Cardon, 1609.

Henry of Ghent. *Tractatus super facto praelatorum et fratrum (Quodlibet XII, quaestio 31)*. Edited by L. Hödl and M. Haverals. Vol. 17 of *Henrici a Gandavo opera omnia*. Leuven: Leuven University Press, 1989.

Honorius of Autun. *Libellus octo quaestionum*. In PL 172, 1185–92.

Hurtado de Mendoza, Pedro. *Disputationes de Deo homine sive de Incarnatione Filii Dei*. Antuerpiae: Apud Martinum Nutium, 1634.

John d'Arbres (Arboreus). *Primus tomus Theosophiae Ioannis Arborei Laudunensis, Doctoris theologi, complectens sanam & luculentam difficillimorum locorum cum veteris tum novi testamenti expositionem, decem libris absolvitur: in quibus lepidissimae sacrorum doctorum sententiae discutiuntur, & multorum haereses revelluntur*. Parisiis: Apud Simonem Colinaeum, 1540.

John of St. Thomas. *Cursus theologicus in Summam Theologicam D. Thomae. Nova editio ad Lugdunensem anni MDLXIII accuratissime expressa, mendisque expurgata. Vol. 8, In Tertiam partem, quaestiones I-XXIV de Incarnatione*. Parisiis: Apud Ludovicum Vivès, 1886.

Juan de Campoverde. *Tractatus de Incarnatione Verbi divini divisus in tres tomos: tomus secundus*. Apud Iulianum Franciscum Garcia Briones, typographum Universitatis Complutensis, 1712.

Juan Sendín Calderón. *R. P. M. Fr. Ioannis Sendin eximii theologi Complutensis, Ordinis minorum de observantia, sacrae theologiae lectoris emeriti, almae provinciae Castellae provincialis ministri, ac supremae Inquisitionis Senatus qualificatoris, opus posthumum*. Edited by Ioannes Bernique et al. Compluti: Ex officina Francisci Garcia Fernandez, & sub illius expensis, 1699.

Justinianus, Benedictus. *Benedicti Iustiniani Genuensis Societatis Iesu in omnes catholicas epistolas explanationes*. Lugduni, 1621.

Lawrence of St. Therese. *Spicilegium theologicum, seu, Difficiliores controversiae selectae ex tertia parte summae Divi Thomae de Vervi Divini Incarnatione discussae et resolutae ad mentem eusdem Angelici Doctoris*. Romae: Ex typographia Iosephi Vannaccii, 1682.

Lessius, Leonardus. *Disputatio de praedestinatione Christi*. In *Leonardi Lesii*

Societatis Iesu theologi opuscula varia in unum corpus redacta, ultima editio denuo a mendis purgata, 563–78. Lugduni: Sumpt. Hieronymi Delagarde, sub signo spei, 1651.

de Lorca, Pedro. *Commentariorum, ac disputationum in Tertiam partem D. Thomae, tomus primus, continens priorum viginti sex quaestionum expositionem.* Compluti: Apud viduam Andrea Sanchez de Ezpeleta, 1616.

de Lugo, Juan. *R. P. Joannis de Lugo Hispalensis, e Societate Jesu, in collegio Romano eiusdem Societatis olim theologiae professoris, nunc S. R. E. Cardinalis; disputationes scholasticae de mysterio Incarnationis dominicae.* Editio ultima. Lugduni: Sumptibus Laurentii Arnaud, Petri Borde, Joannis & Petri Arnaud, 1679.

Lychetus, Francesco. *In tertium Sententiarum Ioannis Duns Scoti Doctoris Subtilis commentaria.* In *Joannis Duns Scoti Doctoris subtilis, Ordinis minorum, opera omnia.* Editio nova juxta editionem Waddingi XII tomos continentem a patribus Franciscanis de observantia accurate recognita. Vol. 14. Parisiis: Apud Ludovicum Vivès, 1894.

Maldonado, Juan. *Ioannis Maldonati Sapharensis, Societatis Iesu theologi, commentarii in quatuor Evangelistas.* Editio postrema. Lugduni: Sumptibus Horatii Cardon, 1615.

Marsilius von Inghen. *Quaestiones Marsilii super quattuor libros Sententiarum.* Vol. 3. [Strassburg: Flach, 1501].

Mastri, Bartolomeo. *R. P. F. Bartholomaei Mastri de Meldula Ordinis minorum conventualium S. Francisci theologi disputationes theologicae in tertium librum Sententiarum.* Editio novissima a mendis expurgata et indicibus necessariis locupletata. Venetiis: Apud Paulum Balleonium, 1698.

de Medina, Bartolomé. *Expostitio in tertiam D. Thomae partem usque ad quaestionem sexagesimam complectens tertium librum sententiarum.* Salmanticae: Typis haeredum Mathiae Gastii, 1580.

de Mendoza, Alfonso. *Fratris Alphonsi Mendozae, ex Ordine Eremitarum D. Augustini, in florentissima Salmanticensium academia, sacrae theologiae Magistri & Vesperarii professoris, quaestiones quodlibeticae et relectio de Christi regno ac dominio.* Salmanticae: Excudebat Petrus Lassus, sumptibus Francisci Martini, 1596.

de Molina, Luis. *Liberi arbitrii cum gratiae donis, divina praescientia, providentia, praedestinatione et reprobatione concordia.* Edited by Johann Rabeneck. Oña: Collegium maximum S. I., 1953.

———. *Ludovici Molinae e Societate Iesu s. theologiae doctoris, & professoris commentaria in Primam D. Thomae partem in duos tomos divisa.* Lugduni: Sumptibus Ludovici Prost haeredis Roville, 1622.

Nazario, Giovanni Paolo. *Commentaria et controuersiae in Tertiam partem Summae D. Thomae Aquinatis.* Bononiae: apud haeredes Ioannis Rossii, 1620.

Opusculum de venerabili sacramento altaris. In *Sancti Thomae Aquinatis doctoris angelici Ordinis praedicatorum opera omnia*, 17:135–76. Parmae: Typis Petri Fiaccadori, 1864.

Pablo de la Concepción. *Tractatus theologici juxta miram D. Thomae et Cursus Salmanticensis ff. discalceatorum B. Mariae de Monte Carmeli primitivae observantiae doctrinam*. 2nd ed. Vol. 4. Parmae: Apud Haeredes Pauli Monti, sub signo fidei, 1725.

de la Parra y Arteaga, Antonio. *Incarnationis arcanum scholastice disputationibus et quaestionibus reseratum, iuxta Angelici Praeceptoris mentem, saepe resolutionibus singularibus expositam*. Matriti: Ex officina Melchioris Sanchez, 1668.

Perlín, Juan. *Apologia scholastica, sive controversia theologica, pro magnae Matris ab originali debito, immunitate, ex sanctis litteris, Conciliis, Patribus, aliisque theologicis argumentorum sedibus ad rem pertinentium diligenter collecta.* Lugduni: Sumpt. Iacobi, Andreae, & Matthaei Prost, 1630.

Peter of Aquila. *Quaestiones in quatuor Sententiarum libros.* In *Petri Aquilani cognomento Scotelli ex Ord. min. in doctrina Ioan. Duns Scoti spectatissimi quaestiones in quatuor Sententiarum libros, ad ejusdem doctrinam multum conferentes.* Edited by M. Constantius a Sarnano. Venetiis: Apud Hieronymum Zenarius, 1584.

Peter of Tarantaise. *Innocentii Qvinti Pontificis Maximi ex ordine praedicatorum assvmpti: qui antea Petrus de Tarantasia dicebatur, In IV libros Sententiarum commentaria.* Vol. 3. Tolosae: Apud Arnaldum Colomerium, Regis, & Acadamiae Tolosanae Typographum, 1652.

Philippe de la Trinité. *Disputationes theologicae R.P. Philippi a Sanctissima Trinitate Carmelitae Discalceati provinciae Sanctae Theresiae; in Tertiam Partem Divi Thomae, complectentes tres Tractatus, Scilicet de Sacrosancto Dominicae Incarnationis Mysterio, de Sacramentis in genere, & de Sanctissimo Eucharistiae Sacramento ex mira eiusdem Doctoris Angelici doctrina collectae, iuxta legitimam Scholae ipsius intelligentiam.* Lugduni: Sumptibus Antonii Iullieron Typogr. & Bibliopolae, in vico Racemi sub signo duarum Viperarum, 1650.

Pigghe (Pighius), Albert. *De libero hominis arbitrio & divina gratia, libri decem, nunc primum in lucem editi.* Coloniae: Ex officina Melchioris Novesiani, 1542.

Prudencio, Juan. *P. M. F. Ioannis Prudentii, Caesar-Augustani, in Sertoriana Academia olim cathedrae Sanctissimi Thomae professoris; nunc in Complutensi Universitate vespertinae cathedrae moderatoris; Ordinis B. M. de Mercede Redemptionis Captivorum et eiusdem ordinis generalis diffinitoris Commentariorum super viginti quatuor primas quaestiones tertiae partis Sanctissimi Thomae tomus primus.* Lugduni: sumpt. Laurentii Anisson, 1654.

The Pseudo-Augustinian Hypomnesticon Against the Pelagians and Celestinans. Vol. 2, *Text edited from the manuscripts.* Edited by John Edward Chisholm. Fribourg: The University Press, 1980.

Rada, Juan de. *Controversiarum theologicarum inter S. Thomam & Scotum, super tertium librum Sententiarum, pars tertia.* Coloniae Agrippinae: Apud Ioannem Crithium sub signo Galli, 1620.

Ragusa, Giuseppe. *Iosephi Ragusae Societatis Iesu theologi, commentariorum ac disputationum in Tertiam partem D. Thomae, tomus unus, sacra incarnati Verbi mysteria pertractans.* Lugduni: Sumptibus Horatii Cardon, 1619.

Raynaud, Théophile. *Christus Deus-Homo sive De Deo-Homine theologia Patrum scholastice examinata & sacris emblematis, allegoriis, & moralibus illustrata ad templorum simul et scholarum usum.* Antuerpiae: Apud Iacobum Mursium, 1652.

Richard of Middleton. *Clarissimi theologi Magistri Ricardi de Mediauilla seraphici Ord. min. convent. super quatuor libros Sententiarum Petri Lombardi quaestiones subtilissimae, tomus tertius.* Brixiae: Apud Baptistam Pellizarium, 1591.

Robert Grosseteste. *De cessatione legalium.* Edited by Richard C. Dales and Edward B. King. Auctores Britannici medii aevi 7. London: Published for the British Academy by the Oxford University Press, 1986.

Rupert of Deutz. *Commentaria in Evangelium sancti Iohannis.* Edited by Rhabanus Haacke. CCCM 9. Turnhout: Brepols, 1969.

———. *De gloria et honore Filii hominis super Mattheum.* Edited by Hrabanus Haacke. CCCM 29. Turnhout: Brepols, 1979.

———. *De glorificatione Trinitatis et processione Spiritus sancti.* In PL 169, 14–202.

de Salazar, Fernando. *Ferdinandi Quirini de Salazar, Conchensis e Societate Iesu theologi, in Complutensi collegio sacrarum litterarum interpretatis, defensio pro immaculata Deiparae Virginis Conceptione.* Parisiis, 1625.

Scheeben, Matthias Joseph. *The Mysteries of Christianity.* Translated by Cyril Vollert. St. Louis, Mo.: Herder, 1954.

Smising, Theodore. F. *Theodori Smising Ordinis fratrum minorum regularis observantiae Provinciae Germaniae inferioris Louanii s. theologiae lectoris Disputationes theologicae de Deo uno.* Antuerpiae: Apud Gerardum Wolffchatium, 1624.

Spinelli, Pietro Antonio. *Maria Deipara thronus Dei, de Virginis beatissimae Mariae laudibus praeclarissimis, sub typo divini throni in Apoc. cap. IV adumbratae: deque pietate ac devotione quae eadem Deipara a nobis colenda est.* Coloniae Agrippinae: Apud Ioannem Busaeum, sub Monocerote, 1663.

Suárez, Francisco. *Commentaria ac disputationes in Tertiam partem D. Thomae.* In *R. P. Francisci Suarez E Societe Jesu opera omnia*, editio nova, a Carolo Berton, cathedralis ecclesiae Ambianensis vicario, innumeris veterum editionum mendis expurgata, adnotationibusque in ultimum tomum relegatis illustrata, vols. 17–18. Parisiis: Apud Ludovicum Vivès, 1860.

Thomas Aquinas. *Commentum in quartum librum Sententiarum magistri Petri Lombardi.* Vol. 7.2 of *Sancti Thomae Aquinatis doctoris angelici Ordinis praedicatorum opera omnia.* Parmae: Typis Petri Fiaccadori, 1852.

———. *Quaestiones disputatae de veritate.* Vol. 22 of *Opera omnia iussu impensaque Leonis XIII. P. M. edita.* Romae: Ad Sanctae Sabinae/Editori di San Tommaso, 1970–76.

———. *Scriptum super libros Sententiarum magistri Petri Lombardi episcopi Parisiensis.* Edited by P. Mandonnet and M. F. Moos. Editio nova. 4 vols. Parisiis: P. Lethielleux, 1929–47.

———. *Summa theologiae.* Vols. 4–12 of *Opera omnia iussu impensaque Leonis XIII. P. M. edita.* Romae: Ex Typographia Polyglotta S. C. de Propaganda Fide, 1888–1906.

———. *Super epistolam ad Romanos lectura.* In *Super epistolas S. Pauli lectura*, edited by Raphael Cai, Editio VIII revisa, 1:1–230. Taurini-Romae: Marietti, 1953.

———. *Super Evangelium sancti Matthaei lectura*. Edited by Raphael Cai. Editio V revisa. Taurini-Romae: Marietti, 1951.

———. *Super primam epistolam ad Timotheum lectura*. In *Super epistolas S. Pauli lectura*, edited by Raphael Cai, editio VIII revisa, 2:211–64. Taurini-Romae: Marietti, 1953.

Thomas of Strasbourg (Thomas de Argentina). *Thomae ab Argentina, Eremitarum Divi Augustini Prioris Generalis, qui floruit anno Christi 1345, commentaria in IIII. libros Sententiarum, hac postrema editione a mendis, quibus passim scatebant, repurgata*. Venetiis: Ex officina Stellae, Iordani Ziletti, 1564.

Vásquez, Gabriel. *Commentarium, ac disputationum in Tertiam partem S. Thomae, tomus primus*. Compluti: Apud viduam Iusti Sanchez Crespo, 1609.

Vicente, Juan. *Relectio de habituali Christi Salvatoris nostri sanctificante gratia*. Romae: Ex typographia Pauli Diani, 1591.

William of Auvergne (William of Paris). *Guilielmi Alverni Episcopi Parisiensis, mathematici perfectissimi, eximii philosophi, ac theologi praestantissimi, opera omnia … nunc demum in hac novissima editione ab innumeris errorum chiliadibus expurgata, instaurata, elucidata, atque sermonibus & variis tractatibus aucta ex m.ss.codd. ut ex praefationibus ad lectorem apertius intelligetur*, 1:593–1074. Londini: Apud Robertum Scott, Biblipolam, 1674.

General

Adams, Marilyn McCord. "The Primacy of Christ." *Sewanee Theological Review* 47, no. 2 (2004): 164–80.

Barden, William. "A Thomist Approach Towards Scotism." *Irish Theological Quarterly* 26, no. 4 (1959): 368–75.

Barth, Karl. *Church Dogmatics*. Translated by G. W. Bromiley et al. Edited by G. W. Bromiley and T. F. Torrance. 4 vols. in 14 books. London: T and T Clark, 2004.

Bavinck, Herman. *Reformed Dogmatics*. Translated by John Vriend. Vol. 2. Grand Rapids, Mich.: Baker Academic, 2004.

Beeke, Joel R. *Debated Issues in Sovereign Predestination: Early Lutheran Predestination, Calvinian Reprobation, and Variations in Genevan Lapsarianism*. Göttingen, Germany: Vandenhoeck & Ruprecht, 2017.

Bonnefoy, Jean-François. "La question hypothétique: Ultrum [sic] si Adam non peccasset… au XIIIe siècle." *Revista española de teología* 14, no. 2/3 (1954): 327–68.

———. *La primauté du Christ selon l'écriture et la tradition*. Rome: Casa Editrice Herder, 1959. Translated and abridged by Michael D. Meilach as *Christ and the Cosmos*. First American edition. Paterson, N.J.: St. Anthony Guild Press, 1965.

Carol, Juniper B. *A History of the Controversy over the "debitum peccati."* Franciscan Institute Publications, Theology Series 9. St. Bonaventure, N.Y.: Franciscan Institute, 1978.

———. "The Absolute Predestination of the Blessed Virgin Mary." *Marian Studies* 31 (1980): 178–238.

———. *Why Jesus Christ? Thomistic, Scotistic and Conciliatory Perspectives.* Manassas, Va.: Trinity Communications, 1986.
Crisp, Oliver D. "The Election of Jesus Christ." *Journal of Reformed Theology* 2, no. 2 (2008): 131–50.
Daguet, François. *Théologie du dessein divin chez Thomas d'Aquin: Finis omnium Ecclesia.* Bibliothèque thomiste 54. Paris: Librairie philosophique J. Vrin, 2003.
Delio, Ilia. "Revisiting the Franciscan Doctrine of Christ." *Theological Studies; Washington* 64, no. 1 (March 2003): 3–23.
del Sagrado Corazón, Enrique. *Los Salmanticenses: su vida y su obra. Ensayo histórico y proceso inquisitorial de su doctrina sobre la Inmaculada.* Pontificia Universidad Eclesiastica de Salamanca. Madrid: Editorial de Espiritualidad, 1955.
———. "Juan Duns Escoto en la doctrina de los Salmanticenses sobre el motivo de la Encarnación." In *De Doctrina Ioannis Duns Scoti: Acta Congressus Scotistici Internationalis,* 4:461–515. Rome: Ercolano, 1968.
———. "El colegio de San Elías y los *Salmanticenses.*" In Rodríguez-San Pedro Bezares, Luis Enrique, *Historia de la Universidad de Salamanca,* Vol. 1, *Trayectoria histórica e instituciones vinculadas,* 687–704. Acta Salmanticensia: Historia de la Universidad 61. Salamanca: Ediciones Universidad de Salamanca, 2002.
Diez, Luis Alberto. "Inéditos mariologicos Salmantinos: El primer teólogo de la Realeza: Pedro de Herrera, OP. (1548–1630)." *Ephemerides Mariologicae* 19 (1969): 418–55.
di Santa Teresa, Enrico. "Il carattere del 'Cristocentrismo, nella tesi dei Salmanticesi sul motivo dell'Incarnazione." *Vita Carmelitana* 3 (1942): 39–56.
Galot, Jean. *Gesù Liberatore.* Florence: Libreria Editrice Fiorentina, 1978. Translated by M. Angeline Bouchard as *Jesus, Our Liberator.* Rome: Gregorian University Press, 1982.
Galtier, Paul. *Les deux Adam.* Paris: Beauchesne et ses Fils, 1947.
Garrigou-Lagrange, Reginald. "Le principe de finalité." *Revue Thomiste* 26, no. 3 (1921): 418–23.
———. "Motivum Incarnationis fuit motivum misericordiae." *Angelicum* 7, no. 3 (1930): 289–302.
———. "De motivo Incarnationis: Examen recentium objectionum contra doctrinam S. Thomae III^a, q. 1, a. 3." In *Acta Pont. Academiae Romanae S. Thomae Aquinatis et Religionis Catholicae,* 7–45. Nova series 10. Rome: Academia Romana S. Thomae Aquinatis, 1945.
———. *Christ the Savior: A Commentary on the Third Part of St. Thomas' Theological Summa.* Translated by Bede Rose. St. Louis, Mo.: Herder, 1957.
Giamberardini, Gabriele. "Due tesi scotiste nella tradizione copta: Il primato assoluto di Cristo e l'Immacolata Concezione di Maria." In *De doctrina Ioannis Duns Scoti: Acta Congressus Scotistici Internationalis Oxonii et Edimburgi 11–17 Sept. 1966 celebrati,* Studia Scholastico-Scotistica 3, 317–84. Rome: Ercolano, 1968.
———. "La praedestinazione assoluta di Cristo nella cultura orientale prescolastica e in Giovanni Scoto." *Antonianum* 59 (1979): 596–621.

Goergen, Donald. "Albert the Great and Thomas Aquinas on the Motive of the Incarnation." *The Thomist* 44, no. 4 (1980): 523–38.
Goudin, Anthony. *Philosophia juxta inconcussa tutissimaque D. Thomae dogmata*. Editio novissima. 4 vols. Pompei: Urbeveteri, 1859.
Gordillo, Mauricius. *Mariologia orientalis*. Rome: Pontificium Institutum Orientalium Studiorum, 1954.
Gracia, Jorge J. E. and Timothy B. Noone, eds. *A Companion to Philosophy in the Middle Ages*. Blackwell Companions to Philosophy. Oxford: Blackwell, 2003.
Gredt, Joseph. *Elementa philosophiae Aristotelico-Thomisticae*. Editio decima tertia recognita et aucta. 2 vols. Barcelona: Herder, 1961.
Hammond, Jay M., Wayne Hellmann, and Jared Goff, eds. *A Companion to Bonaventure*. Brill's Companions to the Christian Tradition 48. Leiden: Brill, 2014.
Harper, Thomas. *The Metaphysics of the School*. 3 vols. London: Macmillan, 1879–84.
Hausherr, Irénée. "Un précurseur de la théorie Scotiste sur la fin de l'incarnation: Isaac de Ninive (VIIe Siècle)." *Recherches de sciences religieuse* 22 (1932): 316–20.
Horan, Daniel P. "How Original Was Scotus on the Incarnation? Reconsidering the History of the Absolute Predestination of Christ in Light of Robert Grosseteste." *The Heythrop Journal* 52, no. 3 (May 2011): 374–91.
John Paul II. *Redemptor hominis*. Acta Apostolicae Sedis 71, no. 4 (1979): 257–324.
Jugie, Martin. *Theologia Dogmatica Christianorum orientalium*. 5 vols. Paris: Letouzey, 1926–1935.
Marcil, George. "Joannes de Rada and the Argument for the Primacy of Christ in His *Controversiae Theologicae*." In *Homo et Mundus: Acta Quinti Congressus Scotistici Internationalis, Salmanticae, 21–26 Septembris 1981*, 137–44. Studia Scholastico-Scotistica 8. Rome: Societas Internationalis Scotistica, 1984.
Martelet, Gustave. "Sur le motif de l'Incarnation." In *Problèmes actuels de Christologie*, edited by Humbert Bouëssé, 35–80. Textes et études théologiques. Paris: Desclée de Brouwer, 1965.
McEvoy, James. "The Absolute Predestination of Christ in the Theology of Robert Grosseteste." In *"Sapientiae Doctrina": Mélanges de Théologie et de Littérature Médiévales Offerts à Dom Hildebrand Bascour O.S.B.*, 212–30. Recherches de Théologie Ancienne et Médiévale, numéro spécial 1. Leuven, 1980.
———. *Robert Grosseteste*. Great Medieval Thinkers. Oxford: Oxford University Press, 2000.
Merl, Otho. *Theologia Salmanticensis: Untersuchung über Entstehung, Lehrrichtung und Quellen des theologischen Kurses der spanischen Karmeliten*. Regensburg: J. Habbel, 1947.
Michel, Albert. "Incarnation." In *Dictionnaire de théologie catholique*, edited by Alfred Vacant et al., 7.2:1445–1539. Paris: Librairie Letouzey et Ané, 1923.
Moiser, Jeremy. "Why Did the Son of God Become Man?" *The Thomist* 37, no. 2 (1973): 288–305.
Mouw, Richard J. "Another Look at the Infra/Supralapsarian Debate." *Calvin Theological Journal* 35, no. 1 (April 2000): 136–51.

Muller, Richard A. *Christ and the Decree: Christology and Predestination in Reformed Theology from Calvin to Perkins*. Grand Rapids, Mich.: Baker Academic, 2008.

Pancheri, Francesco-Saverio. *The Universal Primacy of Christ*. Translated by Juniper B. Carol. Front Royal, Va.: Christendom Publications, 1984.

Pesch, Christian. *Praelectiones theologicae*. 4th and 5th ed. Vol. 4. Freiburg: Herder, 1922.

Pfisterer, Robert B. "El motivo de la Encarnación según los Salmanticenses." Doctoral thesis, Universidad Pontificia de Salamanca, 1950.

Pinna, Hieronymus. *De praedestinatione Chisti et Deiparae secundum Theophanem Nicaenum*. Calari: Società Editoriale Italiana, 1948.

Pomplun, Trent. "Baroque Catholic Theologies of Christ and Mary." In *The Oxford Handbook of Early Modern Theology, 1600–1800*, 104–18. Oxford: Oxford University Press, 2016.

Potvin, Thomas R. *The Theology of the Primacy of Christ according to St. Thomas and Its Scriptural Foundations*. Edited by C. E. O'Neill. Studia Friburgensia: Works Published under the Direction of the Dominican Professors at the University of Fribourg Switzerland New Series 50. Fribourg, Switzerland: The University Press, 1973.

Rahner, Karl. "Christology within an Evolutionary View of the World." Translated by Karl-H. Kruger. In *Theological Investigations*, 5:157–92. Baltimore: Helicon Press, 1966.

———. *Mary, Mother of the Lord*. Translated by W. J. O'Hara. Paperback edition. Wheathampstead, Hertfordshire: Anthony Clarke Books, 1974.

———. *Foundations of Christian Faith: An Introduction to the Idea of Christianity*. Translated by William V. Dych. New York: The Crossroad Publishing Company, 1987.

———. *The Trinity*. Translated by Joseph Donceel. Milestones in Catholic Theology. New York: The Crossroad Publishing Company, 2004.

Richard, Guy M. "Samuel Rutherford's Supralapsarianism Revealed: A Key to the Lapsarian Position of the Westminster Confession of Faith?" *Scottish Journal of Theology* 59, no. 1 (2006): 27–44.

Risi, Francesco Maria. *Sul motivo primario della incarnazione del Verbo, ossia, Gesù Cristo predestinato di primo intento per fini indipendenti dalla caduta dell'uman genere e dal decreto di redenzione*. 4 vols. Brescia: Tipografia Mucchetti & Riva, 1897–98.

Rocca, Gesualdo Maria, and Gabriel Maria Roschini. *De ratione primaria existentiae Christi et Deiparae: Novum tentamen conciliationis sententiae Thomisticae cum sententia Scotistica circa sic dictum motivum incarnationis*. Rome: Officium Libri Catholici, 1945.

Spindeler, Aloysius. *Cur Verbum caro factum? Das Motiv der Menschwerdung und das Verhältnis der Erlösung zur Menschwerdung Gottes in den christologischen Glaubenskämpfen des vierten und fünften christlichen Jahrhunderts*. Forschungen zur christlichen Literatur- und Dogmengeschichte, 18.2. Paderborn: Verlag Ferdinand Schöningh, 1938.

Tanner, Norman P., ed. *Decrees of the Ecumenical Councils*. 2 vols. London: Sheed and Ward, 1990.

Unger, Dominic J. "Franciscan Christology: Absolute and Universal Primacy of Christ." *Franciscan Studies* 2, no. 4 (1942): 428–75.
———. "Christ's Role in the Universe according to St. Irenaeus." *Franciscan Studies* 5, no. 1 (1945): 3–20.
———. "A Special Aspect of Athanasian Soteriology: Part I." *Franciscan Studies* 6, no. 1 (1946): 30–53.
———. "A Special Aspect of Athanasian Soteriology: Part II." *Franciscan Studies* 6, no. 2 (1946): 171–94.
———. "Christ Jesus the Secure Foundation According to St. Cyril of Alexandria." *Franciscan Studies* 7, no. 1 (1947): 1–25.
———. "Christ Jesus the Secure Foundation According to St. Cyril of Alexandria: Part II." *Franciscan Studies* 7, no. 3 (1947): 324–43.
———. "Christ Jesus the Secure Foundation According to St. Cyril of Alexandria: Part III." *Franciscan Studies* 7, no. 4 (1947): 399–414.
———. "The Incarnation—A Supreme Exaltation for Christ According to St. John Damascene." *Franciscan Studies* 8, no. 3 (1948): 237–49.
———. "Christ Jesus, Center and Final Scope of All Creation according to St. Maximus Confessor." *Franciscan Studies* 9, no. 1 (1949): 50–62.
———. "Christ the Exemplar and Final Scope of All Creation according to Anastasios of Sinai." *Franciscan Studies* 9, no. 2 (1949): 156–64.
———. "The Love of God: The Primary Reason for the Incarnation according to Isaac of Nineveh." *Franciscan Studies* 9, no. 2 (1949): 146–55.
———. "Robert Grosseteste Bishop of Lincoln (1235–1253) on the Reasons for the Incarnation." *Franciscan Studies* 16, no. 1/2 (1956): 1–36.
United States Conference of Catholic Bishops. *Doctrinal Elements of a Curriculum Framework for the Development of Catechetical Materials for Young People of High School Age*. Washington, D.C.: USCCB, 2008.
Urrutibéhéty, Chrysostome. *Christus Alpha et Omega seu De Christi universali Regno*. Editio altera. Lille, France: R. Giard Libraire, 1910.
———. *Le Motif de l'Incarnation et les principaux thomistes contemporains*. Tours: Librairie Alfred Cattier, 1921.
van Driel, Edwin Christiaan. *Incarnation Anyway: Arguments for Supralapsarian Christology*. Oxford: Oxford University Press, 2008.
von Balthasar, Hans Urs. *Theo-Drama*. Translated by Graham Harrison. Vol. 2. San Francisco: Ignatius Press, 1990.
———. *The Theology of Karl Barth: Exposition and Interpretation*. Translated by Edward T. Oakes. San Francisco: Communio Books/Ignatius Press, 1992.
———. *My Work in Retrospect*. Translator not given. San Francisco: Communio Books/Ignatius Press, 1993.
———. *A Theology of History*. Translator not given. San Francisco: Communio Books/Ignatius Press, 1994.
———. "Trinity and Future." In *Elucidations*, translated by John Riches, 80–90. San Francisco: Ignatius Press, 1998.
———. Mysterium Paschale: *The Mystery of Easter*. Translated by Aidan Nichols. San Francisco: Ignatius Press, 2000.
———. *Dare We Hope "That All Men Be Saved"?* Translated by David Kipp and Lothar Krauth. 2nd ed. San Francisco: Ignatius Press, 2014.

INDEX

Abulensis, 25, 25n66
Acts of the Apostles, 180
actus purissimus in omni linea, 47, 47n141
ad hominem, 55n155
Albert the Great, xix, 102
Alexander of Hales, xviii, 102, 105n263
Alsted, Johan Heinrich, xxxviii
Álvarez, Diego, 23, 71, 118, 140, 150, 178
Ambrose of Milan, 29, 33, 180
Andrew of Crete, 32
Angeles, Ildefonso, xiii
Anselm of Canterbury, xv, 9n12, 31, 66, 173
Anunciación, Juan de la, xiii, xiv, xxxiv
aptitudinal sign, 104, 104n262
Aquinas, Thomas: generation in, 11–12; in Lorca, xxxiii; Salmanticenses' relationship to, xiv; sin in, xix, 7, 13–14, 26–27, 158–59, 165–66, 174–75. *See also specific works by title*
Araújo, José de, xlii, 23, 71, 74, 140, 150, 170–72
Arboreus. *See* Jean d'Arbres
Aristotle, 5n2, 8n8, 11n15, 58n159, 67n179, 145n11, 147
a simili, 47, 47n140
Athanasius of Alexandria, 28, 28n86, 31, 109n269
Augustine, xxix, 29, 31, 104, 107, 112, 140, 143, 152

Barth, Karl, xxxviiin95, xliii, 145n11
Basil the Great, 28–29
Bavinck, Herman, xxxviii
Becanus, Martin, 25, 150–51
Bede, the Venerable, 152, 152n43
Belluto, Bonaventura, xx

Bernal, Augustín, 26, 135
Bernard of Clairvaux, 30, 32–33, 66, 66n176, 105, 105n263, 107–8
Beza, Theodore, xxxviii
Biel, Gabriel, 24
Billuart, Charles-René, xli–xlii
Bonaventure, xviii–xxiv, 9n10, 13n21, 14n22, 24
Bonnefoy, Jean-François, xliv
Burman, Frans, xxxviii

Cabrera, Pedro de, 23, 74, 165, 174
Caius, 152
Cajetan, Tommaso de Vio, xxvi–xxviii, xxix, xxxii, xxxix, 14n22, 22, 70–71, 73n189, 86–87, 143
Calvin, John, xxxviii, xxxviiin95
Campoverde, Juan de, xxii–xxiii, xlii
Capréolus, Jean, xxiv–xxvi, xxxix, 22, 74, 76
Carol, Juniper B., xxxix, 25n66
Cartagena, Francisco de, 103
Castillo Velasco, Francisco del, 102
Catarino, Ambrogio, 103
chain rule, 116, 116n280
Christ: in Balthasar, xlvi–xlvii; in Barth, xliii; in Billuart, xlii; in Bonaventure, xviii–xix; in Cajetan, xxvi–xxvii, 70, 86; in Capréolus, xxv–xxvi; Church and, 106–7; in Colossians, 14–15; in de la Concepción, xli; in Ephesians, 15; in Frassen, xxviii; in Galot, xlv–xlvi; in Godoy, xxxiv; in John of St. Thomas, xxxv; in Lorca, xxxiii; in Lychetus, xxxv–xxxvi; in Mendoza, xxxvi; merits of, 21, 98, 118–26, 159; in Molina, xxviii–xxix, xxxn62; predestination and, xxi–xxii, xxviii–xxix, xxxii–xxxiii, xxxv–xxxvi, xxxvii, 14–16,

Christ: predestination and (*cont.*)
70–73, 87–88, 94–99, 111–17, 116n281, 118–20, 124; primacy of, xvi–n10, xix, xxi, xxvi, xxxiv, xxxix, xli, xliiin109, xlv, xlvii, 83–85; in Rada, xxiii; in Rahner, xlvi; as Redeemer, xxxii, xxxiv–xxxv, xxxvii, xxxix–xl, xlv–xlvi, xlvii, 73, 81, 84–86, 88, 98–99, 101, 125, 157, 167, 177–78; in Rocca, xliv–xlv; in Roschini, xliv–xlv; in Rupert of Deutz, xvii, 15–16; in Scotus, xx–xxi; in Silvestri de Ferrara, xxxiii–xxxiv; in Suárez, xxin29, xxxii; in Vásquez, xxxii

Chrysostom, John, 29, 29n91, 33, 180, 182–83

Cippullo, Gregorio, 24, 75, 150, 174

citations, xlviii

Clement VIII, 152

Clichtove, Josse van, 103

Colossians, Epistle to the, xlvii, 14–15, 97

Complutenses, 96n229

Complutensian Bible, 152, 152n37

Complutum, 152n37

Comrie, Alexander, xxxviii

Concepción, Pablo de la, xxn25, xli

conceptual stages. *See signa rationis*

condign satisfaction, 7, 7n7

conditioned knowledge. *See* middle knowledge

Cornejo de Pedrosa, Pedro, 23, 71, 150, 174, 181, 181n31

Council of Trent, 143–44

Cursus thelogicus, xiii; authorship of, xiii–xiv

Cyprian, 152, 152n41

Cyril of Alexandria, xvin10, 15, 15n25, 29, 32, 108–11, 109n269

Cyril of Jerusalem, 30

Daniel, Book of, 152

Denis the Carthusian, 24

De veritate (Aquinas), 22, 97

Diez, Luis Alberto, 74n192

Dionysius the Areopagite, 182

divine immutability, xvin10, xvii

end for-the-sake-of-which (*finis cuius gratia*), xxxix, xli, xlv–xlvi, 7, 7n8, 14, 18, 21, 37, 73–74, 82–83, 86–87, 89–93, 95–96, 96n229, 97, 99, 111, 117, 123

end to-which (*finis cui*), xxxix, 7, 8n8, 73, 83, 89–91, 95–96, 96n229, 97

enumeratio partium, 46, 46n139

Ephesians, Epistle to the, 15, 71, 105–6, 115

Epiphanius of Salamis, 30, 106

Erasmus, Desiderius, 152, 152n41

Eriugena, John Scottus, 28n84

Fabri, Filippo, xxviii, 102

falsificare, 42n132

Ferrara, Francesco Silvestri de, xxxiii–xxxiv, xxxivn77, xxxix, 22

Ferry, Paul, xxxviii

final cause, xxxiii–xxxiv, xxxivn77, xxxix–xl, 3n4, 6, 96n229

finis cui. See end to-which

finis cuius gratia. See end for-the-sake-of-which

finis qui, xxxiv, 96, 96n229

finis quo, 96n229

1 Corinthians, 17, 112, 114

1 John, 26, 73, 143

1 Peter, 182

1 Samuel, 32

1 Timothy, 32, 136

Fonseca, Pedro da, 103

Frassen, Claude, xxii, xxviii, 111n270

Galatians, Epistle to the, 27, 41, 180, 182

Galatino, Pietro Colanna, 103, 103n249

Galot, Jean, xlv–xlvi

Galtier, Paul, xliv, xlivn118

Garrigou-Lagrange, Reginald, xxivn37, xliv, 3n4, 96n229

generation, 11–12

Genesis, Book of, 12, 105, 148

glory as a crown. *See* merit

Godoy, Pedro de, xxxii, xxxiv, xxxix, xlviiin132, 23, 44n134, 51, 75, 88, 131, 135, 158, 165, 174

Goergen, Donald, xixn24

Gomarus, Franciscus, xxxviii

Gonet, Jean-Baptiste, xxxiv, xxxix, 23, 75, 150, 174

Gordillo, Mauricius, xvin10
Gotti, Vincenzo, xxiii, xxiiin36, xli–xlii, xliin102
grace, xxiii, xxv–xxviii, 58, 58n159, 70–72, 86–87, 97–98, 118–21, 124–26, 130–31, 130n7, 181n31
Granado, Diego, 26, 75, 137, 139, 151, 178
Gregory of Nazianzus, 28, 31, 36, 42, 180–81
Gregory of Nyssa, 30
Gregory the Great, 32–33, 173
Grosseteste, Robert, xvii, xix, 104n261, 105n264
Guerric of Igny, 30

Hebrews, Epistle to the, 17, 27, 179
Heerbrand, Jacob, 148n18
Heidanus, Abraham, xxxviii
Henry of Ghent, xvii–xviii
Herrera, Pedro de, 74, 74n192
Hilary of Poitiers, 28, 180
Holtius, Nicolaus, xxxviii
Honorius of Autun, xv–xvi, xvin10, xvii, xviin14
Hurtado de Mendoza, Pedro, 103
hypothetical syllogism. *See* chain rule

Immaculate Conception, xxvi, xliv, 58, 100, 162, 169
implicatio, 10n14
Incarnation: in Albert the Great, xix; in Alexander of Hales, xviii; in Anselm, xv; in Aquinas, xix, xixn24; in Araújo, xlii; in Barth, xliii; in Billuart, xli–xlii; in Bonaventure, xviii–xviv; in Cajetan, xxvi–xxvii; in Capréolus, xxiv–xxvi; in Gotti, xxiii; in Grosseteste, xvii, xix; in Henry of Ghent, xvii–xviii; in Honorius of Autun, xv–xvi; in Mastri, xxxvii; as occasioned good, 8–11, 8n10; original sin and, 142–72; in Peter of Aquila, xxii; predestination and, xxi–xxii, xxviii–xxix, xxxii–xxxiii, xxxv–xxxvi, xxxvii, 14–16, 70–73, 87–88, 94–99, 111–20, 124; and remediation of sin, xli, 9, 14, 18, 21, 27, 34, 36–40, 47, 49–51, 56–58, 60–64, 69–88, 113, 162, 179–80; in Rocca, xliv–xlv; in Roschini, xliv–xlv; in Rupert of Deutz, xvi–xvii; in Scotus, xx–xxi, 8n10; without actual sins, 142–72; without original sin, 173–84; without sin, xvii, xl, 5–22, 127–41
infralapsarians, xxxvii–xxxviii
Inghen, Marsilius von, 24
Irenaeus of Lyon, 28, 31, 42, 52, 180
Isaac of Nineveh, xvin10
Isaiah, Book of, 85, 114

Jaime Pérez de Valencia, 103
Jean d'Arbres, 25
Jerome, Saint, 25n66, 29, 39n128
Job, Book of, 39n128
John, Gospel of, 43, 112, 136, 146, 152
John Chrysostom. *See* Chrysostom, John
John Damascene, xvin10, 29
John of St. Thomas, xx, xxxv, xxxvn84, 23, 71
John of the Cross, xxxiv
John Paul II, xlvii
Jugie, Martin, xvin10
Justinianus, Benedictus, 26, 26n77

lapsarian controversy, xxxvii–xxxviii
Lawrence of St. Therese, 24, 75
León, Luis de, xxxiv
Leo the Great, 29–30, 32, 140, 143–44, 152, 152n40
Lessius, Leonardus, 25
locus, 67, 67n179
Lorca, Pedro de, xxxiii, 25, 75, 77, 135, 174
Lugo, Juan de, 26n79
Luke, Gospel of, xlvii, 27, 114, 114n277, 146, 179
Luther, Martin, xxxviii, xxxviiin95, 157, 162
Lychetus, Francisco, xxxv–xxxvi, 102

Madre de Dios, Antonio de la, xiii, xxxiv
Makowski, Ian, xxxviii
Maldonado, Juan, 25, 180–81
Mark, Gospel of, 27
Mastri, Bartolomeo, xxii, xxxvii
material cause, xxvi, xxix, xxxv, xlii, 18, 21, 37, 70, 74, 81–83, 86–87, 95, 99, 117, 123
Matthew, Gospel of, 27, 41, 179

Medina, Bartolomé de, 22–23, 74, 116, 116n281, 150
Mendoza, Alfonso de, xxxvi, 25, 75, 77, 84n212
merit, 18, 77–78, 80n208, 81, 84–85, 87, 93–94, 114–17, 123–24
middle knowledge, xxxi–xxxii, 54, 54n153, 68
Molina, Luis de, xxii, xxviii–xxx, xxxn62, xxxix, xliv, 54n153
motiva totalia et adaequata, 53–54, 53n151
motivum, 3n4

Nazario, Giovanni Paolo, 23, 74–75, 165, 174
neo-scholasticism, xliv
Nicene Creed, xlviii, 30, 30n104, 42, 89

occasioned good, Incarnation as, 8–11, 8n10
On the Motive of the Incarnation: in Middle Ages and beyond, xv–xxxviii; Salmanticenses and, xxxix–xli; after Salmanticenses and today, xli–xlvii
ordinate volens, xx–xxi, xxiv, xxvii–xxix, xxxv–xxxvi, xxxvn84, 16–17, 16n29
Origen, 28, 28n84, 143, 180, 181n28

Pancheri, Francesco-Saverio, xiii
Parra y Arteaga, Antonio de la, 23, 150, 183, 183n35
Pérez, Antonio, 103, 174
Perkins, William, xxxviii
Perlín, Juan, 103–4
Pesch, Christian, xliv
Peter of Aquila, xxii
Philippe de la Trinité, 24, 75, 150
Pierre de Tarentaise, 24
Pigghe, Albert, 103
Piscator, Johann, xxxviii
Pius IX, xliv
Polansdorf, Amandus Polanus von, xxxviii
praecise, 39n128
predestination, xxi–xxii, xxviii–xxix, xxxii–xxxiii, xxxv–xxxvi, xxxvii, 14–16, 70–73, 87–88, 94–99, 111–17, 116n281, 118–20, 124
priority *a-quo*, 19–20, 19n35

priority *in-quo*, 19–20, 19n35
Proverbs, Book of, 3
Prudencio, Juan, 23, 75, 174
Psalms, Book of, 31, 33, 35, 147–48
Pseudo-Augustine, 32, 32n110

Rada, Juan de, xxii–xxiii, xxvii–xxviii, 9n12, 84n212, 92n225, 102, 109n269
Ragusa, Giuseppe, 25, 71, 135, 174
Rahner, Karl, xlvi
Raynaud, Théophile, 26
Redeemer, xxxii, xxxiv–xxxv, xxxvii, xxxix–xl, xlv–xlvi, xlvii, 73, 81, 84–86, 88, 98–99, 101, 125, 157, 167, 177–78
redemption: passive vs. active, 89n220
Reformed theology, xxxvii–xxxviii
repugnantia, 10n13
Richard of Middleton, 24
Rocca, Gesualdo Maria, xliv–xlv
Romans, Epistle to the, 66, 100, 114–15, 115n279
Roschini, Gabriele M., xxivn37, xliv–xlv
Rupert of Deutz, xvi–xvii, xviin14, xviiin18, 15–16, 15n26, 33, 42–43

Sagrado Corazón, Enrique del, xivn4, xxxivn79
Salazar, Fernando Chirinos de, 25
San Juan Bautista, Antonio de, xiii
Santa Teresa, Domingo de, xiii
satisfaction, condign, 7, 7n7
Scheeben, Matthias Joseph, xlii–xliii, xliiin109
scientia conditionata. *See* middle knowledge
Scotism, xx, xxiii, xxxv–xxxvi, 37–53, 68
Scotus, John Duns, xx–xxi, xxii, xxxvn84, 8n10, 9n12, 16, 16n29, 102
Scriptum super librum secundum Sententiarum (Aquinas), 90–91
Scriptum super librum tertium Sententiarum (Aquinas), 22, 107–8
Second Vatican Council, xlvii
signa rationis, xxi–xxii, xxiv–xxv, xxx, xl, 5, 5n2, 19–22, 45–46, 67, 73, 82–83, 93, 122–23, 155–57, 169

Silvestri de Ferrara, Francisco. *See* Ferrara, Francesco Silvestri de
sin: in Anselm of Canterbury, xv; in Aquinas, xix, 7, 13–14, 26–27, 121–22, 144–45, 148–49, 158–59, 165–66, 174–75; in Bernard of Clairvaux, 105; in Bonaventure, 13n21; in Cajetan, xxvi–xxvii; in Frassen, xxviii; in Henry of Ghent, xvii–xviii; in Honorius of Autun, xv–xvi; Incarnation without, xvii, xl, 5–22, 127–41; in Lorca, xxxiii, 77; in Mastri, xxxvii; in Mendoza, xxxvi, 77; in Molina, xxix; predestination and, xx, xxi, xxxvi, 71–73, 98–99, 115–16, 116n281; remediation of, Incarnation and, xli, 9, 14, 18, 21, 27, 34, 36–40, 47, 49–51, 56–58, 60–64, 69–88, 113, 162, 179–80; in Rupert of Deutz, xvii; in Scheeben, xlii–xliii; in Scotus, xx, xxi; in Silvestri de Ferrara, xxxiii; in Suárez, xxxi–xxxii, 53–69, 145–46; in supralapsarian thought, xxxvii–xxxviii
sin, original: vs. actual sin, xl–xli; Incarnation with only, 142–72; Incarnation without, 173–84; originated vs. originating, 162, 162n47
Smising, Theodore, 102
Spindeler, Aloysius, xvin10
Spinelli, Pietro Antonio, 103
Suárez, Francisco, xxin29, xxx–xxxii, 35, 53–69, 55n156, 73n189, 84n212, 93n226, 99n234, 137, 145–46, 150, 178
Summa theologiae (Aquinas): causes in, 3, 37; *Cursus theologicus* and, xiii; generation in, 11–12; good in, 91; Incarnation in, 22; predestination in, 16; primacy of Christ in, 85; sin in, 121–22, 144–45, 148–49, 174–75; will and ends of God in, 6, 34

Super primam epistolam ad Timotheum lectura (Aquinas), 22
supralapsarians, xxxvii–xxxviii
syncategorematic, 58n159
Synod of Dort, xxxviii

Tertullian, 28
Theophylact of Ohrid, 30, 180–81
Thomas Aquinas. *See* Aquinas, Thomas
Thomas of Strasbourg (Thomas de Argentina), 24
Titus, Epistle to, 112
Tostado, Alonso. *See* Abulensis translation, xlviii
Trapezontius, Georgius, 109n269
Twisse, William, xxxviii

Unger, Dominic, xvin10, xvii, xviiin14
universal negative proposition, 42, 42n131
Urrutibéhéty, Chrysostome, xv, xliv, xlivn118

Valencia, Gregorio de, 25, 148, 148n18, 150, 178
Vásquez, Gabriel, xxxii, xxxv, xxxvii, xlii, 25, 44, 66, 71, 73n189, 93n226, 99n234, 135, 150, 174, 174n11
verificare, 42n132
Vicente, Juan, 23, 74, 76–77, 127, 150, 174
von Balthasar, Hans Urs, xlvi–xlvii, xlviin132

Whitaker, William, xxxviii
William of Auvergne, 102, 102n241
Wittich, Christoph, xxxviii

Zwingli, Ulrich, xxxviii, xxxviiin95

On the Motive of the Incarnation was designed in Minion with Hypatia Sans display type and composed by Kachergis Book Design of Pittsboro, North Carolina. It was printed on 60-pound Maple Eggshell Cream B18 and bound by Maple Press of York, Pennsylvania.